Applying Behavior Analysis Across the Autism Spectrum
A Field Guide for New Practitioners
Second Edition

by

Beth Sulzer-Azaroff, Ph.D.,
Kathleen Dyer, Ph.D., CCC-SLP, BCBA-D
Susan Dupont M.Ed., BCBA
Dianne Soucy, M.Ed., BCBA

Candy Mouncey

Library of Congress Cataloging-in-Publication Data
Applying behavior analysis across the autism spectrum : a field guide for new practitioners / by Beth Sulzer-Azaroff ... [et al.].. -- 2nd ed.
p. cm.
Prev. ed. cataloged under author Sulzer-Azaroff, Beth.
ISBN 978-1-59738-036-2
1. Autistic children--Education--Handbooks, manuals, etc. 2. Behavioral assessment--Handbooks, manuals, etc. I. Sulzer-Azaroff, Beth. II. Sulzer-Azaroff, Beth. Applying behavior analysis across the autism spectrum.
LC4717.8.S85 2012
371.94--dc23
2011047767

Cover designer: Amy Rosen
Cover photograph: Steve Liss Photography

© 2012

Sloan Publishing, LLC
220 Maple Road
Cornwall-on-Hudson, NY 12520

Printed in the United States of America

10 9 8 7 6 5 4 3 2 1

ISBN: 978-1-59738-036-2

Applying Behavior Analysis Across the Autism Spectrum:
A Field Guide for New Practitioners, Second Edition

Beth Sulzer-Azaroff , Kathleen Dyer, Susan Dupont, Dianne Soucy and Associates

PART 2
Designing, Implementing, and Functionally Analyzing the Effect of a
Behavioral Intervention   **139**

(Units 1 and 2 from PART 1 can be used here if you are in a new setting)

Acknowledgments

Our friend and colleague, Ellen P. Reese, often found herself paraphrasing B.F. Skinner's famous dictum about the behavior of his laboratory subjects always being right: "The student is always right." We authors of this text couldn't agree more. Given that shared perspective, we set about to field test the initial version of this text. Our dual purposes were 1) to determine how effectively it performed its purported function of preparing applied behavior analysts to shape effectively the behavior of students on the autism spectrum 2) to revise its coverage accordingly. The main result was that for the present edition we interposed a series of steps for ABA trainees to complete before asking them to develop, implement and experimentally analyze the effectiveness of their own original programs. We did that by expanding the manual's coverage to include identifying, organizing, testing and adding a major set of foundational competencies that have been effective in the education of students on the spectrum.

Among the many whose cooperation, support and feedback have encouraged this expanded revision of Applied Behavior Analysis across the Autism Spectrum are the faculty and field practicum students from the Applied Behavior Analysis programs at Elms College, Massachusetts and Eastern Connecticut State University. They deserve our special thanks. We also wish, especially, to extend our appreciation to the students, parents and staff of the River Street Autism Program at Coltsville, who through their words and actions have informed the direction and scope of this revision. Beyond those, several individuals in particular, merit our special thanks:

Tom Parvenski, Director of the River Street Autism Program, CT, who never seems to miss an opportunity to nurture efforts toward improving the quality and effectiveness of its educational programs. No wonder the progress rates of its clientele are so impressive!

Friend and colleague, Dr. Thomas Zane, Director of the Applied Behavior Analysis program at Endicott College, who reviewed and supplied helpful tips on the content and coverage of the competency-based modules.

Greg Smith, Behavior Analyst Extraordinaire at the River Street Autism Program at Coltsville, who spent many many hours videotaping, painstakingly editing, and posting the essential competency observations on the companion website.

Jeff Kupfer, whose personal comments and remarks in the Behavior Analyst (2008), about his experiences in using the first edition of the field guide in his practitioner course at the facility at Lafayette, Colorado, certainly went a long way toward encouraging us to continue refining these materials.

Bill Webber, dream publisher, with a patient "Yes, yes" "Can-do" attitude.

K Camp, a very special young lady well known to us, masterfully, and at a pace outdistancing that of the authors, prepared a number of the clever pictorial illustrations contained in this new edition. We very much appreciate, as well, the patience and support of those of our near and dear families and friends, who have become accustomed to our response, "Soon" to their plaintive inquiry, "When do you think you'll be finished?"

PROLOGUE

To Instructors and In-service Training Supervisors

The Impetus for Preparing this Revised Edition

Four years ago we welcomed you to a new concept in preparing educators and parents to apply behavior analysis with youngsters diagnosed with autism spectrum disorder (ASD), with material designed to extend *applied behavior analysis* (ABA) students' knowledge into actual application. We knew that *saying* did not necessarily equal *doing,* whether in aviation, medicine, or any complex area of application; that being able to recite rules of operation was no guarantee of skill of application. Far more was needed in the form of demonstration, guided feedback of varied forms of feedback and differential reinforcement. To that end we designed and offered a carefully programmed sequence of behavior analytic practice exercises that students or trainees could use to teach children on the autism spectrum. Among others, activities included designing and implementing a behavioral intervention with a student; then functionally analyzing and reporting on progress and results.

Next, as dutiful applied scientists, we put that material to the test by inviting a number of graduate students who had completed their ABA didactic coursework to use the curriculum to guide their practice in an actual school setting. The cooperating program served young students whose ASD was sufficiently severe that their own local public school district's felt they could better profit from more intensive behavioral interventions. Despite skilled applied behavior analysts locally supervising and guiding, the implementation of our program, results were mixed. While certainly our young professionals and their students profited to some extent, we concluded that the steps we had incorporated in our initial program were too challenging. Once again, we found ourselves humbly agreeing with B.F. Skinner's famous maxim, that the study subject is always right—paraphrased here as:

The Student is Always Right!

Consequently, over the past few years, our team has set about to revise, expand and begin field testing the contents of the manual in this current form. More specifically, we have added a major section on mastery of solidly validated foundational behavioral- intervention skills for children on the autism spectrum (Charlop, Schreibman, & Thibodeau, 1985, Dyer, Dunlap, & Winterling, 1990, Hart & Risley, 1975; McGee, Krantz, & McClannahan, 1985, to cite a few), emphasizing, in particular, skills of a pivotal nature (Koegel & Koegel, 2006). Those are designed to be assessed by means of competency-based checklists while the ABA trainee is engaged in teaching particular each particular skill. We have programmed these as instructional tools that both guide our ABA field trainees and, as evidence-based practices, promise to succeed with their assigned students. Each of these programs contains a rational for teaching the particular skill to the child and a checklist for assessing the ABA trainee's instructional performance.

Although the checklists relating to preference, time delay, and incidental teaching have been field tested with trainees in school programs (Dyer & Kohland, 1991; Dyer, Santarcangelo, & Luce, 1991; Dyer, Martino, & Parvenski, 2006; Luce & Dyer, 1995), the others have been field tested on approximately 200 entry level staff during the last decade. While at this point we await strong scientific evidence documenting the extent to which this modified professional curriculum package in its entirety is succeeding as a college practicum training guide, on the basis of informal reports and our own observations, we are convinced that outcomes for the ABA professionals-in-training and the school's students and are much improved. We strongly encourage anyone with the interest in and access to the essential resources to conduct more formal inquiry into the efficacy of this program and would be happy to consult or collaborate with you on such a project.

In this field we move incrementally toward improving our professional instructional and supervisory tools. Our aim is that you, the individual who guides others and/or directly uses the tools we offer in this text, will be contributing toward meeting the universal need for personnel trained in ABA, the only evidentiary-based educational approach shown so far to operate effectively with this population. Join us on this exciting journey. Thrilling discoveries and accomplishments await you along the way!

Your Reinforcers

We who have participated in the field trials of these materials share the common pleasure and satisfaction of having seen our practicum students' and *their* students' progress. About a decade ago, when preparation of this this text was in its early stages, we received an email from one of our ABA students. She was a mother of a boy whose behavior initially had made it almost impossible for the family to go anywhere – shopping, to a restaurant, visiting other family members or friends. Two years later, an email message from her simply stated "_____ began kindergarten *seamlessly* today." At this printing, we're thrilled to report that as a teenager, while not a social butterfly, this same young man excels academically at school, has performed as a cellist with the Minneapolis Youth Orchestra, won a state-wide competition in geography and has piloted a plane.

Information of that sort has more than compensated us for the extra time and effort we have invested in developing, testing and revising this and the other pieces of our *behavioral interventions in autism series.*[a] We trust that by devoting yourself to this pursuit, you will experience satisfaction of a similar nature.

Ongoing Purpose

Our main purpose in assembling and revising this *Practicum Guide* is to help meet the huge global need for personnel and family members trained to apply behavior analysis positively, constructively and skillfully with youngsters on the autism spectrum. The sequence of activities contained within was designed to reinforce 1) trainees' knowledge of ABA *content*—its principles and procedures—as well as 2) *skill in systematically applying and practicing* behavior-analytic based curricula, (including discrete trial and more advanced behavior-analytic (ABA) methods and systems) to analyze and promote clients' learning. We also hope to enable ABA trainees to gain a realistic expectation of what transpires in ASD-education/training programs by exposing them to and providing them the opportunity to gain some hands-on participation. We do not expect them to become fully competent practitioners in this brief period, but instead, steadily to progress toward excellence.[b]

Experiential practicum placements frequently are loosely structured, generally operating on the assumption that following the lead of a skilled mentor in the field provides sufficient training. By contrast, here we have elected to *program* what we teach, and how we teach it, according to solid principles of operant learning.[c] Each step in the process is carefully designed to promote success, both for our field-practicum

---

[a] This practicum originally was field tested as the fourth in a series of distance and face-to-face courses developed to teach *Behavioral Interventions in Autism* to educators and parents of children with autism. Funding for design of the curriculum and field trials was provided in part through a grant to the Eunice K. Shriver Center, University of Massachusetts Medical School, from the U.S. Department of Education, Fund for the Improvement of Post-Secondary Education, Learning Anytime Anywhere Partnership (LAAP) Program, Grant Number: P339B000300. For current information on the complete Internet sequence contact www.umassmed.edu/shriver.

[b] The competency-based *checklists* contained in Part 1 of this practicum curriculum were field tested at the River Street Autism Program at Coltsville, Hartford, CT . A number of the individual trainee-designed educational programs in Part 2 were field tested at the River Street Autism Program at Coltsville, Hartford, CT .

[c] Illustrative video material of the particular skills being taught is available on this book's companion website. To view, visit http://www.sloanpublishing.com/autismspectrum and choose "View vido illustrations." and chose the related page number.

students and theirs. And, as we have established in our field trials, the sequence can be taught both from a distance over the internet, or directly on location.

A Comment to Educational Administrators and Personnel Managers of Educational Programs Serving Students with Autism

The worldwide shortage of educational personnel skilled in behavior analytic applications is acute. One approach many organizations have used is to develop their own staff through collaborative arrangements with colleges and universities. Some larger programs actually have hosted satellite university campuses from their own grounds. There, personnel often are prepared from a distance, over the internet, via group audio-visual conferences and classes or a variety of combinations of those.

Others offer to have their programs host students in practicum and internship positions. These function to develop a pool of potential employees, provided skilled supervisors are available and have time set aside to fulfill that role.

General Student Skills

This field practicum takes trainees beyond the lecture hall into the real world. Its intention is initially to acquaint students of ABA, as participant-observers, with the kinds of activities that behavior analysts carry out in such settings. It should show them what is involved in ABA instructional performance, but not necessarily prepare them to become fully proficient applied behavior analysts. Users of this material will sample what this world is like and how it feels to participate in it in a systematic, though not necessarily complete way. The material is directed toward student participants and on-the-job trainees who already have acquired basic *concepts* in applied behavior analysis to now gain and refine a specific set of *skills*.

We also supply a number of *optional* tools trainees might use to locate and become acclimated to their new field practicum surroundings and to help make them welcome and appreciated by their host organizations. Next, we offer a series of tightly programmed instructional modules for ABA trainees to use to help guide, self-assess, and gain objective feedback on their own and their student's performance. Once ABA trainees demonstrate mastery over those instructional modules, they then move on more independently to design and conduct behavior-analytic-based interventions closely aligned with *their* own student's *individual educational* or *family service plan (IEP or IFSP)*. They are asked to observe and otherwise learn as much as feasible about their student-candidate and plan to intervene by focusing on one or more objectives. The program then supports trainees' performance by enabling them to draw upon their prior knowledge of behavior analytic concepts, methods and research findings to design their own programs to shape their student's behavior gradually toward meeting the objective(s). A wide range of ABA skills are included: assessing *both* adaptive and maladaptive student behavior and its functions within the environment, then observing, instructing, recording, measuring, graphing, analyzing and communicating the results of those instructional efforts. In general, by designing and beginning to test out their own original programs, trainees are led to see how the various key elements of those intensive ABA methods they already learned about in didactic coursework, fit together into a whole.[d]

---

[d] Notice the omission in this text of objectives related to preventing, assessing, and correcting severely maladaptive behaviors. A separate text designed for that purpose is in the conceptual stage.

Your Role as Trainer or Supervisor

First, we assume you yourself have proficiency and experience in ABA and share an enthusiasm for promoting performance excellence among the students you are training and supervising. Perhaps you are a *Board Certified Behavior Analyst* with an advanced degree or are on your way to becoming certified. You may be employed as a regular or adjunct faculty member of a college or university,[e] as a consultant to programs or directly within a program. (If yours is the latter arrangement, you should be able to combine the roles of *instructor, supervisor* and *field facilitator* into one.)

In the present situation, we imagine you are working with trainees who have convinced you of their prior attainment of prerequisite knowledge; that they can *talk the talk* of ABA. Your job is to guide and support them as they *walk the walk* of ABA skills. That requires considerable behavior analytic expertise and skill of you, especially because this sequence is both challenging and involves a solid investment of your and your students' time.[f]

You, as supervisor, probably will need to schedule **at least** *a half to an hour a week observing and supplying feedback to each practicum student you have agreed to supervise, and at a minimum, another hour or two each week discussing the material, reviewing assignments, and offering guidance and suggestions individually or in a group.*

In the field trials of the material on which this manual was based, we found that most trainees, especially those electing to participate as distance learners, often had children diagnosed with autism of their own and/or were employed or attending school full or part-time. Faced with heavy demands on their time, energy and material resources, students in such situations, especially, need your ongoing guidance and constructive support. Given those challenges, your main responsibilities, then, are to assist each ABA student by:

- Becoming individually acquainted with them; with the concerns they share in common with their fellow trainees and their own personal challenges, special abilities, and interests.
- Assisting in organizing their assignments and scheduling their preparation and implementation of the check-listed programs they are to implement and assess during the first portion of their field experience.
- Carrying out or assigning to a qualified staff member the responsibility for observing, scoring and, if necessary coaching the ABA trainee's correct implementation of the programs contained in part I of this manual.
- Serving as or guiding them toward obtaining and consuming relevant research literature and other resources.[g]
- Stimulating and directing them toward undertaking challenging yet achievable goals.
- Mentoring or designating another qualified staff member to mentor practicum students while they plan, design, conduct, evaluate and report on their progress with their individual ABA programs.
- Shaping their progress with their students toward those goals through judicious combinations of positive feedback, reinforcement and minimal prompting.

---

[e] If your students wish to obtain college credits for this experience, some formal arrangements will need to be made with a local or distance institution of higher learning that offers courses in applied behavior analysis. [See websites for: 1) the *Association for Applied Behavior Analysis International*: http://www.ABAinternational.org , 2) the *Behavior Analysis Certification Board*: http://www.BACB.com and 3) The Cambridge Center for Behavioral Studies http://www.behavior.org for listings of programs.]

[f] Current professional Behavior Analysis Certification Board guidelines[f] indicate that field *practicum students* will spend a minimum of 1,000 hours (Board CertifiedAssociate Behavior Analyst (BCaBA[©]) or 1,500 hours (Board Certified Behavior Analyst (BCBA[©]) in supervised independent fieldwork.

[g] Among the most useful sources we have found are *Google Scholar* and the *Journal of Applied Behavior Analysis* websites

- Encouraging them to interact productively with their peers, either by scheduling regular on-site or distance face-to-face group meetings or discussions.
- Developing a supportive and understanding mentor relationship with them, permitting them only to move on to each next step after they have demonstrated the high quality performance demanded by a mastery-based program.

How This Manual Is Designed to Work

This manual is designed to be *flexible*, though the sequence you and your student(s) follow should be planned in advance. For instance, in *Unit 1*, we provide a sample schedule and a blank form that the two of you might elect to use to tailor your joint activities to match given circumstances, such as skipping training in skills previously demonstrated as having been mastered, or steps already taken, subtracting non-relevant teaching modules or adding study of additional concepts or skills, and so on. Once the process is underway, you may find it necessary to alter the plan. If so, that is acceptable, assuming the decisions are arrived at jointly and in writing (e.g., you design a new schedule and progress chart).

For College Course Instructors

Level. We have offered comparable courses at the advanced undergraduate (usually for honors students) and masters and/or doctoral-level students, after they have completed at least some basic coursework in the concepts and methods of applied behavior analysis.

Group Size and Time Allotment. If you are a college instructor coordinating a group field practicum as a formal course assignment, we recommend you limit the *size of your group* to no more than seven or eight. Depending on the actual number of course participants, the qualifications, skills, and willingness and available time of participating field supervisors, if you are to meet the responsibilities demanded by this program, you will want to budget the amount of time you usually would when teaching a three-semester-credit college seminar for each of two semesters or three quarters. Typically, we have found ourselves spending about 1–2 hours per ABA student per week. This, of course, varies as a function of your students' levels of skills and commitment.

Credits. College, program and student schedules vary considerably, as do licensing and certification requirements. While the model presented here was designed to describe a two-semester or three quarter field experience, credits can be modified by adjusting the workload. For instance, students may wish a full time placement, in which case they might double up on assignments, or on the number of students with whom they work or the hours they assist other personnel in ABA-related activities.

Other Reinforcers for Yourself and Your Supervisees. If you are a qualified supervisor, according to *Behavior Analysis Certification Board* guidelines, your trainees probably should be able to use their completion of this programmed sequence to fulfill a portion of the *supervised field experience* requirement. Also, depending on your own qualifications (e.g., a doctorate), it might be possible to negotiate an adjunct appointment for yourself at a local college or university to deliver the program as a course for credit. Alternatively, perhaps you could investigate opportunities and conditions for awarding *continuing education credits* for those of your staff already certified as Associate or fully Board Certified Behavior Analysts. Again, check the BACB website.

Adjusting Assignments. Possibly this is a student's first major field experience. Other trainees may be employed in their practicum settings; or are parents working at home with their children. In such cases, some assignments will be irrelevant or unnecessary for specific people. Then you should feel free to alter their assignments as outlined in Unit 1, and excuse them from the requirements related to locating and becoming familiar with the organization.

Schedule. You may wish to use the schedule of assignments included in the *Week 1 Introduction* as presented, especially if you are working with distance learners. For instance, in that version, we allowed time for students to locate a site and local "Field Facilitator." If your trainee currently is associated with an intact ASD (autism spectrum disorder) educational program, though, those assignments should not be necessary. Also, learners' backgrounds and program schedules vary from one to another. So, if appropriate, modify dates and assignments accordingly. In such instances, use our schedule as an illustrative model for your own version.

Site-based Supervision. Field practicum trainees often are good candidates for subsequent employment at their practicum sites. Consequently, attracting qualified and enthusiastic students and helping them hone their applied skills in ways consonant with local circumstances can be advantageous for a program. Undoubtedly, though, assignments and schedules will need to be adjusted to complement those of the program.

Who Is the "Field Facilitator?"

The field facilitator is a person willing to host practicum students, but who has yet to acquire advanced skills in behavior analysis. Field facilitators perform a vital role as host and local mentor. More specifically, after initial contacts are made between the site administrator and practicum student, and with his or her own training-program supervisor's agreement that s/he may take the time to perform this function (about an hour a week), the "field facilitator":

- welcomes and orients the practicum student to the site and its program
- aids him or her to identify and become well acquainted with a student on the autism spectrum by locating instructional space and material, sharing records and other background information, facilitating live observations and video recording (under strict conditions of confidentiality)
- assists and agrees to the selection of an instructional objective for the selected child
- reviews local site standards of acceptable professional performance with the practicum student
- assesses the field-practicum student's professional performance twice during the semester
- interacts with the practicum supervisor, who may well be operating at a distance from the training institution

The Field Facilitator is *not* expected to be a subject matter or application expert or trainer in behavior analysis. That is the function played by trained local supervisors or the course instructor.

If no university-based supervisors are available in the locale, one alternative is to enlist qualified site-based program personnel as supervisors. Program personnel with advanced degrees in applied behavior analysis, adjunct college faculty or *Certified Applied Behavior Analysts* may serve in the role of instructor/field supervisor. Another option is to identify staff members who lack advanced ABA skills to serve as "Field Facilitators" (see box containing information about the field facilitator). Additionally, these supervisors or instructors need to contract in advance with their own managers if they are to invest a portion of their time on the job in this activity.

Grading/Evaluating Performance. The grading system we illustrate in this manual is founded on the concept of mastery learning. Regardless of the content, coverage and sequence you design, we strongly encourage you to adopt a system that makes student progress dependent on matching standards of excellence at each step along the way. Sometime this means a student falls short of completing the sequence within the designated period. In such cases, we have assigned an *incomplete*, until all standards have been met. Although apparently we prefer requiring skill mastery for a system of personnel preparation of this sort, your circumstances may demand a different approach. In that case, you may need to adjust your assessment scheme to meet your own local situation.

For Distance Instructors

If you are teaching this practicum from a distance, the internet will allow you to many options. You can review all of your students' products, including assignments and video recordings and transmissions, interact with them individually, as well as within a group format by means a discussion board or other group distance-communication program. Probably it would be difficult for you to assist your students to affiliate with a program, though, and you may not be available to supervise them on-site in real time. The concept of the *field facilitator* has been designed to overcome the obstacles posed by such a situation. The field facilitator does not require your level of expertise in applied behavior analysis but does accept responsibility for monitoring and managing the practicum students' professional conduct on-site, and for guiding and supporting them through the logistic mazes they may encounter. As a distance instructor, *you will need to contact each of your student's field facilitators early in the sequence to express your appreciation for their willingness to help, and afterwards, maintain contact with them at least on a social level several times during the semester.*

In-service Instruction

Many organizations providing educational services to clients on the autism spectrum hire personnel to perform at different levels of skill and responsibility. Some, for instance, may be employed as "shadows" or aides; others as classroom or specialized teachers, possibly licensed, or increasingly, Board Certified (or Board Certified Associate) Applied Behavior Analysts. As suggested above, with some minor adjustments in the nature and scheduling of assignments, you may use this manual as an in-service training tool to develop or hone the skills of regularly employed staff. For example, it has been suggested to us that therapists with fairly good experience in following programs but who generally lack foundation skills might gain by learning some of the underpinnings of the work they do. Also, the experience might be useful for personnel needing background work to prepare for graduate school or for personnel who hope to become qualified to supervise others.

Use of the Material

This manual is designed to serve as the main resource for this field practicum experience. Its contents are proprietary. The authors and publisher do grant permission for you and your students to copy worksheets and forms for own personal use, but ***not the main text, without express written permission of the authors and publisher.***

Other Material Resources

Your students/trainees are asked to have access to video recording equipment and the means for transmitting video materials. They also may find it to their advantage to purchase a copy of the American Psychological Association's *Publication Manual*, to subscribe to one or more especially relevant journals in the field and/or to be supplied with access to a professional library.

Discussions

If you are responsible for preparing more than one field practicum student, we suggest you schedule time each week for either face-to-face or internet group discussions. (Otherwise meet individually with your single student.) Among other advantages, we have found that such group discussions provide students with a sense of belonging to a community of peers with shared experiences. Group members often exchange information about useful resources, are mutually supportive and gain valuable practice by communicating informally on this topic.

Mentoring

Just as the emphasis in this practicum material is to *shape* skillful performance through differential reinforcement, you should attempt to do the same interpersonally with your own practicum students. *Be generous with your use of positive feedback for performance excellence as well as for evidence of progress.* Limit *correcting* to serious situations, such as those posing potential danger to people or interference with programs. Be friendly and communicate on matters of mutual interest and concern. Serve as a resource person, assisting participants to locate papers, audio-visual materials and so on. Encourage them to do the same with their peers.

Video Recording

Throughout, students are asked to prepare a series of video recordings. The purposes are multiple: If yours is a distance-learning course, the videos can serve as a source of reliability by demonstrating that they have affiliated with a program, 2) are observing and working with a child, and 3) are attempting to implement the instruction they have selected/designed. They also provide you and the ABA student with opportunities to observe and help shape their own progress and may even informally display growth on the part of their own students with ASD.

To avoid having this feature of the program becoming too time consuming for you, we ask your students to choose brief portions of the best examples of their teaching to share with you. If you see to it that they adhere to this guideline, they will teach themselves to detect their own improving performance, and you will have more opportunities to provide them with positive feedback. You should not necessarily assume that the clips validly represent *your* student's teaching at other times and places, nor *their* student's learning.

Additional Suggestions

 Notes about the topic at hand are distributed to instructors or supervisors throughout this manual. Some weeks you will feel like a juggler keeping many balls up in the air. *By reviewing the entire manual in advance and scheduling your time accordingly, you will avoid having to work under pressure.*

Consumer Satisfaction

College-based coordinators generally recognize that hosting students requires an investment of time from programs or families. Those hosts surely will appreciate periodically receiving personal notes or calls from you. It is a good idea to introduce yourselves in the beginning, and to thank them for their cooperation and support at the end of the semester. Such social niceties also should increase their willingness to invite other students to join them in the future or even increase the likelihood of your being considered as a job candidate. (We also ask similar practices of our students, as you will note, in the beginning, middle and end of the course.)

To Administrators, Trainers, Supervisors and/or Managers

The laws of behavior apply to everyone: typically developing children and those with special needs; adults in all walks of life; and even non-human animals. Everyone's behavior increases in rate when reliably followed by an event or item of current reinforcing value for the individual and it diminishes after a while when reinforcers are no longer forthcoming. When people experience particular combinations of consequences, they also learn when, where, why and how to respond or not.

A major portion of your role as a trainer/supervisor is to help bring out the best in the associates or parents you are advising or supporting. Using a behavior analytic approach will support your accomplishing this aim. In fact, considerable research has demonstrated this to be the case among a cross-section of the population: parents, teachers, production workers, human service, commercial and restaurant personnel, executives and scientists.[h,i] In other words, what works with children with autism also works with us and everyone else.

Assuming you already have had considerable experience in applying behavioral interventions directly with children, you may well be in the position of wanting to try out the model with a staff member, associate, aide, teacher, student specialist, parent, other adult (or even yourself). That is fine—and completely appropriate for the purposes of this course.

A Note to On-Site ABA Staff Trainers

If, as a qualified behavior analyst, developing ABA skills among your program's staff is one of your functions, you might:

1. Provide ongoing in-service training by reviewing basic ABA concepts with staff, preferably combined with assigned readings.

2. Use this field practicum guide as a basis for assisting staff to design and conduct their own ABA-based interventions.

An example would be a concept like the importance of identifying and using functional reinforcers. You could assign study questions and a reading from a book, such as Bondy & Sulzer-Azaroff's *The Pyramid Approach to Autism Education (2002)*,[j] have them demonstrate mastery of the concepts via a quiz or interview and then assign them to assess reinforcers for a particular student. They might then include that approach within the proposal contained in this guide and you could mentor as the process unfolds.

3. Manage the process on an ongoing basis by observing, recording data samples of teaching performance, supplying constructive feedback and reinforcing progress.

If you choose to take that route, basically all you will need to do is to make some adjustments in the assignments:

- Where you see the terms "child" or "student" or "child or student with autism," you will need to substitute another more appropriate to your situation: "parent," "teacher," "aide," etc.
- Some portions of assignments, such as most of the material on skill-training in Part One may not be applicable. In that case, just write *N/A* with a sentence or phrase explaining why.
- When in doubt about how to translate any specific assignment to accommodate your adult "client," contact your instructor.

---

[h] See the *Journal of Organizational Behavior Management* for numerous others. http://www.haworthpress.com/web/JOBM/
[i] Also see chapters on Organizational Behavior Management in J. Austin & J. E.Carr (eds.): (2000) *Handbook of Applied Behavior Analysis*. Reno Nevada: Context Press.
[j] Pyramid Educational Products, Newark, DE.

The flow diagram below summarizes the key steps in the practicum process.

Flow Diagram of ABA Field Internship Practicum Process

```
┌──────────────┐
│ Locate site  │
└──────┬───────┘
       ▼
┌──────────────────┐     ┌──────────────┐     ┌──────────────────┐     ┌──────────────┐
│ Identify field   │     │ Observe,     │     │ Arrange,         │     │ Negotiate    │
│ supervisor or    │ ──▶ │ assist in    │ ──▶ │ implement,       │ ──▶ │ own          │
│ facilitator;     │     │ program      │     │ demonstrate      │     │ student(s)   │
│ while honing     │     │              │     │ mastery of       │     │ for full     │
│ skills as a      │     │              │     │ competency-      │     │ behavior     │
│ team player      │     │              │     │ based checklists │     │ analytic     │
└──────────────────┘     └──────────────┘     └──────────────────┘     │ intervention │
                                                                        └──────────────┘
```

Locate site

Identify field supervisor or facilitator; while honing skills as a team player

Observe, assist in program

Arrange, implement, demonstrate mastery of competency-based checklists

Negotiate own student(s) for full behavior analytic intervention

Select objectives

Observe, analyze
- behavioral patterns
- contextual conditions
- other antecedents
- other consequences

Read literature

Design program

Choose Reliable Measures

Apply Intervention

Demonstrate fidelity of intervention

Under baseline & intervention: Observe, record, graph, analyze behavior

Submit weekly progress reports

Adjust program as needed

Prepare and present report

Applying Behavior Analysis Across the Autism Spectrum
A Field Guide for Practitioners in Training

Introduction

Unit One
Becoming Oriented to Your Field Setting

"Oh good! The meeting hasn't started yet," Rosa drops into one of the staff meeting- room chairs at the Walden School, mops her brow, and heaves a sigh of relief.

"What's happenin'?" Jeb inquires.

"A never-ending freight train—seemed like over a hundred cars. From here on in, I take the long way around, over the bridge—the way you suggested, Allie. Lucky you, living on this side of town."

Just then, Ginger, the Board Certified Behavior Analyst field coordinator, arrives. "Ah, you're all here. Great!" she smiles. "Since we toured the school together last week and met the teachers, behavior analysts and support personnel, today, I'd like to spend some time discussing your general impressions; answering whatever questions you have now and describing our plans for the semester in a little more detail. And, as mentioned last time, each of you will be assigned to particular students and begin the process of getting to know them better. So, your impressions, first?"

"Seems like a great place!" Jeb offered. "It's not the first time I've visited a school with kids on the autism spectrum. I expected to hear lots of noise—screeching, banging, teachers shouting and looking frazzled!"

"I agree," Allie added. "The first program I visited, scared me. Lots of the kids howling; teachers too. Made me wonder why I was considering working in this field. Here, it's different. So much more peaceful; and practically everyone's on task. I'm wondering why such a striking contrast? "

Ginger can't hold back a smile of satisfaction. "What do you guys think might be different here?"

Jeb raises his chin. "Couldn't be the way you guys run the program, by any chance, could it? Like applying behavior analytic principles and procedures and such?"

All chuckle; nodding their agreement. In assigning students to field sites, their ABA professor had mentioned they tried to match student interests with assignments to particular programs. Locations were selected from those in the region that best applied behavioral principles. He considered Walden one of the best.

"So, now for our reinforcers. Shall I begin by telling you mine?" Ginger offers.

Agreement all around.

"First of all, I volunteered to be coordinator of our ABA student interns because I know how much folks like you can contribute. Previous interns have helped out by assisting teachers in various ways and, eventually, by participating in and designing their own successful educational activities for our clientele. Sure, it does take some of my time and I worry a bit about maintaining our high standards, but when I think of how badly kids on the spectrum need the best available teaching practices if they are to move toward mainstream society, I feel as if these efforts just have to pay off in the long run."

"Now, how about you folks?"

"Well," Rosa volunteered, "as I mentioned last time, I have a cousin on the spectrum. She's eight years old now. By the time she was two and a half, my aunt and uncle were at their wits end; didn't know how to handle her tantrums;

thought she'd never learn to talk. Then after trying out a few, they finally found a program for her; one that looked like it would work out. At first they brought her tantrums under control by teaching her to communicate what she wanted and needed. Now, she can talk and is learning to read. They even took her to Disney World last summer. Seemed like a miracle to me. So, when I visited over spring break, they invited me to come along to her school. I asked the behavior analyst where she had gotten her training. She mentioned our program at the U. Long story, short—here I am! I'm guessing my reinforcers probably are fairly obvious—doing the most I can to help people, especially kids, to learn and achieve their best."

"And you, Jeb?"

"You know, I grew up in a tough neighborhood, with lots of bad stuff going on. Had a Grannie who was determined for me to succeed, though. She was smart; but she was tough. Read to me and told me stories until I got hooked on books. Took me places—museums, the library; got me into sports. 'You're going to make something of your life,' she told me over and over again. The coach of our neighborhood basketball team—he spent lots of extra time with me too, and said I'd make a good teacher or coach; the way I helped the younger kids learn to shoot and defend."

"So how did you get from coaching B-ball to ABA?" Rosa wondered.

"One of those kids I coached, I learned later on, was high-functioning autistic. His Mom kept thanking and thanking me for teaching her boy how to shoot baskets. Told me I had lots of patience. Then, in my junior year in college, in this course in ed. psych—you know—for my P.E. major, Prof showed me a few papers on behavior analysis and sports. Got me hooked!"

"Your turn, Allie," prompted Ginger.

"Ever since taking A.P. Psych in high school, I wanted to be a psych. major. By my senior year at the U., fortunately I was an honors student and because of that could register for the ABA graduate-level sequence. What appealed to me was the combination of science-based conceptual, analytic and applied aspects. Not only would I be able to learn that material, but would have hands-on practice in applying the principles based on behavioral science. Couldn't wait to 'get my hands wet!'"

"This conversation has been very helpful" Ginger observed. "Now that I know a little more about each of you, I think arranging your assignments will be easier."

Now it's your turn. Fill out form 1.1 and share the information about yourself with your field supervisor and any fellow ABA trainees.

Form 1.1

Field Participant Information

Your Name _____ Date _____

Contact information (email/postal address &/or phone) _____
_____

Program at which you are receiving (have received) your formal training in ABA:
_____

The stated purpose of your field assignment:
General goal(s) _____
_____

Specific objectives (if articulated):
_____
_____
_____
_____
_____
_____

Number of hours expected to participate on-site per week _____ Number of weeks _____

Your academic mentor's name and contact information _____
_____

Tell us something about your general background. _____
_____
_____
_____

What attracted you to the field of applied behavior analysis in the field of autism?
_____
_____

What would you like to learn about the clientele in this setting? _____
_____
_____
_____

What would you be interested in knowing about your field supervisor(s)? _____
_____
_____
_____

Say what you would be interested in learning about this organization and its other staff ?
(Or family and its members?) _____
_____
_____
_____

Form 1.1, page 2 of 2

Your Name _____

What would you be interested in knowing about fellow students on field assignment at this or other locations? _____
_____
_____
_____

Pose your questions in a group setting or privately with your field supervisor. Summarize and comment on your findings.
_____
_____
_____
_____
_____
_____
_____
_____

Search, discover and summarize the answers to your questions by asking your field supervisor and others at the setting. _____
_____
_____

a) Ask you field supervisor to review his or her expectations of your performance at this field site.
b) List these here or attach a "contract"
_____
_____
_____
_____
_____
_____

After being briefed by your field supervisor as to his/her expectations of you, what further questions do you have? _____
_____

On request, *submit copies of this completed form to your training program supervisor, and/or field supervisor. Save a copy for yourself in a folder dedicated for this purpose.*

Accomplishing Client Assignments

"Jeb, I think we've got the assignment for you—the nine to ten-year-olds. I'm thinking how that group has a few students you'll enjoy working with. One's a small guy, Scott—fairly high functioning for our population, and he seems to really enjoy physical activities. He's good at them; but put Scott in with a group of peers and he's lost. Team play is well beyond him, because he lacks the necessary social skills, like gaining entry into a group, taking turns, accepting and acting on suggestions from the teacher or Herb, our P.E. specialist."

"All right! I've got my group!"

"Great! Assuming his teacher, Polly and coach agree, you probably will be able to begin by assisting with discrete trial teaching in the classroom and during group games and coaching sessions."

"Yeah! Right on."

"So Rosa—we can really use some help with the younger kids—four and five-year-olds. Some are verbal; others aren't. You'd probably be helping out with various incidental and discrete trial teaching, along with other class activities. How does that sound to you?"

"Pretty much as I'd expected—and hoped. I know that reading about and mastering the descriptions of behavioral procedures is hardly the same as actually practicing them; and I can't wait to try them out."

"And, Allie, you voiced particular interest in functional assessments and verbal behavior. So I think we have just the group for you. It's a small class, including some youngsters with challenging behaviors. Their verbal skills are limited, though they're improving, and some occasionally flip out, especially when they can't get what they want fast enough. They'll teach you what you hope to learn know about behavioral functions, and then some."

Complete Form 1.2 now. While adhering to the ethical guidelines, as set out by your professional organization, share the information about your field assignment with your academic supervisor and your fellow field practicum students. Remember, though, otherwise to respect your client's and associates' rights to privacy, along with those of the personnel at your field site. When sharing information with your fellow students at other locations, rather than using actual client or staff names outside of the field setting—use a pseudonym instead.

That task completed, Ginger describes the way they will proceed.

"So now, you have your schedules and assignments. Here is a packet of materials for each of you."

She then distributes a set of materials containing performance expectations for field practicum students like themselves (see below). Included are an overview, policy statement and procedures for field practitioners to follow. Also various forms: standard (Table 1.2) or alternate (Table 1.2 alt) unit by unit assignments and recording forms, an individual contract form for those wishing to modify the suggested schedule (form 1.3 standard and alternative progress charts (Tables 1.4 and 1.4 alt),and a list of the professional skills they will be expected to practice (Table 1.6).

Form 1.2

(*Please share this completed form with your academic supervisor and with your field supervisor*)

Your Name_____ Date _____

Your own contact information (address, email and/or phone)
_____
_____

Your academic supervisor's contact information (name, email and/or phone)
_____
_____

Name and mailing address of field placement
_____
_____
_____

Name and contact information for your field supervisor
_____
_____

Please add any questions and/or concerns below:
_____
_____
_____
_____
_____
_____

Field Practicum Overview and Policies

So, welcome to a new experience as you enrich your capabilities as a teacher of or service provider for children with autism. While typical field experiences are defined by the number of hours participants spend at a site, this manual provides you with something much more specific: a carefully programmed sequence of activities related to the application of behavior analysis to the teaching of children with a diagnosis of ASD. By progressing satisfactorily through this sequence of activities, you will markedly enhance your ability to apply behavior analysis (ABA). As you know, ABA has been demonstrated to be effective in thousands of single-case studies and the sole approach found through controlled field trials, to outperform others with this population (e.g., Cohen, Amerine-Dickens, & Smith, 2006; Lovaas, 1987. Please also refer to our reference section at the end of Part 1, for the evidence base for each of the foundational competencies we include). To discover for yourselves, do join us on this exciting journey. Thrilling discoveries and accomplishments await you along the way!

Your Reinforcers

You may well be participating in these field activities to meet the eligibility requirements for taking a behavior analyst certification examination, to receive course credit or meet the requirements for a degree or specialty certification, and/or to be able to obtain a letter of recommendation for a job or admission into a graduate training program. But we presume you are pursuing an even more important reinforcer: to become more proficient in applying behavioral interventions with youngsters with autism.

Purpose

Our main purpose in assembling this *Practicum Guide* is to help satisfy the huge global need for personnel and family members capable of applying behavior analysis (behavioral interventions) intensively and skillfully with youngsters on the autism spectrum. We have designed the *content* of this sequence of practicum activities to teach you not only *how* to apply behavior analytic (ABA) procedures and principles, and have also incorporated ABA-based methods in our own design of the assignments.

What does that mean? Experiential field practicum placements often are loosely structured and operate on the assumption that following the lead of a skilled mentor is a sufficient field experience. By contrast, we have elected to program *what* we teach and *how* we teach it; that is, according to solid principles of operant learning. And we enable you and your supervisors or instructors to monitor and guide your performance with detailed feedback and reinforcement along the way. Each step in the process is carefully designed to promote success—your own and the student(s) you yourself are teaching during this experience.

We assume you will be working on-site or possibly from a distance, under the supervision of a Board Certified Behavior Analyst,[1] or someone with at least equivalent credentials. If necessary, you also may be asked to identify someone at your practicum site to serve as your "field facilitator," who will support your efforts on location. (The role of the field facilitator is described in detail later on.)

General Participant Skills

Assuming you already have a solid background in applied behavior analytic *concepts and principles (i.e., can **say** or recite ABA principles and rules),* we have designed this field experience to help you gain an extensive set of actual *skills; that is, you will be able to **do** applied behavior analysis.).* Included are locating and becoming acclimated to your new field practicum surroundings and using tools to help make you feel welcome and remain appreciated by your host organizations. In Part 1, you will learn foundational behavioral intervention skills by implementing pre-programmed, competency-based instructional modules, and your progress will be verified via competency-based checklists. These skills include the basics of discrete trial intervention, incidental teaching, prompting and prompt fading, incorporating choice and preference, task-analyzed training, and running written programs.

In Part 2, you are asked to identify and teach a youngster on the autism spectrum to achieve one or more objectives closely aligned with his or her *individual educational* or *family service plan (IEP or IFSP).* Then you will draw upon your prior knowledge of behavior analytic concepts, principles and methods and on current research findings to program, implement and document the steps you and your student(s) are to take toward achieving those objectives. This will include a wide range of ABA skills: among others, assessing behavior and the environment, observing, instructing, recording via paper and pencil and video, graphing, analyzing, and communicating the results you obtain.

---

[1] If you have difficulty locating a skilled supervisor, you might seek local or distant university faculty teaching ABA or refer to the Behavior Analyst Certification Board (www.bacb.com) for lists of Certified Behavior Analysts in your region. At this printing, the number of *supervised field experience* hours required of a candidate to be eligible to sit for the certification examination is half of that required for candidates whose experience was simply *mentored*.

What Is the Role of Your Instructor or Supervisor?

Your (usually academic) instructor/supervisor probably is confident that you possess considerable prerequisite knowledge; that you can *talk the talk* of ABA. At this point his or her job is to guide and support you as you *walk the walk*, by:

- Serving as a resource person, guiding you to locate and consume relevant research literature.
- Monitoring and providing feedback and differential reinforcement on your progress through the steps in this program
- Stimulating and directing you toward undertaking challenging—yet achievable—goals.
- Coaching you as you progress with your students toward those goals through judicious combinations of positive feedback, reinforcement and minimal prompting.
- Encouraging you to interact productively with your peers, either by scheduling regular face-to-face group meetings or distance internet discussions.
- Developing a supportive and understanding mentor relationship with you, while allowing you to progress from one step to the next on the basis of high quality performance.
- Assigning and reporting your grade, if applicable, to your academic program.

How This Manual Is Designed to Work

Given that the content of this manual is intended to be *flexible*, you probably will participate in a good many of the following activities:

Attending and Participating in Meetings. If there are several members in your field experience group, we trust you will assemble weekly for group discussions, either with your common academic advisor and/or your local practice supervisor. You also will need to meet individually with your supervisor (in-person or over the internet), preferably weekly, or at a minimum, bi-weekly, for a specified minimal amount of time. (Refer to current BCBA Guidelines).

Assignments. This may or may not be your first practicum experience. Perhaps you are employed in your practicum settings; or maybe you are a parent working with your child at home. Consequently, some assignments will be irrelevant or unnecessary for you. If you believe that to be the case, discuss with your supervisor the possibility of being excused from those particular requirements. If you have an interest in becoming certified as a behavior analyst, please also be certain to review current guidelines to determine any restrictions related to the client you select for your field experience, number of hours participating, and other specifics.

Schedule. The assignment schedule included in the first unit is suggested, not carved in stone. Because program schedules may vary from one to another, you might, if appropriate, arrange with your instructor/supervisor to alter assignments, completion due dates and so on. Assuming your supervisor agrees, you also may decide either to modify our suggested schedule or to develop one of your own.

Grading. We believe you should be permitted to progress only when each step you take along the way matches objective standards of excellence. That being the case, if you are enrolled in a credit-bearing course, you may not be able to complete the sequence within a single academic year. If this happens in your case, your supervisor/instructor, at his or her discretion, may decide to award you an *incomplete* until you have met all pre-set required performance standards.

Materials. **This manual is proprietary and the main text may not be reproduced without the author's and publisher's permission.** You should feel free, however, to copy worksheets and forms (which are available on the publisher's website at www.sloanpublishing.com/sulzer) for your own personal use.

Discussions. As mentioned earlier, try, if possible, to participate in a discussion group with the others enrolled in your practicum group. That should enrich your experience by supplying you with a sense of belonging to a community of peers, and allowing you to share resources, exchange experiences, and practice communicating informally on topics of relevance.

Remember, though, unless you have been granted written parental and teacher permission to do so, to avoid identifying your students by name or displaying their images during your discussions with your fellow students. Just as our ABA student trainees and Ginger, the Walden School coordinator, are becoming better acquainted, before going any further, you should introduce *yourself* to your own field supervisor and any other ABA trainees assigned to your field facility. Rest assured, you have a lot in common with one another. *First,* obviously you have arrived at this point inspired with a passion for teaching and supporting the progress of students with autism and related conditions. Although your work demands intense energy, patience, and consistent, skillful practice, you also appreciate its rewards: seeing your students reach their current personal-best levels of functioning. You also realize that your students' progress can impact positively on the lives of their classmates, teachers, families and the members of their communities.

Second, we assume you have demonstrated your mastery of didactic coursework content by scoring very well on quizzes and examinations covering a set of well-established behavior analytic concepts, including principles and rules of practice relating to effectively and ethically educate students with autism. A partial list of these includes:

1. identifying students' learning needs
2. specifying constructive instructional objectives, especially those pivotal to more efficient learning
3. choosing and using behavioral measures
4. graphing results
5. defining and describing a set of basic behavior-change concepts, principles and methods, including:
   a) reinforcement
   b) differential reinforcement
   c) shaping
   d) prompting
   e) fading
   f) extinction
   g) punishment*
6. graphing results
7. analyzing the function of specific patterns of behavior and the contexts that affect them
8. stating rules and guidelines for designing and/or selecting behavioral-instructional plans, including those founded on discrete trial, incidental and other formal and naturalistic teaching methods
9. explain and provide examples of reinforcer-based behavior-change procedures to enable students to:
   a) increase rates of a behavior, especially concentrating on student engagement in simple and complex academic, verbal, social, recreational, self-care and other classes of behavior
   b) acquire new and more complex behaviors
   c) broaden or narrow the conditions under which the behavior of concern is to occur
10. recording, graphing and analyzing data
11. continuing or altering methods based on the results of data analysis

Third, you recognize the importance of conducting yourself in a professional manner, including understanding and *consistently adhering to established ethical standards.*[2] Meeting ethical standards can seem daunting, but for many of us, they parallel rules we follow in other facets of life. By striving toward excellence in your work (among others, adhering to schedules, preparing adequately, completing written work according to professional standards of grammar, punctuation and spelling, submitting it in a timely fashion, keeping current with progress in the field through continuing education, reading professional journals, being active in national and local organizations, and collaborating productively with associates, parents and professionals), you show you are well on your way toward meeting these standards.

---

* A familiarity with the concept of punishment, how it works, and its side effects is essential for anyone functioning in the role of an applied behavior analyst. Because strongly coercive methods can engender undesirable spin-offs and require numerous *ethical* safeguards, though, we suggest new practitioners practice analyzing the *function(s)* of unwanted behaviors instead (which we plan to teach you to do under professional guidance in a field manual on the topic currently in preparation) and then teach new alternative (often communicative) behaviors to enable that student to use more pro-social ways to gain those reinforcers.

[2] See the *Behavior Analyst Certification Board Guidelines for Responsible Conduct For Behavior Analysts*© http://www.bacb.com

Lest you panic, we DO NOT assume you are thoroughly skillful in behavior analytic *applications*, just that you know an extensive set of rules *related to* applying behavior analysis. You probably have not formally practiced, designed, conducted, and monitored full ABA programs under the expert supervision of a credentialed behavior analyst. That is the main purpose of *this* experience, which is to guide your actual *application of* behavior analytic practices and methods with students on the autism spectrum. Among many other activities in **Part 1** of this program, you will:

- Review the components of high-quality professional conduct
- Observe one or more students with ASD in action
- Implement foundational intervention competencies, including
  - Incorporating preference and choice
  - Discrete trial interventions
  - Training of functional skills sequences
  - Prompting and prompt fading techniques
  - Incidental teaching

Then, in **Part 2, you will**
- Record and analyze the functions of some of those student's behaviors
- Identify meaningful instructional goals and objectives
- Select and use live and/or DVD recording methods
- Familiarize yourself with state-of-the-art research related to what you hope to teach
- Design, apply, monitor, and at least partially analyze and communicate in writing the effectiveness of your own instructional sequence

Perhaps you want to know something about those of us who are guiding you. We who have prepared these activities are a team of ABA specialists who share your passion for this field: experienced teachers, communication specialists, curriculum designers and developers, researchers, and behavior change agents. We are convinced that scientifically derived behavioral principles and methods apply not only to students with autism spectrum disorder (ASD), but are fundamental to shaping the way all of us behave. If you remain vigilant during your supervised passage through this material, you will see many instances in which we apply behavior analytic principles such as differential reinforcement, shaping, chaining, prompt fading, and many others. Now, let us focus on the specific objectives of this program more precisely.

The Purpose and Objectives of This Program

You now recognize that beyond mastering the ability to "talk the talk" of applied behavior analysis, you need, to learn skillfully, through hands-on experience, to "walk the walk" as a behavior analyst. *Your practice should be supervised by a qualified behavior analyst, thereby helping to assure your conformance with behavior analytic principles, ethical standards, and exemplary rules of professional conduct.* With the help of your instructor and/or supervisor, upon the successful conclusion of the program, you will have demonstrated your ability to:

- arrange your practicum site, if necessary, by making contact with and planning to participate at a field practicum site in which applied behavior analytic practices are used to serve people on the autism spectrum. (See Table 1.1 for roles and functions of participants.)
- obtain local, or, if necessary, long-distance assistance if your supervisor or instructor is not on-site, by identifying and enlisting the help of a behavior-analytic friendly individual who is regularly available to act as your *field supervisor or field facilitator*
- become familiar with the nature of the site program by observing and analyzing its operation
- identify your students(s) by obtaining permission to work with one (or more)
- learn about your students' histories and challenges by:
  - reviewing their records
  - investigating the contingencies influencing their behavior
  - observing and analyzing their behavioral patterns, along with the contextual conditions and other transitory and durable antecedent events and consequences affecting them
- in collaboration with the teacher, choose and use the series of pre-programmed materials included in this manual (Part 1) to practice teaching toward particular instructional objectives

- in collaboration with the teacher and your ABA supervisor, choose new appropriate educational objectives for a particular student(s): (Part 2 of this manual)
- become better prepared effectively to teach toward specific objective(s) by familiarizing yourself with published literature relevant to those objectives.
- given appropriate permissions, promote your student's attainment of the selected new objective(s) and design or choose a promising ABA intervention program to apply
- assess students' progress by choosing valid and reliable measures of the behavior(s) of interest.
- maintain the integrity with which you implement the procedures.
- after assessing baseline performance, promote your students' progress toward the chosen objective(s) by applying your intervention.
- assess the impact of your intervention(s) by observing, recording, graphing and analyzing the behavior(s) of interest under baseline and intervention conditions.
- maintain your instructional activities as planned.
- optimize the power of your intervention(s) by preparing and submitting weekly progress reports to your supervisor.
- with input from your supervisor, carefully plan promising data-based adjustments to the program.
- begin your program report by preparing a written *preliminary draft,* including research-based rationales for choosing the objectives and methods, results, and a discussion and conclusion, including future recommendations.
- place a record of your program in the student's portfolio.
- prepare a final report.
- inform the student's team and/or your classmates, as appropriate, by presenting an oral presentation of your teaching program and its results.
- hone your skills as a team player by following through with your responsibilities, being supportive as you collaborate and communicate with your fellow students, and responsive to comments and suggestions during interactions with your supervisor and/or field facilitator, teachers, parents and your instructor.
- in general, to be able to use applied behavior analytic strategies to monitor and promote students' progress toward selected objectives, you will commit to investing a particular minimum number of hours per week[3] working under the direction of your *instructor* or *supervisor[4],* with input from your field facilitator and other site personnel (if applicable).

Formalizing Roles and Functions of Participants

In this kind of activity, all participants must clearly understand their obligations and one another's expectations. You need to see to it that you and your site hosts (*site facilitator, supervisor,* and/or *host teacher/teaching parent*) complete several forms covering your respective roles and responsibilities within the first week or two of your practicum.

---

[3]If becoming certified as a Board Certified Behavior Analyst (BCBA) or Board Certified Associate Behavior Analyst (BCABA) is your goal, we suggest you check *http://www.BACB.com* for definitions and current requirements and guidelines. If you are registered as a student in a formal university course, you and your instructor need to arrange the number of hours you will spend on-site, the schedule and nature of your supervision, and the number of credits you should receive contingent on satisfactory performance.

[4]**Supervisors or instructors** probably will plan additional hours for trainees to devote to outside preparation, group discussions and other activities. Below, we provide more detailed information on the course objectives, equipment, materials, activities and assignments. Further s*uggestions* are included in the Preface and as *footnotes.* We suggest you remind your students/trainees to take note of and follow relevant footnote guidelines.

Your Role as a Participant

Specifically, you will need immediately to:
1. provide your instructor[5] or supervisor with a copy of the materials related to the expectations related to your functioning.
2. arrange a follow-up meeting right away with your on-site supervisor or facilitator. During the meeting, emphasize that as a participating trainee you are there to learn, and when called upon, to be helpful. You are not there to judge the program or any of its features.
3. Then clarify:
   - Your role as practicum participant.
   - The role of the instructor or supervisor with whom you will work, including the form of supervision (group or individual).
   - The role played by the supervisor or facilitator in the program: teacher, aide, and/or parent(s), and their ability and willingness to comply with the requirements needed to enable your successful completion of this experience.
   - The kinds of general information you will collect and the types of behavioral data and recordings you anticipate gathering
   - What you are hoping to learn by working with the facilitator.
   - Any mutual advantages to cooperating person(s) during and at the end of the semester.
   - Your own anticipated contributions to the process.

In the event you have *advanced experience* in applying behavioral interventions with children, or occupy a senior position in your organization, you may negotiate with your instructor and field supervisor to alter some of the requirements for this sequence or you may prefer to apply this model with a staff member, associate, aide, teacher, student specialist, parent, or other adult (or even yourself) as your client. That is fine, and completely appropriate for purposes of this practicum.

If you choose to work with an associate or parent, you will need to make some adjustments in the assignments, including:
   - Substituting appropriate labels for your participants (instead of *child*, another more appropriate term, such as *parent, teacher, aide*, etc.).
   - Omitting all or portions of assignments not applicable to your situation. In such instances, enter *N/A,* and add an explanatory sentence or phrase.
   - When in doubt about how to adjust specific assignments to suit your adult learner, contact your supervisor or instructor.

The Instructor-Supervisor's Role

By monitoring your progress and helping to shape your evolving skills, your supervisor or instructor supports your developing competence as an applied behavior analyst. Assuming you submit your completed assignments on schedule, s/he should review each as quickly as possible and return it to you with constructive commentary. S/he may ask you to revise and resubmit your assignments until they match standards of acceptability. (More will be said about this in the *Performance Assessment and Grading* section.) Supervisors and instructors are expected to practice what ABA preaches, so it is reasonable for you to count on them to reinforce your progress. In most cases, careful preparation and adherence to guidelines will keep requested revisions to a minimum. Instructors also will follow similar practices when reviewing the visual material you submit throughout the course.

---

[5]Instructors of field practica, who are assigning these materials to 3 or more students, may request examination copies from the publisher.

Table 1.1 Summary of Roles and Functions of Participants

Role	Person	Function
Field Practicum Student/trainee	You, the student enrolled in this course or in-service training program.	Having previously mastered a broad range of *applied behavior analytic* (ABA) concepts, you will complete the activities contained in this field practicum guide at levels acceptable to your instructor.
Field Practicum Instructor[6]	A qualified individual with expertise in teaching and/or in-service training of personnel in behavioral interventions in autism.	Selects curriculum, guides, serves as a distance or on-site instructor, resource person and evaluator of your performance and products. May also act as an on-site or distance *Supervisor*.
Field Practicum supervisor	A person with expertise in serving clients on the autism spectrum and skill in supervising students and/or on-site personnel.	Observes practicum student's performance either directly on-site or electronically from a distance, coaches and supplies performance feedback. May also serve as *Instructor*.
Field Facilitator	An individual, who may or may not have expertise in ABA, but is involved directly with students with autism at the site: a lead teacher, program manager, care provider, parent or other.	In the absence of an on-site behavior analyst to supervise the student, supports and enables the behavior analysis student to fulfill practicum requirements. Cooperates with Instructor, if student enrolled in a course, and assesses the behavior analysis student's professional conduct.
Student or Field Practicum Student	The child or adult client with a diagnosis of autism spectrum disorder or related condition.	Learns and progresses as a function of the supervised actions of the practicum student.

Assignment Summary and Schedule

The standard program is designed to span an academic year.[7] After familiarizing themselves with their field sites, practicum students are expected to complete the basic set of pre-programmed, validated assessment and instructional programs with assigned client-students. These assignments should be satisfactorily completed within ten to 15 weeks, with mastery of the skills demonstrated by meeting the stated criterion standards for each one.

---

[6] We assume instructors and supervisors are skilled in applying behavior analysis among students on the autism spectrum or other special difficulties and preferably they are credentialed as Board Certified Behavior Analysts (BCBAs or BCBA-D's) through the Behavior Analysis Certification Board (http://www.bacb.com). *Instructors* arrange in advance with students and their higher education programs the number of course credits to award, and the approximate amount of time to be spent working on site per week. We have found the amount of time the supervising instructor spends each week per trainee can take from about 3 to 8 hours, depending on the number of credits for which the student has registered, student entering skills and specific assignments, including reading work submissions, providing positive, supportive, constructive feedback, reading and commenting on re-submissions until they reach standards of acceptability, posing discussion topics either during weekly team meetings or internet discussion boards, responding to new topics posed by group members, and sharing resources, current events and materials in the field. *Supervisors* regularly observe the field student in action in real time or via recorded DVD images or tapes and/or by visiting on-site bi-weekly, coaching by providing supportive, constructive feedback as merited.

[7] **Supervisors/instructors**: Depending on your situation, the suggested schedule can be rearranged.

Each set of assignments includes one or more of the following:

- Assisting at the site
- Assessing student performance
- Assessing own performance
- Assessing the environment
- Implementing particular teaching protocols toward pre-specified levels of mastery
- Interviewing
- Observing
- Analyzing results of observations
- Reviewing records
- Conducting library research

- Participating in discussions with other students and your instructor
- Arranging instructional environments
- Collecting data
- Graphing data
- Teaching skills
- Analyzing data
- Revising teaching or management practices
- Other activities integral to effective practice of ABA in field settings

Initially you will complete various forms documenting your arrangements for this experience. Included are permissions and consent agreements. Then, during the first quarter or semester, after familiarizing yourself with your fellow students, colleagues, supervisors, and specialized personnel, you prepare to and implement a set of assessment and instructional programs until you achieve pre-set mastery levels.

During the second quarter or semester, after completing that basic series of assessment and intervention activities, you then will choose an ABA goal for a particular student (or other client) and begin to design your own assessment and intervention program. That program will be directed toward enabling the client to achieve a particular instructional or behavioral objective. Once you have had ample time to implement, evaluate and, if necessary, revise and teach or re-teach toward your objective, you will be asked to complete both a *Preliminary* and a *Final Project Report*. Those reports will contain a comprehensive description of the data-based teaching project you conducted with each of your students. Evaluations of those reports combined with your field supervisor's or facilitator's ratings of your professional conduct on-site will contribute to your overall performance evaluation.

The *Unit-by-Unit Schedule of Activities and Responsibilities* (*Table 1.2*) lists each of those suggested activities. You need to complete each set by the designated week. Your supervisor/instructor then will review your products and provide constructive, timely feedback.[8] If others are participating in the field experience, also allot about an hour a week to face-to-face or distant team discussions. We include suggested weekly topics, though your instructor/supervisor or teammates may introduce or substitute others. (The blank *Alternate Table 1.2* may be used as a basis for preparing that modified format.) Finally, periodically you will encounter an occasional *tutorial*, designed to refresh or amplify your prior knowledge or skill set.

Adjusting Particulars of This Course to Your Individual Circumstances

Most participants will progress in the standard way, by completing one set of programmed assignments per week. Individual circumstances, though, may require alternative schedules. This depends on your situation and the nature of the assignments. If you are employed at the field site or perhaps teaching your own or someone else's child at home, some of the early assignments and forms (such as finalizing your site location) will not be relevant. *We suggest you discuss and formalize your altered schedule with your instructor or supervisor before moving on.* S/he may assign some supplementary work or automatically award you credit, allowing you just to move on to the next relevant assignment. (See the individual contract form, *Form 1.3.*) If relevant, you still should join your group or classmates and instructor in weekly discussions of scheduled topics.

---

[8]**Instructors; supervisors:** The material in this text was designed and field tested with students taught and supervised under both traditional practicum conditions as well as from a distance over the Internet. *By familiarizing yourself with the manual's content in advance, you will be able to decide which, if any assignment, scheduling, or grading policies you may wish to adjust. We strongly suggest you schedule time during each unit to review student materials and provide timely, heavily positive, and constructive feedback.*

Recording Your Progress

Students usually find it reinforcing to keep track of their progress. Refer to the *progress charts, Tables 1.4 and 1.5* (or an altered set of charts, prepared in agreement with your instructor and/or supervisor) to see an easy way to do this. Each time you complete an assignment, simply fill in (or X) the boxes next to that assignment and above the week indicating how far you are into the course. You should see the darkened boxes forming an upward pattern of accomplishment. We have outlined each box according to its suggested due date. But you can move more rapidly. Getting ahead of that "rate line" or pattern will be to your advantage. As an added "motivator," you may wish to copy the chart on heavy paper and post it in a place you will view daily, such as the refrigerator door or on the bathroom mirror.

About Professionalism

Treating people with autism generally is a team effort, with all members sharing a common interest in seeing the student succeed. Within the ABA field, though, different paths may or may not lead toward the same destination. To avoid working at cross-purposes, we urge you to choose a common course of action, one firmly based on *hard scientific evidence.*

If you are working with team members who are unsophisticated in applying behavior analytic methods, you have a real opportunity to set a good example. Remember, though, to respect and learn from the others' experiences and in general to earn and retain their mutual trust and respect by checking first and then doing what you can to help. Skills we consider especially important in this area are listed in Table 1.5, *Professional Skills to Be Assessed by Your Field Facilitator.* To support your progress here, if applicable, your on-site supervisor or field facilitator is asked to rate your performance as a professional at least twice: during and/or following your completion of Segment One (pre-programmed instruction) and during and/or at the end of the year. In preparation we suggest you:

1. Review the skills contained in this list.
2. *During the first week of the practicum,* give that individual a copy of the list to cue which performances they will be asked to look for and assess during Units 8 and 15 in Part 1 of the practicum, and Units 21 and 28 during Part 2 of the practicum.

Table 1.2. Unit-by-Unit Pre-programmed Activities and Assignments PART 1
Suggested Schedule of Activities

Indicate your Unit by Unit Assignments. Also budget at least 1 hour per unit for *discussions;* from 1-4 hours for *tutorials.*

Activity #	Abbreviated Title of Activity	Form	Abbreviated Title of Form	Time Estimate (in hours)
1.1	Pacing Adjustment (optional)	1.1	Individual Contract	0–1
2.1	Finalizing Arrangements	2.1	Contact information	0–10
2.2	Acquainted; Agreements	2.2,.3, 4	Field Facilitator, Instructor Agreements	0–10
2.3	Description Field or Home Setting	2.5, .6	Description: Setting	2
2.4	Recording and submitting DVD	2.7, 2.8, 2.9	Parent, Admin. DVD consents, Cover Sheet	2–4
3.1	Observe use of preference assessment	3.1	Guided Observation 1: Preference	1
3.2	Assisting Teachers	3.2		
3.3	Preference Assessment Checklist	3.3, 3.4	Preference Assessment Checklist, Preference Scoring Form	2–4
4.1	Social Responsiveness checklist	4.1, 4.2	Social Responsiveness Data Form, Social Responsiveness Checklist	1–3
4.2	Observe discrete trial training and prompting	4.2	Guided Observation 2: DTI and Prompt	1–3
5.1	Collect student response data	5.1	Collecting student response data	2
5.2	Discrete trial training checklist	5.2	Discrete trial checklist	1–2
5.3	Observing prompts across the day	5.3	Prompts Across Day	1–2
6.1	Most-to-Least Prompting Checklist	6.1	Most-to-Least Prompting Checklist	1–3
6.2	Most-to-Least Prompting Data	6.2	Most-to-Least Prompting Data Form	1–3
7.1	Graduated Guidance Checklist	7.1	Graduated Guidance Checklist	1–3
8.1	Least-to-Most Prompting Checklist	8.1, 8.2	Hand Washing Task Analysis, Least-to-Most Prompting Checklist	1–3
8.2	Least-to-Most Prompting Data Collection	8.3	Least-to-Most Prompting Data Collection Form	1–3
8.3	Field Facilitator Assessment	8.3	Field Assessment	1/4
9	TAKE A BREAK			
10.1	Time Delay Checklist	10.1	Time Delay Checklist	1–2
10.2	Observe shadowing	10.2	Guided Observation Shadowing	1–2
11.1	Identify shadow opportunities	11.1	Identify Shadow opportunities	1–2
11.2	Shadowing Checklist	11.2	Shadowing Checklist	1–2
12.1	Preferred Activity and Choice Checklist	12.1	Preferred Activity and Choice Checklist	1–2
13.1	Incidental Teaching	13.1	Incidental Teaching Checklist	1–2
14.1	Setting up the Environment	14.1	Getting ready to run a program	1–2
14.2	Collecting and calculating data	14.2	Collecting and calculating data	1–2
14.3	Running a Program Checklist	14.3	Running a Program Checklist	1–2
15.1	Final Field Facilitator Assessment	15.1	Field Facilitator Evaluation	1/2
15.2	Student Evaluation of Experience			< 1 hr

Alternate Table 1.2. *Optional Pacing Adjustments. (Estimated time 0–1 hours)*

Indicate your Week-by-Week Assignments. Also budget at least 1 hour per week for *discussions;* from 1–4 hours for *tutorials.*

Activity #	Abbreviated Title of Activity	Form	Abbreviated Title of Form	Time Estimate (in hours)

Form 1.3 Individual Student Contract

Individual Student Contract

Your name: _____ Date: _____

Your instructor's or supervisor's name _____

College/University _____ Department _____

Course registration #_____ Number of registered credit hours _____

Adjusted Schedule

Original Schedule	Proposed Schedule	Reason(s) for Modifying the Suggested Schedule
Week	Week	
1		
2		
3		
4		
5		
6		
7		
8		
9		
10		
11		
12		
13		
14		
15		

Additional comments (including ways of amending the contract).
From you

_____

_____

From your instructor or supervisor

_____

_____

_____   _____   _____
Student signature   Instructor's signature   Witness's signature

_____   _____   _____
Date   Date   Date

Table 1.4. Progress Chart for Completion of Standard Weekly Assignments PART 1

Directions: Put an X in the box next to each assignment and above the date when completed. Allow enough time to read/study tutorials, and for discussions (record across bottom row).

Form	Item															
15.2	Evaluation of Experience															
15.1	Field Facilitator Evaluation															
14.3	Running a Program Checklist															
14.2	Collecting and Calculating Data															
14.1	Getting Ready to Run a Program															
13.1	Incidental Teaching Checklist															
12.1	Preferred Activity and Choice Checklist															
11.2	Shadowing Checklist															
11.1	Identify Shadow Opportunities															
10.2	Observe Shadowing															
10.1	Time Delay Checklist															
8.4	Field Facilitator Assessment															
8.3	Data Collection Form															
8.2	Task Analysis															
8.1	Least-to-Most Prompting Checklist															
7.1	Graduated Guidance Checklist															
6.2	Most-to-Least Prompting Data															
6.1	Most-to-Least Prompting Checklist															
5.3	Prompts Across the Day															
5.2	Discrete Trial Checklist															
5.1	Collecting Student Response Data															
4.3	Guided Observation															
4.2	Social Responsiveness Checklist															
4.1	Social Responsiveness Data Form															
3.3-4	Pref. Assessment Checklist and Scoring															
3.2	Assisting Teachers															
3.1	Guided Observation Preference															
2.7-9	Film consents and sheet															
2.5, .6	Description Setting															
2.2-4	Agreements															
2.1	Contact information															
1.1	Individual Contract (optional)															
	Unit Discussions															
	WEEK	1	2	3	4	5	6	7	8	9	10	11	12	13	14	15

Field Activities

Field activities are formal assignments designed to walk you through teaching a series of programs designed by others; then you developing, implementing, measuring, evaluating, revising and reporting the results of a comprehensive teaching program with a child. More specifically, initially you will act as a participant-observer, expected, among other activities, to systematically observe student and instructor behavior in a school, home or

Table 1.5. *Skills Covered in the Professional Skills Assessment*

Field Practicum Student's Professional Skills
Is friendly (regularly looks directly at, smiles, greets people individually) and reinforcing (follows others' actions with positive social consequences)
Listens respectfully (waits while they talk; responds to the point)
Clarifies confusions about roles and practices right away
Gives and responds with positive and constructive feedback
Is flexible (adjusts to new conditions)
Is helpful in the program and does more than is expected
States plans and expectations clearly
Undertakes responsibilities and plans time carefully
Meets responsibilities s/he has undertaken
Schedules time realistically
Completes responsibilities on schedule
Is prepared in advance of instructional sessions
Strives for excellence in written and oral communication
Is patient with his or her student(s)
Works productively with his or her student(s)
Makes a point of thanking people who go out of their way to help

community setting, review student records, and then practice by implementing a range of previously designed and packaged instructional programs. Later, after consulting with other team members and interviewing parents and professionals, you will be asked to select tentative functional objectives for an individual student, and to conduct narrative recordings and A-B-C analyses. Once you have collected sufficient information, you will finalize your teaching objective(s), choose behavioral measures, review relevant journal articles, select or design, then implement sound teaching strategies based on the research literature and your own familiarity with effective behavior analytic strategies. In addition, you will DVD-record and review those recordings of your teaching sessions, graph and evaluate student progress and report your results. No, these are not *all* hands-on assignments, but after you become fluent in conducting behavior-analytic based instruction, they do represent the mix of background research, team-based planning, implementation, analysis and evaluation that characterize effective professional practice of applied behavior analysis.

Unit Preparation

Advanced preparation is critical. This manual includes a set of instructions, guidelines and forms for you to complete each unit. Take a moment now to see what to expect. You will be wise to review the material specific to a given week well in advance of that unit. This will allow you time to schedule activities such as visiting online or actual libraries, meeting with personnel or parents, obtaining permissions, or duplicating or otherwise preparing materials.[9] We have provided a very rough estimate of the time you might expect each activity to take. Realize, though, that individuals and conditions undoubtedly vary.

---

[9] The authors give permission to users of this manual to copy *forms* for their own personal use, but not the text material itself.

Discussions

One of the special components of this program is its emphasis on connecting our ABA field-practicum students with one another, if at all possible, providing them with a sense of community. Whether in person or over the Internet, opportunities to share information and mutually support one another have proven invaluable to students who have previously completed this practicum.

The backgrounds of members of your class or group may be relatively uniform or quite diverse. Regardless, the combined experiences and exchanges enable you to join together as a cohesive team and to gain insight into the many facets of working effectively with clientele across the autism spectrum.

A remark from an actual student

"What I liked about the discussions was hearing the variety of different comments from my classmates. You get ideas you may not have thought of on your own."

Ethical standards pertaining to privacy and confidentiality must be maintained during any discussions with people beyond your site. Do not mention actual names of client-students, families or other identifying information. Use pseudonyms or keep references generic (my student, his/her parent etc.). Your instructor or supervisor may offer a few comments to initiate discussions, and to ensure adequate coverage of relevant topics.

In this sequence we ask (require) you to:
- respond at least once to one of the topics and/or your instructor's and/or classmates' comments
- offer at least one original comment each week

Course Equipment and Materials

Making DVD Recordings Field Assignments[10]

Whether they are on-site or not, the minimum[11] of 11 required DVD-recording assignments for Part 1 and five for the latter half of Part 2 will allow supervisors or instructors to assess, show examples and provide feedback on your developing level of skill. If you are working at a distance, DVD technology, such as Skype© or Ooo-Voo©, offers a satisfactory substitute for on-site supervision, by allowing your instructor to observe your sessions and provide you with feedback.[12]

DVD recording on a disk or memory stick offers other benefits as well, including allowing you and your instructor the opportunity to review and analyze each session outside of the "real time experience." Your own independent analysis may permit you to detect those of your skills in need of improvement, missed opportunities

---

[10] We thank Richard K. Fleming for providing and allowing us to use this material.

[11] Instructors should check current BACB specifications for the amount of live or distance observation required and adjust assignments accordingly.

[12] As online live streaming DVD transmission becomes increasingly cost efficient, distance instructors may wish to substitute that medium for recorded and/or live observations. In such cases, though, we suggest preserving at least a portion of the images as a basis for follow-up feedback and as a basis for monitoring improvement over time.

or student responses overlooked during the actual session. That review, for instance, might reveal your timing (or mis-timing) of prompt or reinforcer delivery contingent on a shift in the child's movements or expression that need to be addressed.

To protect the privacy and confidentiality of the child, her/his family and the organization providing the practicum opportunity, you need to approach the DVD recording process with great care. Before beginning this step of your field experience, you must obtain written consent from the child's parent(s) to record your sessions, and, based on its privacy policies, from the site provider. Adhering to the stated consent conditions is an essential component of your ethical responsibilities. "Informed consent forms" are included within Unit 2.

Certain logistic guidelines must be considered for DVD recording as well:

1. You need to obtain adequate equipment and supplies to complete the various assignments. Check with your instructor and test the compatibility of your equipment in advance.
2. You may require someone else to operate the recorder/camera to permit effective tracking and recording of your own and the child's actions and to operate the zoom function, if available.
3. If no one is handy to assist, you can capture the necessary footage by mounting the camera on a tripod within a confined area. We suggest you experiment with the angle and positioning of the tripod to assure yourself of your ability to capture the teaching interaction safely and clearly.
4. To simplify handling, you may wish to transfer your recorded DVD material onto a compact disk or other memory device.

Probably you will need to plan your video recording in advance of Unit 3, when you are asked to produce the first one. Then you will be making a video of yourself for each of the 11 competencies in Part1. See the full DVD schedule for, displayed in Table 18.1 for the DVD schedule in Part 2.

Following each DVD submission, your supervisor or instructor will review the recording and provide you with written, and/or, in-person feedback. *In case s/he wishes to use or copy this material for other purposes, s/he should obtain your explicit written agreement, along with that of the program administrator and the client's parent(s).*

Recommended Texts

 All the instructions and forms you will need are contained in this manual. Unless your instructor plans otherwise, the *Publication Manual of the American Psychological Association*[13] *is* the only assigned text for this program. Many students, however, have found it useful to subscribe to one or more journals that publish high quality scientific behavior analytic studies applied to children with autism.[14]

Performance Assessment[15]

Note: You are expected to turn in each written and recorded assignment on or before the due date, unless you have contracted otherwise in advance with your supervisor or instructor. In the event of a serious emergency, you will be responsible for contacting that individual to negotiate an adjustment in the schedule.

Your evaluation or grade in this field experience will be based on the four groups of activities summarized in Table 1.6. Note that the grading methods differ for each activity, depending on the nature of the task.

Minimum standards for mastery of field assignments generally are set at 90% complete and correct. Your supervisor or instructor will read each assignment, supply merited positive comments and suggestions for improvement and let you know when you have achieved mastery standards. To allow him or her adequate time to review your work and you to maintain a healthy pace, please revise and re-submit your material quickly.

If you are enrolled in a course for a grade, see the suggested grading policy displayed in Table 1.6. It proposes one way your instructor might choose to weight each set of activities.

The final project should be graded for accuracy and thoroughness of coverage. Remember, during Unit 13 of Part 2 you will have prepared and submitted a draft report, and then received instructor feedback. You will have submitted your graphed data by Week 27. Therefore, your instructor probably will want to weigh your responsiveness to his or her suggestions heavily when assessing the quality of your final report. You should be awarded full credit for your contribution to *discussions,* provided you do two things *each week*: 1) say something relevant and novel; 2) offer at least one response or comment on a prior offering.

---

[13] To order online: www.apa.org/books/

[14] One favorite is the *Journal of Applied Behavior Analysis* (JABA) which will allow you a student discount. Check out JABA http://seab.envmed.rochester.edu/jaba/index.html and other behavior analytic journals on the web. Many display sample articles.

[15] Again, **instructors** should read these *suggested* grading standards carefully and make any desired changes in advance of initiating the practicum. As supported by considerable research (e.g., P. H. Raymark & P. A. Conner-Greene, "The Syllabus Quiz" (2002), *Teaching of Psychology, 29*, 286–288) we strongly suggest instructors quiz their students over the contents of the syllabus at the beginning of the course.

Table 1.6 Suggested Grading Policy

PART 1

Activity	How many?	How graded	Relative weight
Competency-Based Checklists	11	Meets mastery standards set by instructor or revises to acceptable level, or excused from assignment	60%
Field Assignments	15	Standards for mastery achieved, using feedback on draft report for revisions	20%
Discussions	14 [§]	Contribute and respond	15%
Professionalism	2 reports	Field facilitator ratings	5%

PART 2

Activity	How many?	How graded	Relative weight
Field assignments	42	Meets mastery standards set by instructor or revises to acceptable level, or excused from assignment	60%
Final project	1	Standards for mastery achieved, using feedback on draft report for revisions	20%
Discussions	14 [§]	Contribute and respond	15%
Professionalism	2 reports	Field facilitator ratings	5%

[§] Does not include vacation week

As described earlier, your *professional skills* will be evaluated by using mid-term and final *field supervisor or facilitator assessments*.

The evaluations, responses and recognition provided by your instructor, along with input and encouragement from your fellow students, will furnish you with ongoing feedback. As mentioned earlier, many students enjoy the process of filling in their weekly progress charts. The realization of your own client(s)'s progress, though, should be the biggest reinforcer of all.

We anticipate that within the next few weeks, you will state your willingness to adhere to the standard program or contract with your instructor for the specific activities you will have agreed to perform between now and the end of the first phase of this field experience. Afterward, during the second phase, you will be asked to design, implement, and experimentally analyze a particular intervention with a student/client and to report on that project orally and in writing to the relevant staff.

Take a few minutes to thumb through the packet. Notice how early on you begin—by assisting the classroom teacher (Form 3.2). As a participant-observer, this will familiarize you with the setting in which you will be working; acquaint you with the personnel and the students in the class. Also, it will enable the students to become accustomed to your presence.

In particular, review the set of checklists, and the explanations of how they are to be used.

Note how in the first part of this workbook you will be demonstrating a basic set of core competencies deemed essential for effectively teaching students with autism. You'll accomplish those by planning and implementing work sessions with one or more particular students. Please prepare yourselves at this point, by reading about our plans for you; specifically:
- how you are expected to participate
- the standards for accomplishing particular tasks
- and not only what *we,* but also you and your client-students should gain from this experience.

As a coming attraction, take a peek at the list of core competencies you will be expected to master and demonstrate during the first phase of this sequence. If possible, try to address specific objectives for three or more students of varying abilities. In so doing, you will become more skillful at displaying how successfully you can generalize these core competencies across students.

Core Discrete Trial Training Competencies for ABA Professionals in Training
- Assessing *Preference*
- Promoting *Social Responsiveness*
- Applying *Discrete-Trial Teaching*
- Using *Most-to-Least Prompting*
- Using *Graduated Guidance*
- Using *Least-to-Most Prompting*
- Using *Time Delay Prompting*
- *Shadowing*
- *Incorporating Preference* and *Choice within Programs*
- *Applying* Incidental Teaching
- *Running* a Program

Unit 1 Discussion Topics

 1. Describe yourself and your experiences in this field. If this is an electronic course, post your picture along with your narration. Even if you have done that in earlier courses, your classmates and instructor will appreciate your reminding them what you look like.

2. Share the highlights of courses you have taken that relate to this one. Tell us what you found most interesting, helpful and/or useful in your previous courses on applied behavior analysis in autism education. What good stories do you have to report?

3. Why have you elected to participate in this practicum experience? What do you hope to gain from it?

4. Add a question of your own about the purposes and/or operation of this practicum experience.

*Generally you should participate in each discussion **at least twice** each week. Try to respond to at least one question, and then comment on others' contributions and/or add a new piece of information of your own.*

Now, back to our story—-having explained the way the Walden School practicum is expected to operate, Ginger suggests: "Let's take a short tour of our facility, so you can see the lunchroom, gym, outdoor playground, administrative and nurse's office and the rest. Then, I'll introduce you to your supervisors. Maybe today, but surely during your next visit, you'll have a chance to observe your students, their teachers, and the behavior analysts in action; also to review your students' records. The teachers are busy every second, so save any questions for them until break times. Meanwhile, the other behavior analysts, Herb and Ilona, and I should be able to answer any immediate specific questions."

Following the tour, Ginger turns our three aspiring behavior analysts over to Herb and Ilona, who discuss with them the importance of their integrating smoothly into their classrooms. Herb counsels, "After I introduce you to the staff, you want to remain as unobtrusive as possible, so as not to distract the students. The watch-word—that is 'watch-phrase'—is for you to 'fade into the woodwork,' until the actions you'll be called upon to perform are clear. That doesn't mean, though, that you have to remain still throughout the session; just that until your roles are more clearly defined you don't distract the ongoing educational activities."

"Yes, in fact, there will be times this week when you actually can be helpful" Ilona adds. "I've brought along a packet of materials you can add to your folders. It describes your very first assignment."

Unit 2
The Big Decision
Finalizing Your Practicum Setting: Key Players and Your Role

Having been oriented by Ginger and introduced to the personnel with whom they will be collaborating, our team of three practicum students returns to the Walden program the following week to finalize their arrangements and prepare to participate in their respective activities.

"So," remarks Ginger. "How are your guys feeling about your assignments?"

"Excited," remarks Jeb.

"Me too," Rosa adds. "Its one thing to spend a few hours with my cousin, and something quite different actually to be taking on real responsibility for successfully teaching with the kinds of kids we see here."

"That's only natural," Ginger consoles her. "Some of the issues you've already seen here can be daunting. But try not to be too worried. We are fortunate in having a highly trained and skillful staff who will help you all along the way."

"That seems true enough. From the bit I've seen in the way youngsters are treated here, even when they fly off the handle, I'm impressed," Allie remarks. "I feel as if I'm going to learn so much from the students and staff!"

"Amen to that!" Jeb adds. "Can't wait to get going!"

At this point, they, as we, need to review our own perspectives, because our chosen work poses similar challenges. When teaching people on the autism spectrum, generally we work as a team with a shared determination and willingness to invest what it takes to produce positive progress. That means planning, preparing, executing, and evaluating the success of our plans. This week we will begin to lay the groundwork for our own adventure: applying behavior analysis with students with autism[16].

Unit 2 Objectives

We assume you have completed formal coursework in or otherwise mastered information about applied behavior analysis in the autism field, along with its principles, practices, and other key features. Consequently, by the end of this week you should be able to identify and describe your own and other participants' roles and your field setting by:

1. contacting a school administrator or parent by mail or email, followed by a telephone call, obtaining permission to conduct your ABA teaching practicum at their site.
2. identifying your role and anticipated tasks by generating an introductory letter.
3. securing contact information for advocates or supervisors.
4. with the help of the administrator, identifying an individual at the site who will facilitate your participation. This person may be the administrator, behavior analyst, teacher or another designated person.
5. generating a confidentiality agreement with this administrator and/or parent.
6. stating the roles and responsibilities of key parties.
7. describing the instructional setting, including but not limited to, program mission and purpose, population, program activities and instructional strategies and features.

---

[16] Or in some cases with someone else, like a teacher, aide, parent, or specialist within the system.

Activity 2.1 (Estimated time: 0–10 hours)
Finalizing Practicum Site Arrangements

> **Note: For students already affiliated with a site.**
>
> By now, many of you already have an available practicum site. Teachers and other educational personnel currently working with children with ASD may wish to integrate the practicum as an extra during their regular teaching duties; but they still will need to obtain the required permissions and complete each of the activities requisite for the course. Parents may choose to conduct practicum activities in or outside of their homes
>
> *Please obtain your instructor's okay if you already have a site, and as a result, feel you do not need to complete this assignment.*

Written Requirements: Sample letter
Objectives: To identify and describe key participants, you will:

1. Contact a school, workshop administrator, or parent by mail, email or phone to describe your purpose. Then follow up, preferably via a face-to-face meeting to obtain permission to conduct your ABA teaching practicum at their site.
2. Generate an introductory letter identifying your role and anticipated tasks.

> **Note:** Making final arrangements for your practicum site before the end of the next week is essential. If, after following the instructions below, you need help or direction in searching for a practicum setting, contact your instructor right away.

Instructions

1. Consider contacting one or more of the administrators of the following:
   - the school or preschool your child attends
   - another school or preschool serving children with autism
   - a community organization that includes students with autism, such as scouts, recreational centers, sports teams, riding schools, day camps and so on.
   - A sheltered worksite

2. Immediately write a letter to the senior administrator or director of the organization. It is wise to direct all communication to specific individuals. If you are not aware of or able to access the name of your contact person, call the program and inquire before sending out any contact information. Compose your own message, or if you like, you can modify or directly use the sample letter below (Figure 2.1).

3. In the letter, *say* you will contact them, and then *be sure to* follow up with a phone call to schedule an appointment with the administrator.

Figure 2.1

A Sample Letter to Send to the Administrator of the Organization

Your address

Date

Dear (Senior Administrator),

Allow me to tell you of an exciting opportunity we may find mutually beneficial—to your program as well as to me. I am enrolled as a student at _____ in a course entitled "Field Practicum in Behavioral Analysis." The course is designed to enable students to gain proficiency in the practice of applied behavior analysis (ABA) among clients with autism spectrum disorder. As you probably know, scientific studies have demonstrated these methods to be especially effective with this population.

Although my fellow students and I have solid knowledge of many important ABA concepts, now we need to begin to put that knowledge into practice. Consequently, we have been asked to locate a program serving a clientele with autism spectrum disorder, and to volunteer to participate in specific ways. Under the supervision of our ABA instructor, a person with advanced training and considerable experience in this field, and a volunteer local supervisor, identified by yourself, we are asked to spend a minimum of six§ hours a week at the site for purposes of:

1. identifying one or more students
2. practicing applying behavioral instruction by implementing a pre-selected set of discrete-trial training programs
3. after gaining fluency in implementing discrete-trial instruction, analyzing the need for and selecting novel constructive instructional goals or objectives suited to each student and approved by his or her primary educator (and/or parent)
4. using an *all positive approach* to design and teach the student(s) to progress toward those objectives
5. Choosing or designing behavioral measures of the behavior of interest
6. collecting performance data to track the students' progress and as a basis for
7. making sound revisions in the process
8. incorporating indicated data-based revisions in the plan
9. preparing a report summarizing the project
10. submitting the report to our instructor
11. assisting in other ways, as mutually determined

The program asks little of you and your staff, other than for your assistance in helping us identify a child with whom to work and an adult (i.e., a "field facilitator") to handle local arrangements related to our weekly assignments. While, as I'm sure you know, we cannot guarantee success with a student, we do promise to make our best efforts.

I shall follow up this letter with a telephone call during the next few days.

Sincerely yours,

§ Number of hours may vary, depending on the number of credits for which you are registered.

Activity 2.2 (Estimated time: 0–10 hours)
Becoming Acquainted with One Another and Obtaining Participant Agreements

Written Requirements: Forms 2.1, 2.2, 2.3 and 2.4

Objectives: To identify and describe key participants and your role as a participant and participants' roles, you will:

1. identify advocates or supervisor's contact information.
2. with the help of the administrator, identify an individual at the field setting who will facilitate your participation. This person may be the administrator, teacher or another designated person.
3. generate a confidentiality agreement with this administrator and/or parent.

Instructions

Your initial contact with site personnel and clear communication of your intentions underlie a successful practicum experience. The following guidelines can assist you:

1. Schedule a meeting (beginning *and* ending time) with the *senior manager* of the organization (or parent, if this will be a home program) to become acquainted with one another and to describe why your work will benefit them.

2. Practice first, then during the meeting remember to:
   - introduce yourself and explain your interest in the field of Applied Behavior Analysis in Autism in general and this program in particular
   - review the purpose of your practicum
   - discuss how the host program will benefit from your participation
   - talk about your personal hopes, interests, preferences and any concerns or personal limitations which might affect your performance

3. Request the administrator identify and obtain the agreement of a teacher or other member of the staff to serve as your *field facilitator* and find out *when, where* and *how* to contact that individual.

4. End the meeting on time and thank your host for this learning opportunity.

5. Follow up with a brief note summarizing the meeting and thanking your host once again.

6. Schedule a similar meeting with your field facilitator. Show your instructor or supervisor and your field facilitator the list of standard responsibilities listed in Table 2.1. Discuss any necessary changes to these roles.

> **Note:** See also Activity 2.3. Time permitting, you may complete that activity during this meeting as well.

7. After meeting with the senior manager or parent(s) and your field facilitator, please complete these *four* forms:
   - Contact Information (Form 2.1)
   - Confidential Agreements among
     - Student
     - Field Facilitator
     - Supervisor/Instructor (Forms 2.2–2.4.)

Completing these forms is essential if you are to proceed with your practicum. Remember to keep copies of all forms and give or send the originals to your instructor or supervisor. Pose to them any questions or concerns related to the course or the assignments.

Table 2.1 Responsibilities of Cooperating Individuals

Field Practicum Student	• Attend the program at least six[17] hours a week (except for your break) over the 28-week span, according to the program's schedule. • Complete all weekly assignments on schedule. • Conduct with a student an instructional program that is aligned with his or her individual educational or family service plan and participate in program activities in other ways, to be mutually determined.
Field Facilitator	Support the practicum student's participation in program by: • helping the behavior analysis student to identify a child in the program to whom to teach a mutually acceptable skill • allowing the student to teach toward the particular skill, under the supervision of his or her distance learning instructor • inviting the student to participate in other ways, to be determined mutually between field facilitator and student • assessing the student's professional demeanor twice during the practicum
Instructor and/or Supervisor	Maintain regular weekly contact with the practicum student to guide, coach and assess that student's performance (e.g., assign weekly tasks, evaluate and comment upon the quality of products and skills).

Note: For students choosing alternate locations or clients:

- *If you are working in the student's home, the parent may function as the field facilitator.*
- *If you are a "parent instructor" for your own child, find someone who can be available to assist in DVD or data recording, teaching strategies requiring facilitators, etc.*
- *If your focus is on an adult service provider or manager, his or her supervisor or manager may play the role of field facilitator.*
- *If you are the supervisor, trainer or manager, simply explain that on the form.*

---

[17] Number of hours may vary, depending on the number of credits for which you are registered. If you anticipate applying for certification as a Board Certified Behavior Analyst, consult the BACB website for current hourly requirements.

Form 2.1 Contact Information

Note: *All identifying information contained in this agreement will be distributed only to the named key parties and kept confidential, unless otherwise agreed to in writing by all of the individuals involved.*

(Please print or type)

Name of Field Practicum Student	Address
Phone number	Best times to call
Email address	Fax number
Name of Course Instructor	Email address of Course Instructor
Phone number	Best times to call
Name of field setting (with permission of senior administrator)	Field setting address
Phone number	Best times to call
Email address	Fax number
Name of Senior Administrator	Name of Field Facilitator
Types of DVD recording or transmitting devices you have available	Other important information

Form 2.2

Field Facilitator Agreement

I agree to allow _____ (name of field practicum student) to participate in our program for a minimum of _____ hours a week for ___ weeks and in keeping with the program's schedule. During that time s/he will conduct instructional programs with one or more students[18] and possibly participate in our activities in other mutually determined ways. I understand this field practicum student's instruction will be supervised directly by _____or from a distance by _____ (instructor), a qualified Instructor associated with _____ (name of college, university or other organization).

Further, I understand this student will adhere to the BACB Guidelines for responsible conduct, and any other local professional confidentiality policies in reference to his or her student. Although s/he may discuss aspects of the instruction with her/his instructor privately or classmates during formal group discussions, s/he will withhold any identifying information, such as names, addresses and so on.

I also agree to help this student *identify* one or more students and/or clients in our program to teach toward specific learning objectives endorsed by the child's regular teacher and parent(s), *record* and *report on progress* in writing to his or her instructor and to *obtain appropriate permissions* for DVD recording and sharing these DVDs in confidence with his or her instructor.

Further, I agree to complete three interim and one final rating form that includes a set of the practicum student's professional skills, such as friendliness, attendance, timeliness, helpfulness and cooperation.

_____   _____   _____
       Print Name   Signature   Date

Please add any questions or comments below:

---

[18]More advanced practicum students may elect to develop a program for staff, parents or other service providers.

Form 2.3

Student Agreement

I agree to attend the _____ program for a minimum of ____ hours a week, in keeping with this program's schedule, for ____ weeks. During that time I will follow a set sequence of activities, including observing and conducting discrete trial instruction, designing and conducting an original student-tailored instructional program for one or more selected students [or parent(s), staff member(s) or other care-giver(s)]. That program will be aligned with the objectives of the students' individual educational (IEP) individual service or family service plan.

I understand that my behavioral instructional activities will be supervised locally or from a distance by _____ (print name of instructor/supervisor), who is affiliated with _____ (name of organization).

Further, I agree to adhere to professional confidentiality policies in reference to my student(s). Although I may discuss aspects of the instruction with my instructor privately or with my classmates during formal group discussions, I will not share any identifying information, such as names, addresses and so on.

Further, I agree to participate in routine activities in other ways, as mutually determined by my host(s) and myself. I plan to attend the program punctually and regularly, except when emergencies arise, in which case I shall notify my *on-site supervisor* or *field facilitator*, _____, the person serving as a liaison at your site.

At the end of my participation, I will prepare a report on my experiences and submit it to my instructor and to this program. I also understand that my field facilitator will provide feedback to my instructor and/or supervisor concerning my professional skills.

_____   _____   _____
Date   Print Name   Signature

Form 2.4

Supervisor and/or Instructor Agreement

I agree to supervise and coach _____, a student participating in a supervised field practicum, directly/ from a distance (circle one). This will involve:

- specifying weekly assignments
- reviewing the student's weekly products, including, for instance, records, forms, DVDs, graphs and so on
- commenting privately on his or her contributions to the discussion
- assessing and grading his or her weekly and end-of-term performance
- providing him or her with guidance, feedback and merited reinforcement
- requesting periodic assessments from the Field Facilitator on this student's performance as a professional

Further, I agree to adhere to professional confidentiality policies in reference to my student's client. Although, for instructional purposes, we may discuss aspects of my student's case privately or during formal group discussions, I shall withhold any identifying information, such as names, addresses and so on, and do my best to see to it that the others comply similarly.

Others (to be determined)

_____

_____

_____

_____ _____ _____
        Print Name   Signature   Date

Activity 2.3 (Estimated time: 1 hour)
Description of Field Setting

Written Requirements: Form 2.5 or 2.6

Objective: To identify and describe your field setting, you will:

1. state the roles and responsibilities of key parties.
2. describe the instructional setting, including but not limited to, program mission and purpose, population, program activities and instructional strategies and features.

Instructions

1. Two sets of forms are attached. One (Form 2.5) is for students conducting their practicum activities in a group setting outside of the child's home. The other (Form 2.6) is for those working in the home or community. Use the one appropriate to your situation.
2. This activity assumes you did not yet obtain necessary permissions or agreements during your first meeting with the senior manager of your practicum site. If all forms have been completed and submitted to your instructor and there is a clear understanding of your intentions and involvement at the site, then it may be appropriate to proceed to the Discussion at the end of this week's assignments. Nevertheless, it is suggested that you review the remaining instructions to be sure "all your bases are covered."
3. Show the attached form to the manager or parent and record their responses for later transcription.
4. Privately transfer the answers to the attached form. Complete only those parts for which the program director and/or parent has given consent.
5. Submit the completed form to your instructor for feedback.

Form 2.5 (p. 1 of 3)

Description of Field Setting

Your Name _____ Instructor's Name _____ Date _____

Please obtain the permission of the program manager before: 1) completing each item, and 2) sharing this information with your instructor.

1. Identifying Information

Program Name (or pseudonym)

_____

Program Administrator _____

Address _____

Phone Number _____ Email address _____

Name of field facilitator _____

Email address of field facilitator _____

Program website address, if any _____

What is the program's vision, purpose or mission? (**Note**: Many programs will have an existing written statement for you to use. If so, attach it. Some of these are very brief, though, so feel free to expand upon it if necessary for our purposes.)

_____
_____
_____
_____

2. Population: Who is served?

- Ages _____
- Description of population served (common diagnoses, frequency of maladaptive behavior, inclusion of typically developing children, etc.) [19] If the program has a brochure or other printed description, you may wish, with permission, to send that along.

_____
_____
_____
_____
_____
_____
_____

---

[19] Attach, with permission (or scan, mail or fax) copies of printed brochures or web-pages

Form 2.5 (p. 2 of 3)

Your Name _____ Instructor's Name _____ Date ____

3. Staff positions (list titles and a one-sentence description of roles where possible)

_____
_____
_____
_____

- Typical staff-to-child ratio for instruction (include individual and group sessions, as appropriate)_____
_____

4. General description of program activities (In a few paragraphs, describe a typical day. You may attach additional pages if necessary.)

_____
_____
_____
_____
_____
_____
_____
_____
_____
_____
_____
_____
_____
_____
_____
_____
_____
_____
_____
_____
_____
_____
_____

5. Instructional Approach

Some programs follow a well-defined intervention model, which governs how teaching is structured and carried out. Others take a more mixed or eclectic approach to teaching design. Briefly describe what you have learned about this program's approach.

_____
_____
_____
_____
_____
_____
_____
_____
_____
_____
_____

Form 2.5 (p. 3 of 3)

Your Name _____ Instructor's Name _____ Date _____

6. Comment on how completely you think our practicum objectives can be met in this program.

_____
_____
_____
_____
_____
_____

7. Special program features (if any)

_____
_____
_____
_____
_____
_____

8. Parental involvement (Do parents also conduct systematic teaching programs in the home and community as part of this program's activities or participate in other ways?)

_____
_____
_____
_____
_____

9. Other comments

_____
_____
_____
_____
_____
_____

Form 2.6 (p. 1 of 2) Alternative Assignment

**Description of Home or Field Setting
(For Students Conducting Their Practicum in the Home or Community)**

Your Name _____ Instructor's name _____ Date _____

Please obtain the permission of the key participants before completing each item and sharing this information with your instructor.

1. Identifying Information

Briefly describe location: urban, suburban, rural; access to educational and social services

_____
_____
_____
_____
_____
_____

2. Location and contact information

Please obtain permission before completing these sections. Otherwise leave blank.

Parent's or Manager's initials or name (with permission) _____

Address _____

Phone Number _____ Email address _____

Name of field facilitator or helper _____

Email address of field facilitator or helper _____

Name (with parental permission) or pseudonym of student with a diagnosis of ASD
_____

Name or pseudonym of parent (with permission) if other than self _____

Fax Number _____ Email address _____

Other means of contacting _____

Other participants in teaching program and their relationship to student _____
_____
_____
_____

Major goals or objectives of Individual Family Service Plan
_____
_____
_____

Form 2.6 (p. 2 of 2)

Your Name _____ Instructor's Name _____ Date _____

3. Instructional setting
- Describe the location in the residence in which teaching may take place

_____
_____
_____

- Is an area set aside for instruction? _____

- Identify the roles and functions of others present (Include other children, family members, home teachers, care-givers and so on)

_____
_____
_____
_____
_____
_____

- Times available for conducting program without interruption

_____
_____

- Plans for avoiding unanticipated interruptions

_____
_____

- Other things that might help or hinder instruction?

_____
_____
_____
_____
_____

- Additional comments or concerns

_____
_____
_____
_____

Activity 2.4 (Estimated time: 2–4 hours)
Recording and Submitting a DVD[20] or Directly Streaming of Ongoing Teaching at Your Practicum Site

Well-designed practicum courses designed to teach and support the correct use of behavioral procedures typically include observation and feedback from qualified instructors or trainers. DVD-recorded observations have several added advantages: Both student and instructor can view and review any segment of interest. Practicum students can observe their own recent teaching interactions more objectively than while they were concentrating on teaching. Instructors can supply very precise feedback, guidance and reinforcement by indicating exactly the moment to which they are referring. And, when courses are offered from a distance, DVD images in action permit direct supervisory observations across the miles.

There are 17 DVD taping assignments spread throughout this course (There are 11 in Part 1 and 6 in Part 2).

Written Requirements: Forms 2.7, 2.8 and 2.9

Objectives: To execute a DVD production in your student's instructional setting, you will:

1. obtain administrative, teacher and parental consent for filming participation.
2. carry out a film recording of teaching interactions for each training checklist according to the **CHECKLIST TRAINING PROTOCOL.**

> **Note:** Please check with your instructor in advance regarding the compatibility of your equipment. For instance, as the technology for producing and streaming images over the Internet becomes simpler and more economical, you may have the opportunity to use that medium instead; but be certain your instructor can receive it.

Instructions[21]

1. Review the attached consent forms.

2. Meet with the child's parent, preferably in the company of the field facilitator to:
   - Review Form 2.7 with the parent
   - Provide the parent with a copy of the form
   - Answer any questions you can, and/or direct the parent to your instructor if s/he has more questions.

3. Make *three* copies of the signed consent form:
   - send the original signed copy of the form to your instructor
   - give a copy of the form to your Field Facilitator
   - keep one copy for your own files

4. Repeat steps 1 to 3 with the *Administrator/Director Consent Form.*

---

[20] Streaming video may (preferably) be used to permit instructors to provide rapid feedback. Nevertheless, if feasible, the session also should be recorded for more precise feedback and future reference.

[21] Richard Fleming, Ph.D., composed these guidelines on video recording consent and methods.

Form 2.7 (p. 1 of 2)

Consent to Participate in Video Recording &/or Transmission
Parent Form

Program Title: *Field Practice in Behavior Analytic Interventions in Autism*
Sponsor _____

Person(s) contacting parent(s) _____

In this practicum course, participants are expected to work directly with students with autism either in their homes or an educational setting. Supervision by a person skilled in the application of behavioral procedures also is required.

Purpose of Video Recording and Transmission in this Project
Any effective practicum course for trainees who are learning to perform behavioral interventions with children with autism requires that their performance be recorded from time to time while they apply their skills with students. There are two main advantages to this: The practicum students are able to 1) observe themselves during the teaching process, and 2) receive feedback from their qualified instructor.

Procedures
During this 13-Unit course, the practicum participant working in your home, or at an educational site, is required to film 11 3-5 minute segments in which he or she is shown conducting a teaching session with your child. Either you, or a designated teacher with whom the participant is working, will do the DVD filming. DVD-recorded teaching sessions will be expected to show how well participants have prepared instructional materials, provided instructions and prompts, given positive reinforcement, corrected errors, and accurately recorded your child's progress. All teaching sessions will focus on *skill acquisition*, addressing objectives upon which you and your child's team have agreed earlier. *Participants in this course are asked not to apply interventions designed directly to address maladaptive behavior or to use any aversive/punitive consequences.*

Once each DVD-recording is made, the participant will give or mail it to his or her instructor. The instructor will review the recording, provide detailed comments to the participant, and return it to him or her. Written comments will not include your child's last name or any other identifying information.

For instructional purposes and under conditions of strict confidentiality, other members of the participant's practicum team may view and analyze the recording as a group.

Benefits and Risks
This project is designed to enable your child to benefit from the participant's teaching. While it is hoped that this DVD filming procedure will result in better teaching interactions, there is no guarantee the process will provide additional benefit to your child. One extremely small potential risk is that a DVD-record could be lost in the mail. We and our students will use a mailing service that provides documentation about when and by whom each recording was sent. Another potential risk is that your child will become upset *because* of the recording process itself. Accordingly, if your child shows any discomfort associated with the DVD filming procedure, it will be discontinued, and attempted again at another time, using the same criterion for discontinuation.

Form 2.7 (p. 2 of 2)

Consent to Participate in Video Recording and Transmission
Parent Form

Your Rights

It is important for you to know that:

Your consent for videorecording and transmission, following the procedures described above, is voluntary.

You may discontinue your participation and withdraw your consent at any time by contacting _____, the program director.

You will be told about any new information or changes in the project that might affect your consent for participation.

Your decision about whether or not to participate will in no way jeopardize your future relations with the sponsoring organization.

Confidentiality

Instructor comments and other written information associated with the DVD-recordings will be identified only by code; your child's identity will not be revealed. Without your expressed permission, DVD-recordings will not otherwise be shared, and they will be erased within 6 months of the end date of the practicum course. Results of this project may be shared through progress reports to the organization sponsoring this course, publication in professional journals and presentations at professional conferences. Your child's identity will not be revealed in any report, publication or presentation.

Questions

Please feel free to direct any questions you may have about this project, or about your child's participation, to the project director _____. Call collect at _____.

Consent to Participate in this Project

Child's name: _____

The purpose and procedures of this project and the risks and benefits that might result have been explained to me. I have had the opportunity to ask questions of the project contact, and all of my questions have been answered. I agree to give consent for the above-named individual to participate in this project. I understand that I may end his/her participation at any time. I have been given a copy of this consent form.

Your name: _____   Relationship to Child: _____
        (Print)

_____   Date: _____
    (Your Signature)

Form 2.8 (p. 1 of 2)

Administrator/Director Consent Form

Project Title: *Field Practicum in Applying Behavior Analysis in Autism*
Sponsor: (Name of Sponsoring Behavior Analytic Training Organization):

_____

Contact Information:
(Name of Training Program Manager or Coordinator):

_____

We appreciate your willingness to host a student studying ABA interventions in autism at your facility. In this practicum course, our students are expected to work directly with pupils with autism either in their homes or an educational setting. Supervision by a person skilled in the application of behavioral procedures also is required.

Purpose of DVD filming in this Project
Any effective field practicum course for trainees who are mastering behavior analytic skills requires that they be able periodically to review their own performance while teaching via reviewing video recordings from time to time. There are two main advantages to this: The practicum students are able to 1) observe themselves during the teaching process, and 2) receive feedback from their qualified instructor.

Procedures

During the initial 13 Unit course, the trainee is asked to film 11 3-5 minute segments in which he or she is shown conducting a teaching session with the child. DVD recording will be done by the designated teacher or *Field Facilitator* with whom the participant is working, or another volunteer associated with the program. DVD-recorded teaching sessions will be expected to show how well participants have prepared instructional materials, provided instructions and prompts, given positive reinforcement, corrected errors, and accurately recorded the child's progress. All teaching sessions will focus on *skill acquisition*, addressing objectives that the child's team previously agreed upon. Interventions will not directly address *maladaptive behavior* or use aversive/punitive consequences.

Once each DVD-recording is made, the participant will give or securely package and mail completed DVD-records to his or her course instructor. The instructor will review the recording, provide detailed written feedback comments to the participant, and return it. Written comments will not include your agency's or the child's last name, or any other identifying information. A sample of DVD-recordings may also be sent to, and reviewed by, _____ for project evaluation purposes.

Benefits and Risks

This project is designed for the child to benefit from the teaching the participant provides. While it is hoped that this DVD filming procedure will result in better teaching interactions, there may be no additional benefits associated with DVD filming. One small but potential risk is that a DVD-recording will be lost in the mail. We and our trainees will use a delivery system that ensures documentation about when and by whom each recording was sent. Another potential risk is that the child will become upset *because* of the DVD filming itself. Accordingly, if the child shows any discomfort associated with the DVD filming procedure, it will be discontinued, and attempted again at another point, using the same criterion for discontinuation.

Form 2.8 (p. 2 of 2)

Administrator/Director Consent Form

Your Rights

As a program administrator, it is important for you to know that:

Your consent for supporting DVD filming, following the procedures described above, is voluntary.

You may discontinue your agency's participation and withdraw your consent at any time by contacting the training program's director or manager.

You will be told about any new information or changes in the project that might affect your consent for participation.

Your decision about whether to participate will in no way jeopardize your future relations with the _____ organization.

Confidentiality

Instructor comments and other written information associated with the DVD-recordings will be identified only by code; the child's identity will not be revealed. DVD-recordings will not otherwise be viewed, except, under strict confidentiality conditions for teaching purposes among our trainee's practicum group. Unless separately negotiated with you, the recordings will be erased within 6 months of the end date of the practicum course. Any evaluations of the effectiveness of this training may be shared with funding agencies or through publication of findings in professional journals and presentations at professional conferences. Unless written permission is supplied by your agency, the parent, and our trainee, the identity of your agency or of the child will not be revealed in any report, publication or presentation.

Questions

Please feel free to direct any questions you may have about this project, or about your agency's or the child's participation, to _____ (contact information above). Call collect.

Consent to Participate in this Project

Practicum Participant: _____

Child's name: _____
The purpose and procedures of this project and the risks and benefits that might result have been explained to me. I have had the opportunity to ask questions of the project contact person, and all have been answered. I give consent for the above-named practicum participant and child to participate in this project. I understand that I may end our agency's participation at any time. I have been given a copy of this consent form.

The name and address of your agency:

_____
_____
_____

Phone number: (____)_____ Fax Number: (____)_____

Email_____

Your name: _____   Your title: _____
        (Print)
_____   Date: _____
(Your Signature)

Form 2.9 (p. 1 of 2)
Instructional Setting DVD Recording

DVD Cover Sheet

Your Name_____ Instructor's Name _____

Date___/___/___ Location of recording site_____

Time recording started _____ Stopped _____

Initials or pseudonym of student _____

1. Check roles of people present:

☐   Parent ☐ Regular classroom teacher ☐ Aide or assistant
☐   Other personnel (specify)

2. Provide any special instructions for your instructor related to playing this DVD-recording.

Explain_____
_____

3. Describe how the environment is arranged to support the activity, (e.g., time of day, arrangement of furniture, materials, other resources, number of children present, what they are doing, the ratio of adults to children) and any other aspects of the learning environment.
_____
_____
_____
_____

4. What are the objectives of the ongoing lesson or activity?
_____
_____
_____

5. State the skills, or target responses, being taught (see Mini-Tutorial for review).
_____
_____

6. Give a behavioral definition of the target responses being taught, including all key features.
_____
_____

7. Describe the procedures used to teach the skills, or target responses (e.g., what shaping procedures were employed?)
_____
_____
_____
_____
_____

Form 2.9 (p. 2 of 2)

8. What reinforcers were used and how did the children respond to them? Please describe.

_____
_____
_____
_____

9. Explain other pertinent ongoing activities that may have affected learning conditions, (e.g., lunch was currently being prepared on the other side of the room).

_____
_____
_____

10. On the attached page, please identify the specific time and number on the disk counter or footage number and write a brief phrase to indicate what is happening during the DVD recording.

11. Add any further comments or questions you may have for your instructor.

_____
_____
_____
_____
_____

Unit 2 Discussion Topics

Note. *Confidential, professionally responsible discussions with your peers and instructor are an important aspect of your practicum experience. Please go to the Behavior Analysis Certification Board website (www.bacb.com) for the current ethical guidelines regarding confidentiality.*

Both face-to-face and virtual (Internet-based) group discussions can help you to:

1. confidentially share your actual experiences; and in so doing, allow you and your team or classmates to become familiar with numerous examples of ABA concepts, principles and practices. This, as you recognize, facilitates generalization.
2. solve problems as a group, which will better prepare you to function as a team member.
3. share events of current interest: News or magazine articles, technical papers and research reports, television programs, websites and so on.
4. develop your ability to effectively communicate your perspectives and describe your experiences.
5. gain a sense of community with your fellow classmates.
6. describe the nature of the setting in which you will be carrying out your practicum activities. (Only mention names if permission formally given.)
7. if you have already identified your student or client, share your reasons for selecting him or her. (Remember to respect confidentiality. Use pseudonyms or other neutral identifiers.)
8. talk about reasons why issues of confidentiality are so important. Share your own experiences related to this topic.
9. discuss the value you can you see in recording and submitting DVD recordings for:
   - your student
   - yourself
   - your instructor
   - your student's family

And don't forget to listen to or read and respond to others' contributions. That will bring cohesion to your group and allow you to teach and learn from one another.

This page is intentionally blank.

PART 1
FOUNDATIONAL BEHAVIOR INTERVENTION SKILLS

Competency-Based Checklists

Teaching Core Competencies

During the past half-century, leading researchers and teachers (e.g., Koegel & Koegel, 2006; Lovaas, 1987; Cohen, Amerine-Dickens & Smith, 2006). have developed, applied, functionally analyzed and conducted wide-scale assessments of the impact of numerous programs designed to enable youngsters on the autism spectrum to gain valuable skills. Given how powerfully effective these programs have been shown to be, in Part One of this manual we have elected to begin your applied training by assigning you to teach a set of these to one or more students. After you have demonstrated your mastery of the skills necessary to implement those programs, we then move on to the second portion of this curriculum, in which you will undertake a more independent role as an applied behavior analyst by designing a behavioral intervention to apply with a given student. Here we describe the first portion in more detail.

Competency-based Checklists

For the first part of this workbook, you will be demonstrating core competencies necessary to teach students with autism. You will set up sessions working with a student, and a supervisor will observe you working with your student. You will demonstrate the following competencies during your sessions:
- Preference Assessment
- Social Responsiveness
- Discrete Trial Teaching
- Preference and Choice
- Most-to-Least Prompting
- Graduated Guidance
- Least-to-Most Prompting
- Time Delay Prompting
- Shadowing
- Incidental Teaching
- Running a Program

SAYING AND DOING
THE CHECKLIST TRAINING PROTOCOL

Part 1–Oral Checklist: Before working with your student, your supervisor will implement a checklist-based program that will ask you to describe the rationale and the procedure for implementing the competency. Being able to describe what you are doing, and why you are doing it, is essential for you to be able to communicate clearly among all the important people in the student's life.
- First, you will want to be able precisely and simply to explain what you are doing to the student's caregivers, as they eventually will be carrying over some aspects of the intervention for generalization.
- Second, you will need to be able to describe what you are doing so you can eventually train others.
- Third, we need a common language among colleagues and practitioners for efficient communication.

For this reason, your supervisor will question you orally about the content and process of teaching the particular skill at hand. S/he will immediately acknowledge correct responses and correct any inaccurate responses. Your supervisor then will re-administer the oral portion of the checklist until your oral descriptions reach pre-set criterion levels.

Part 2–Performance Checklist. After passing the oral portion, you will be asked to demonstrate your ability competently to instruct up to three students. As we know, being able to accurately describe what you should be doing is no guarantee that you will be able actually to perform the skill precisely. Therefore you will be provided with opportunities to practice each skill until you can do it correctly. To learn how to execute the skill, you will follow these steps:

1. Watch your supervisor or other trained adult provide a live or videotaped demonstration of how to teach each particular skill.
2. Take data on the student's performance while you observe the above demonstration. Next, compare your results with those of the trainer, and repeat this scoring exercise until you achieve 80% interobserver agreement.
3. With an adult partner, role-play teaching the competency.
4. Practice the competency with a student in the trainer's presence, while receiving ongoing feedback.
5. Continue practicing the skill on your own, using the checklist to self-monitor your performance.
6. Submit a DVD of your best performance of that instructional competency to your supervisor.
7. Your supervisor will review the DVD. If necessary, s/he will schedule one or more sessions to observe you working with the student,* providing you with feedback sufficient to allow you to satisfactorily demonstrate your competency.

*We recommend you work with approximately three students of varying abilities to demonstrate generalization of teaching core competencies across clients.

Unit 3
Assessment of Student Preference and Class Participation

 Allie and Rosa enthusiastically agree when their field supervisor requests help on the playground. They noticed that Samuel has isolated himself in a quiet corner, pouring gravel back and forth from container to container. Allie calls out, "Samuel, come here! I'll push you on the swing!" Samuel pays no attention and continues pouring the gravel back and forth.

Just then, Herb, the gym teacher, walks onto the playground with the giant bubble making wand. He proceeds to make huge, gorgeous bubbles that float out over Samuel's way. Samuel notices them floating nearby and runs over to Herb, who gladly allows him to take a turn.

Allie asks Herb for his secret to engagement.

"It's all about figuring out what the kids like—their reinforcers in the moment. Finding that special item or activity is 90% of the work. Then, the rest is easy!!"

"I'm beginning to see that if we identify or create currently effective reinforcers, we'll be able to use more positive methods for motivating kids," Allie observes. "I remember learning that if we develop programs using motivators or reinforcers to increase positive behavior, we won't have to target as many programs to decrease unwanted behavior."

"Yeah, I remember that too. But I thought Samuel would love the swings and he paid no attention to them. He clearly loved the bubbles though. How do we figure out what any kid actually likes?" Allie questions.

Interrupting herself—she ponders, "Now, wait just a sec. Something about preference assessment??"

"Right," Rosa smacks her hand to her head. "Data! If we want to identify an effective reinforcer for a child, we need to observe and take data on student responses to items and activities."

"How do teachers assess preferences here at Walden?" Allie wonders.

"Tell you what," Herb, suggests. "Let me show you a DVD of the procedure we generally use—the *Preference Assessment*. After you watch it we can talk about the method and then you guys can try the assessment yourselves."

Unit 3 Objectives

By the end of this unit, you should be able to identify core deficit behaviors that are exhibited by students with autism; identify how preference is used to increase social responsiveness, engagement, and learning; and conduct a preference assessment by:
1. observing your student and describing behaviors associated with social, behavioral, and communicative deficits that are characteristic of individuals with autism.
2. observing strategies that incorporate the use of preference to increase engagement, responsiveness and learning.
3. consulting with your student's teacher to develop a list of tasks pertaining to classroom participation.
4. conducting preference assessment and implementing **THE CHECKLIST TRAINING PROTOCOL.**

Activity 3.1 (Estimated time: 1 hour)
Use of Preference in the Practicum Setting

Tools: Form 3.1

Preparation: For this assignment, using Guided Observation Form 3.1, you will:

- **First**: Observe and document behaviors exhibited by your student that are characteristic of persons with autism. Focus your observations on communicative, social, and repetitive behaviors exhibited by this student.
- **Second**: Observe an instructor conducting a preference assessment (if you do not have a live observer, please view the demonstration on our companion website).
- **Third:** Observe how preferred activities are used to establish the instructor as a reinforcer.
- **Fourth:** Document how the instructor is using student preferences to motivate the student in areas of learning, engagement, and social responsiveness.

These activities will assist you when you conduct your own preference assessments, social responsiveness sessions, and eventual teaching sessions that are ahead.

Form 3.1 (pg. 1 of 1)

Guided Observation 1
(To be completed in conjunction with Field Assignment 3.1)
Your Name _____Date_____
Indicate the day(s)_____ and time(s)_____ you are attending this location each week.

1. Autism definition
List behaviors that seem to suggest that this student might have a diagnosis of autism:

- Communicative Behavior

- Social Behavior

- Repetitive Behavior

2. Preference Assessment
How did the therapist identify possible motivators for the student during the preference assessment?

Did the student readily engage in any activities without being prompted to do so? If so, which activities?

Did the student resist having any activities removed? If so, what were they?

Did the student reach or request for items that were out of reach? If so, what were they?

Did the student exhibit positive affect such as smiling, laughing, or looking engaged or absorbed with any activities? If so, what were they?

3. Incorporating Preference in Teaching New Skills
Did the preferred items and activities used by the therapist seem to motivate the student? Why or why not?

What behaviors showed you that the student was engaged with the item? Not engaged?

Activity 3.2 (Time: To Be Arranged–TBA)
Becoming Familiar *Firsthand* with Ongoing Educational Activities by Assisting Teachers and/or Teaching Parents as Requested

Written Requirements: Form 3.2

Objective: To describe how you will assist in the instructional setting, you will list tasks pertaining to your classroom participation after consulting with your student's teacher

Instructions:
While awaiting feedback from your instructor on Activity 3.1 and afterward, you should use your time profitably by offering to help staff or parents. Activity 3.2 prepares you. Although the specifics may change from week to week, complete the form for now.

Before you begin teaching independently, though, wait until your instructor gives you the go-ahead. Then you will be ready to initiate instruction on your chosen objective.

1. You already have explored the student's main objectives and discussed these with the teacher or parent. Now talk to that person about ways you might be of help during ongoing educational activities. The important thing here is for you to *avoid initiating any help before obtaining the teacher's go-ahead.* Why? As you probably realize, the types of lessons and the way they are arranged for children with autism can be quite subtle and complex. For instance, with the best of intentions an observer might unwittingly interfere with a pre-designed plan. Here's an example: The objective is to have the child practice orally *requesting* "juice," in the absence of any contrived prompts.

 *The juice container is on the counter. A little boy points to the pitcher. Not receiving any juice, he begins to jump up and down and cry. A well-meaning Good Samaritan might come along, pour the juice and give it to the child. So much for that lesson for this day!*

2. Below we list a number of ways you might help, *after being adequately briefed by the teacher*. On Form 3.2, check those you agree to perform. But don't feel restricted to these. Add others you have negotiated with the teacher(s) and submit the form to your instructor.

Organizing snacks, materials or toys for lessons	Cleaning table tops, dishes or toys after use	Duplicating formal lessons for purposes of generalization
Shopping for snacks or materials	Guiding children to the bathroom, water fountain	Reading stories to the group
Putting away leftovers, re-shelving materials or toys after lessons	Guiding students from behind during lessons	Participating in or leading group games
Greeting students at bus	Helping dress them on departure	Others. List:

Form 3.2

Assisting Teachers and/or Teaching-Parents as Requested

Your Name _____ Date _____ Instructor's Name _____

After discussing ways in which I might help, we decided upon the following:
(If you are the teacher or teaching-parent, simply check N/A _____ here)

Form of Assistance	Details
• Organizing snacks, materials or toys for lessons	
• Shopping for snacks or materials	
• Putting away leftovers, re-shelving materials or toys after lessons	
• Greeting students at bus	
• Duplicating formal lessons for purposes of generalization	
• Participating in or leading group games	
• Cleaning table tops, dishes or toys after use	
• Guiding children to the bathroom or water fountain	
• Guiding students from behind during lessons	
• Helping dress them on departure	
• Reading stories to the group	
• Others. List:	

Activity 3.3 (Estimated time 2–4 hours)
Preference Assessment Checklist

An essential beginning step in working with any student with autism is to identify preferred activities and materials that can be used as reinforcers and stimuli to increase engagement.

Tools: Preference Assessment Checklist (Form 3.3) and Preference Assessment Scoring Form (Form 3.4).

Objective: Conduct preference assessment and implement **THE CHECKLIST TRAINING PROTOCOL**

Part 1–Oral Checklist: Before working with your student, your supervisor will administer the oral portion of the checklist that will be provided by direct questioning. Incorrect responses will be immediately followed with corrective verbal feedback. Your supervisor will re-administer the oral portion of the checklist until you can describe the competency at criterion levels.

Part 2–Performance Checklist:
Preparation:
1. Select items and activities to bring to the preference assessment. Some suggestions for initially identifying items include:
   - Asking the student what they like (if appropriate)
   - Asking familiar caregivers what the student likes
   - Watching the student and observing what s/he does for long periods of time without being prompted
   - Identifying the type of sensory feedback the student gains from self-stimulatory behavior, and providing toys and activities that provide similar feedback
   - Assessing reinforcers that serve the same function as problem behavior
     - o IF PROBLEM BEHAVIOR SERVES ESCAPE FUNCTION—assessing activities that allow escape from task, such as "Go play," taking a break in a tent or going to reading area
     - o IF PROBLEM BEHAVIOR SERVES ATTENTION FUNCTION—assessing activities that provide attention, such as smiles or high fives
   - IF ALL ELSE FAILS, identifying the type of self-stimulatory behaviors the student engages in and assessing those as reinforcers.
   - Remember to consider items and activities from all senses, including seeing, touching, hearing, smelling, and moving.

Form 3.1

PREFERENCE ASSESSMENT CHECKLIST
Part I: Oral Checklist

Instructions:

Supervisor scores appropriate box for each item. Part 1 of checklist is administered by direct questioning.

	+/-
Describes the importance of assessing/identifying potential reinforcers:	
a) Reinforcement results in maintenance/increase of behaviors and skills	
b) No reinforcer = no lesson	
c) Reinforcers constantly change	
PERCENT CORRECT	

CRITERIA FOR PASSING: 100% CORRECT SUPERVISOR RE-ADMINSTERS CHECKLIST IF BELOW 100%

Part 2: Performance Checklist

Instructions:

Supervisor administers Part 2 of checklist by observing the specified behaviors. For each item involved in the observation, the supervisor scores a (+) if the behavior occurs, a (-) if the behavior does not occur. For observed behaviors, administer the checklist three times, and preferably across three students.

Preparation Step: Sets up environment prior to calling the student by:	+/-
a) removing distracting items from student's reach, vision and hearing, and placing items to be assessed in bin out of sight.	

CRITERIA FOR PASSING: 100% CORRECT   SUPERVISOR RE-ADMINISTERS CHECKLIST IF BELOW 100%

	Item 1	Item 2	Item 3	Item 4	Item 5
Performs a preference assessment by:	**+/-**	**+/-**	**+/-**	**+/-**	**+/-**
a) introducing objects/activities to student one at a time.					
b) demonstrating how object can be manipulated.					
c) recording whether student manipulates object for more than 15 seconds or consumes edible.					
d) recording whether student resists when object is taken away.					
e) recording whether student reaches for object within 3 seconds when placed up to one foot away directly in front of student.					
f) recording whether student exhibits positive affect while manipulating object (e.g. smiles, laughs, or looks absorbed).					
Performs "mini-assessments" throughout session to determine continued potency of reinforcers by:					
a) following student's interest by assessing items that the student requests, reaches for, and/or watches intently.					
b) assessing items that the student, upon presentation, ceases stereotypy.					
c) placing new items in an array and asking student to choose, or by performing steps are above with the single item.					
Totals					
PERCENT CORRECT	_____ /45 x 100 = _____ %				

CRITERIA FOR PASSING: 90% CORRECT SUPERVISOR RE-ADMINSTERS CHECKLIST IF BELOW 90%

Choice Step: After conducting initial assessment, determines final choice by:	Score +/-
a) presenting the three highest rated items to student, and ranking items that are chosen as most to least preferred based on order of student selection.	

CRITERIA FOR PASSING: 100% CORRECT SUPERVISOR RE-ADMINSTERS CHECKLIST IF BELOW 100%

Form 3.4
Preference Assessment Scoring Form

Score a + for each preference behavior student exhibits

Assessed Item/Activity	Engage/ Consume	Resist	Reach	Positive Affect

LIST ITEMS WITH 3 OR MORE +'s

1. _____

2. _____

3. _____

4. _____

5. _____

RANKING: Present 3 highest ranked items, and ask student to select items, and rank as most-to-least preferred:

1st CHOICE _____

2nd CHOICE _____

3rd CHOICE _____

Unit 3 Discussion Topics

1. How would you normally go about exploring the likes and dislikes of typically developing children? How is that different from the formal preference assessment you observed? Why do you think this is done differently for children with autism?
2. It is commonplace to hear that students should be internally motivated to do work. Why do you think educators in the field of autism use preferred objects and activities as extrinsic motivators?
3. Of what value would it be for students participating in a practicum experience like this to assist personnel with routine activities? What precautions do you think would be important to follow? Add any illustrative examples you might have experienced.

Unit 4
Social Responsiveness Training

 Jeb was trying to get to know eleven-year-old, Samuel. When he asked Sam the usual social questions about where he lived or about his family, Samuel just closed his eyes and his face went flat. One day, Ashley, Samuel's teacher, came in the room and gave Sam a fist bump, exclaiming "It's Sam the man! Hey, let's play our finger game before we start!"

Jeb watched in amazement as Samuel and Ashley played a finger 'break dance' game for a few minutes. Samuel laughed with Ashley, who kept coming up with new and creative finger-break dance moves. After a few minutes of play, Ashley started her work session, and Samuel continued to smile and look at Ashley even after Ashley initiated instruction. Throughout the session, whenever it looked as if Sam might just be starting to drift off a little, Ashley returned to the finger break-dancing. In this manner, the two remained involved in the lesson until its successful conclusion.

When, later on, Jeb attempted finger break-dancing with Samuel, the boy briefly responded to him as well. The entire episode taught Jeb that "Social Responsiveness Training" was not just fun and games. Rather, because social withdrawal is a core deficit in autism, it can serve a critical role in each student's treatment.

Noticing Jeb's successful attempts to engage with Samuel, Ashley mentioned that when everyone in the kids' lives—their parents, brothers and sisters, friends and teachers—all participate in this kind of treatment, youngsters begin to avoid less and to approach new people to whom they are introduced.

Unit 2 Objectives
By the end of this week, you should be able to conduct a social responsiveness training session, collect reliable data on social responsiveness, and identify teaching strategies in the instructional setting by:

1. conducting a social responsiveness training session, collecting data, and implementing
    THE CHECKLIST TRAINING PROTOCOL.

2. observing and describing discrete trial teaching strategies used with your student.

Activity 4.1. (Estimated time: 1–3 hours)
Social Responsiveness Checklist

Tools: Social Responsiveness Data Form (Form 4.1) and Social Responsiveness Checklist (Form 4.2).

Instructions: To conduct social responsiveness training, you will first identify a preferred activity. Sometimes identifying an activity that a student with ASD both likes and that be done with two people can be challenging. It helps if you can find a therapist, friend or family member who has a good rapport with the student and note what activities they do with the student. In addition to the type of activity, note the types of body movements, affect, level of enthusiasm and physical proximity that others have found to be successful.

When you are first getting to know a student, expect to try up to 10–15 activities before finding the activity that the student likes, bring a big box of things to try, and go through activities at a rate of 30 seconds or a minute per activity.

HINTS FOR IDENTIFYING A PREFERRED ACTIVITY:
- Try activities that can be done with two people. Examples include:
  o Singing a song
  o Clapping games such as pat-a-cake
  o Drawing together
  o Reading a book
  o Movement activities, such as swinging, jumping, dancing
  o Taking pictures
  o Playing dress up
- Choose activities that the child cannot do without your participation
  o Blowing bubbles
  o Therapist making funny faces or noises
  o Therapist turning on a toy that only operates for a short time
  o Putting on a funny mask or hat
  o Playing with a puppet

WHEN CONDUCTING A SOCIAL RESPONSIVENESS SESSION:
o Remember to have fun!
o Remember that acting silly is ok!
o Some students like unpredictable movements, it keeps their attention and interest.

Instructions: Implement the **CHECKLIST TRAINING PROTOCOL**

Form 4.1

SOCIAL RESPONSIVENESS CHECKLIST
Part 1: Oral Checklist

Instructions:
Supervisor scores appropriate box for each item. Part 1 of checklist is administered by direct questioning.

	+/-
Describes importance of conducting social responsiveness sessions:	
a) Engaging in student-directed activities typically results in an increase in the student's social approach behaviors which may then more easily generalize to novel persons in the student's environment.	
PERCENT CORRECT	

CRITERIA FOR PASSING: 100% CORRECT SUPERVISOR RE-ADMINISTERS CHECKLIST IF BELOW 100%

Part 2: Performance Checklist

Instructions:
Supervisor administers Part 2 of the checklist by watching an actual teaching session or digital recording or a video of a teaching session, and observing the specified behaviors during the lesson. For each item involved in the observation, the supervisor scores a (+) if the behavior occurs, a (-) if the behavior does not occur. For observed behaviors, administer the checklist one time. If time allows, re-administer across three students.

Preparation Step: Sets up environment prior to calling the student by:	+/-
b) removing distracting items from student's reach, vision and hearing, and placing items to be assessed in bin out of sight.	
PERCENT CORRECT	

CRITERIA FOR PASSING: 100% CORRECT SUPERVISOR RE-ADMINISTERS CHECKLIST IF BELOW 100%

Implements social responsiveness procedure by:	+	-	N/A
a) conducting a preference assessment.			
b) continuing to engage student in preferred activity when initiation (i.e. following the student's lead) and preference behavior is displayed.			
c) reassessing for preference and re-engaging student in newly preferred activity when boredom or avoidance behavior is displayed.			
d) giving a minimal of verbal directives. (Safety directives are allowed—e.g. 'Don't throw that rock!')			
e) narrating the student's activity (e.g. 'You're going down the slide!') or narrating one's own activity (e.g. 'I'm going down the slide!').			
f) asking questions related to the student's preferences (e.g. 'Do you want to play tag?').			
g) having fun! (e.g. playing peek-a-boo, making funny noises or faces, etc.)			
h) trying to be unpredictable to encourage greater attention from the student.			
Totals			
PERCENT CORRECT		_____%	

CRITERIA FOR PASSING: 90% CORRECT SUPERVISOR RE-ADMINISTERS CHECKLIST IF BELOW 90%

Data Collection: Demonstrates ability to collect data appropriately by:	+/-
a) matching own data with that of the experienced instructor (scores 1-5 on social responsiveness data sheet).	

CRITERIA FOR PASSING: 100% CORRECT SUPERVISOR RE-ADMINISTERS CHECKLIST IF BELOW 100%

Form 4.2

SOCIAL RESPONSIVENESS DATA SHEET

(To be completed in conjunction with Field Assignment 4.1)

Your Name_____Instructor's Name_____Date_____

Indicate the day(s)_____ and time(s)_____ you are attending this location each week.

Directions: After each 5-minute session, assign a rating of 0-5 of the child's overall social responsivity. The rating scale is as follows:

0	The child tries to leave the therapy setting, throws tantrums, kicks, screams, throws materials around the room, cries, pushes the activity away, or refuses to engage in the activity.
1	The child remains in the therapy setting, but does not engage in the activity; and behaviors consists primarily of vocalizations and motor behaviors unrelated to the activity such as yawning, rocking, loud tapping and so on.
2	The child engages in the activity, but tends to get fidgety, and there are frequent moments of staring or inattention. The child does not seem to be happy or particularly unhappy.
3	The child engages in the activity, but there are moments of inattention and unresponsiveness.
4	The child responds to the activity and the person willingly. There are frequent moments of looking at the task and/or the person with the child.
5	The child smiles, laughs appropriately, and seems to be enjoying self, and the child is alert and involved in the activity and the person, indicated by frequent eye contact with the person and the activity materials.

Student Name	Date	Score	Comments
Student 1			
Student 2			
Student 3			

Activity 4.2 (Estimated time 1–2 hours)
Observe Discrete Trial Training

One of the most fundamental teaching strategies with students with autism is the discrete trial. You have most likely learned about discrete trial training with various modes of prompting in your coursework. For this assignment, you will be observing one or more teachers conducting discrete trial lessons with a variety of students, and will identify as many different prompts as you can.

Written Requirements: Form 4.3

Objective: Observe a discrete teaching session and identify components of discrete trial and modes of prompting.

Instructions:

With the input of your Field Facilitator, choose at least 3 students to observe during direct instruction:
- Arrive at the scheduled time with Form 4.2, a pencil or pen, and a clipboard.
- Complete Form 4.2 by listing the program name during which you observed a discrete trial, components of the trial, and describe prompt seen. For example, if you notice a teacher providing full physical prompts while working with a student, you would list "hand-over-hand assistance during zipping of coat" under the section "Full Physical."

Form 4.3

Guided Observation 2
Discrete Trial Instruction/Prompting Strategies
(To be completed in conjunction with Field Assignment 4.2)

Your Name_____Date_____

Indicate the day(s)_____ and time(s)_____ you are attending this location each week.

Choose three instructional programs for a particular student or student(s). Refer to the lesson plan and the step (specific behavior targeted). Complete the form below for each program. Observe the instructor implementing the program.

1. Discrete Trial Instruction: List the steps of the discrete trial instruction that you are observing.

- How did the instructor establish attending?

- What was the targeted instruction (cue, S^D)?

- What was the targeted correct response?

- If prompts were used, described them.

- What were the reinforcers? For prompted responses? For unprompted responses?

- What were consequences for incorrect responses?

2. Observe a variety of students involved in programming. List the types of prompting strategies you observe and the programs in which they were used.

Full Physical

Faded Physical

Gestural

Model

Verbal

Faded Verbal

Pictoral

Textual

Shadow

3. Please note any other comments or observations about the discrete trials you observed here.

Unit 4 Discussion Topics

1. How did the lessons that you observed differ from other lessons that you have seen in other settings with other populations of students?
2. Some instructors find it a difficult transition when making the shift from directing the instruction to following a student's lead during social responsiveness sessions. What was your experience with this?
3. What helped you gain higher levels of social responsiveness from your student?
4. Did you have any difficulty gaining social responsiveness with your student? If so, why do you think that happened?
5. What social approach behaviors did your student demonstrate?
6. Do you think this social responsiveness intervention is important? Why or why not?
7. The evidenced-based literature states that the discrete trial is an effective teaching tool. Based on your observations, do you agree or disagree? Why or why not?
8. Why do we use prompting strategies with our students?

Unit 5
Discrete Trial Instruction

One afternoon Rosa was observing Abby, the youngster newly assigned to her, in the Kindergarten classroom.

Rosa noticed that the Kindergarten teacher, Mrs. McKenney, was trying to teach Abby names of colors. She would put out the crayons, and ask Abby to take a blue one, or a yellow one, or an orange one. Each time Abby chose the wrong crayon, the teacher would say something like, "Oh, you picked red instead!" or "Oh, that's not yellow, that's blue." She then would allow Abby to color—an activity Abby favored—and would move on with the lesson.

All the other students in the group seemed to be able to identify at least eight basic colors, whereas Abby seemed to label them randomly. Mrs. McKenney said they had been working on colors with Abby for a long time (just red, yellow, and blue), yet she wasn't sure if the child was capable of identifying them with any consistency. Her helper, Mrs. Simon, also tried teaching Abby color names, but was working on black and white only.

When Rosa joined the group, Mrs. McKenney was delighted to pass along the color-naming task to her, reasoning that would be a perfect assignment. Rosa was excited at the prospect, but felt unsure about how best to go about it. She would ask her field supervisor, Ginger, for advice.

Ginger told Rosa she would be pleased to show her how to teach a child a specific discrimination. She should learn to do this in a manner that would be clear and help the child figure out whether or not her actions were right or wrong, simultaneously allowing the teachers to monitor progress.

They decided they would begin by presenting Abby just one color, red. After removing all other extraneous materials from the work area, they would present just one red crayon, saying "Take red." Then they would place a hand over Abby's hand and guide her to take the red crayon. Once she grasped the red crayon, they would tell her "Great job!", and allow her to color for about 5 seconds. They would repeat this sequence multiple times, gradually fading out their physical prompts from one trial to the next, until Abby was able to do this 3 times in a row with no prompting at all!

On returning to the kindergarten Rosa put the plan to the test, and wonder of wonders, it worked! Excitedly she declared to Ginger during their next meeting, "Wow, I taught Abby to identify the color red!"

"Not so fast," said Ginger. "Are you sure she is not simply choosing red because that was the only possible choice?" So, they decided to pair another crayon, a green one, with the red crayon, and repeat the instruction "Take red." At first, they would prompt Rosa to take the red crayon. Soon they were able to fade their prompts, and even add crayons of additional colors, until Abby was able to choose the red crayon in the presence of up to 4 other colors. They collected data to allow them see whether she really was able to do this with 90% accuracy.

Eventually, Rosa used this same method to teach additional colors, until, when presented with up to 4 choices, Abby was able to identify 4 different colors, with an accuracy level of over 90%.

Unit 5 Objectives

Assuming you have completed formal coursework in or otherwise mastered information about applied behavior analysis in autism educational practice, along with its principles, practices, other key features, by the end of this week you should become familiar with the specific aspects of discrete trial teaching by:

1. identifying what constitutes a correct response and collecting student response data.
2. conducting a discrete trial training session following the **CHECKLIST TRAINING PROTOCOL.**
3. observing a teaching session and identifying various types of prompting strategies the teacher used during the session.

Activity 5.1 (Estimated time 2 hours)
Collecting Student Response Data

As you begin to work in an applied behavior analysis setting, you will be expected to collect student-response data. To do this well, you will read a written program to identify the correct response and the teacher cues that precede that response. In addition, you will practice collecting student response data.

Tools: Form 5.1

Objectives: To observe a teaching session and collect student response data, you will:

1. with the input of your field facilitator, choose a student to observe during a structured teaching session.
2. with the help of the student's teacher, or your field facilitator, choose three instructional programs to observe. These programs should have comprehensive lesson plans available to review, and require trial-by-trial accuracy data.
3. upon review of the lesson plan, for each program, list the objective, current set (target) and a description of a correct response.
4. complete Form 5.1. You will include information gathered from the lesson plans, and will be observing the teaching session and collecting data while observing.

Preparation

1. Schedule 1–2 hours to observe one student in an actual site. (If you do not have an actual site, observe the DVD video on this texts companion website).
2. Observe the student working on prescribed instructional programs.
3. Arrive at the scheduled time equipped with:
   - Form 5.1
   - A pencil or pen
   - A clipboard

Form 5.1
Collecting Student Response Data

Your Name _____ Dates _/ / & / /_   Instructor _____

Observe a teaching session and choose three objectives that will be taught during the session. Complete the assignments below for each of the objectives:

Objective #1
1. What is the objective? _____
_____

2. What is the correct response? _____
_____
_____

3. Collect trial-by-trial data for a total of 10 trials:

Trial	1	2	3	4	5	6	7	8	9	10
+/-										

4. Compare your data with the teacher. Are your data points similar? Y / N

Objective #2
1. What is the objective? _____
_____

2. What is the correct response? _____
_____
_____

3. Collect trial-by-trial data for a total of 10 trials:

Trial	1	2	3	4	5	6	7	8	9	10
+/-										

4. Compare your data with the teacher. Are your data points similar? Y / N

Objective #3
1. What is the objective? _____
_____

2. What is the correct response? _____
_____

3. Collect trial-by-trial data for a total of 10 trials:

Trial	1	2	3	4	5	6	7	8	9	10
+/-										

4. Compare your data with the teacher. Are your data points similar? Y / N

Activity 5.2 (Estimated time: 1–2 hours)
Discrete Trial Instruction Checklist

Now that you have observed discrete trial teaching programs, it's your turn to try. During this assignment, you will practice incorporating a lesson using discrete trials.

Tools: Discrete Trial Checklist (Form 5.2)

Objective: Conduct a discrete trial training session following the **CHECKLIST TRAINING PROTOCOL**

Instructions:

With the input of your student's teacher or field facilitator, choose a student with whom you can practice implementing discrete trials. With their assistance, choose three instructional programs that you can implement with the student. These programs should have comprehensive lesson plans available to guide you, and should incorporate discrete trials as a teaching strategy. **THE PROGRAMS YOU CHOOSE SHOULD BE BASED ON SKILLS THE STUDENT HAS MASTERED ALREADY.** This provision will increase the probability that the student will be successful during your lesson, and therefore, help you yourself to maintain your focus on delivery of instruction and reinforcement. In addition, this will substantially decrease the probability that you will need to insert prompts. (If a response requires considerable prompting, please have your supervisor help you with this skill or choose an easier lesson).

Form 5.2

Discrete Trial Checklist

Part 1: Oral Checklist

Instructions:

	+/-
1. Describes components of discrete trial instructional sequence:	
S^D, Prompt (if needed), Response, Consequence, Inter-trial Interval	
2. Describes four benefits of using discrete trial teaching:	
a) Each discrete trial provides a clear, concise instruction.	
b) Discrete trials clearly indicate the elements of a correct response.	
c) Given that each component of the discrete trial is clearly defined, the method supports consistent teaching across instructors.	
d) Discrete trials permit the instructor to monitor students' progress by evaluating rates of learning for each new skill.	
PERCENT CORRECT	

Supervisor scores appropriate box for each item. Part 1 of checklist is administered by direct questioning.

CRITERIA FOR PASSING: 100% CORRECT SUPERVISOR RE-ADMINISTERS CHECKLIST IF BELOW 100%

Part 2: Performance Checklist

Instructions:

Supervisor administers Part 2 of the checklist by observing an actual teaching session, a digital recording or a video of a teaching session, and observing the specified behaviors for the first ten trials of the lesson. For each item involved in the observation, the supervisor scores a (+) if the behavior occurs, a (-) if the behavior does not occur. For observed behaviors, administer the checklist one time. If time allows, re-administer across three students.

Implements discrete trial procedure by:	Score first 10 trials									
	+/-	+/-	+/-	+/-	+/-	+/-	+/-	+/-	+/-	+/-
1. obtaining student's attention before presenting the instruction.										
2. providing the steps of the discrete trial in the appropriate sequence.										
3. providing a clear and concise discriminative stimulus (S^D).										
4. allowing student 5 seconds to respond (unless otherwise specified in the individual lesson plan).										
5. providing student with appropriate consequences:										
a) contingent on behavior										
b) immediate										
c) consistent (unless during maintenance phase)										
d) unambiguous										
6. prompting the desired response, if necessary:										
a) prompts provided following the S^D										
b) prompts effective in evoking the desired response										
c) prompts faded systematically										
7. maintaining inter-trial intervals at 3 seconds or less in duration										
Totals										
PERCENT CORRECT	_____ %									

CRITERIA FOR PASSING: 90% CORRECT SUPERVISOR RE-ADMINISTERS CHECKLIST IF BELOW 90%

Activity 5.3 (Estimated time 1–2 hours)
Prompts Across the Day

As you begin to teach using the methods of applied behavior analysis, you will find you often need to use a variety of prompting strategies. Probably you have learned in your coursework about various modes of prompting. For this assignment, you will be observing one or more teachers conducting lessons with a variety of students, and will identify as many different prompts as you can.

Written Requirements: Form 5.3

Objective: Observe a teaching session and identify modes of prompting.

Instructions:

- With the input of your field facilitator, choose at least 3 students to observe during direct instruction. Observing students during times when they require shadowing to increase independence would be especially beneficial.
- Arrive at the scheduled time with Form 3.3, a pencil or pen, and a clipboard.
- Complete Form 3.3 by listing the program name during which you observed a specific type of prompt, and describe each prompt you saw. For example, if you notice a teacher providing full physical prompts while working with a student, you would list "hand-over-hand assistance during zipping of coat" under the section "Full Physical."

Form 5.3 (p. 1 of 1)

Your Name _____ Dates _//_ & _//_ Instructor _____

Indicate the day(s) _____ and times _____ you are attending this location each week.

Prompts Across the Day: Observe a variety of students participating in instruction. List modes of prompts you observe and the programs in which they were used.

<u>Full Physical</u>
1.

2.

<u>Faded Physical</u>
1.

2.

<u>Gestural</u>
1.

2.

<u>Model</u>
1.

2.

<u>Verbal</u>

1.

2.

<u>Faded Verbal</u>

1.

2.

<u>Shadow</u>

1.

2.

<u>Other prompts you may see</u>:

Unit 5 Discussion Topics

1. What do you feel was the most effective part(s) of the lessons that you observed?

2. How did the student respond to the lessons?

3. If you have worked in a public school, what challenges would you anticipate in conducting 1:1 sessions in that setting?

4. Under what circumstances do you think prompting would be most helpful? When do you think it would be least helpful?

5. Would you agree with the following statement "The prompting strategy you use will vary across students and tasks?" If you agree, why? If you do not agree, why not?

Unit 6
Most-to-Least Prompting

Jeb, the new practicum student, was eager to begin teaching.

He decided to start with something very functional for Abby. On the girl's Individual Educational Plan (IEP), he noticed that Abby was learning how to use a napkin to wipe her hands clean. Having noticed that Abby usually soiled her hands considerably while she ate, Jeb figured that helping Abby wipe her hands would make her appear more presentable when she ate at local restaurants, something her family enjoyed doing.

Thinking this would be a pretty easy task, Jeb sat down with Abby while she was eating her lunch. Whenever Abby's hands became soiled, Jeb said "Abby, wipe your hands." Abby never responded appropriately. So Jeb attempted different things. One day, he tried to demonstrate to Abby by wiping his own hands. On other days he would hand Abby a napkin and Abby would tap her hand with the napkin and then put it down. After three weeks, progress remained at a standstill.

In response to a plea for help, Jeb asked Ginger, his Field Supervisor, for help. Ginger responded by demonstrating the more systematic most-to-least prompting system. The two also agreed to give Abby added opportunities to practice the hand-wiping skill by practicing in her classroom.

Ginger gave Abby a very messy tuna fish sandwich, and began with a full physical prompt, placing her hand over the girl's and helping her use the napkin to wipe the mess off her hands. This method prevented Abby from making any errors and allowed her to enjoy the success of having clean hands. They then practiced this routine three times, after which Ginger began to fade her prompt by reducing the amount of pressure she placed on Abby's hands. By the next day, Ginger had faded the partial physical prompt to a gestural prompt; and after several more days, she was able to remove the prompt all together, as all rejoiced in Abby's now consistently clean hands.

Unit 6 Objectives

By the end of this week, you should be able to provide the student(s) the opportunity to be successful by implementing most-to-least prompting. You will learn how to gradually fade the prompt so that your student responds to the targeted stimulus by:

1. Collecting accuracy data on prompted and unprompted student responses during most-to-least prompting.
2. Conducting most-to-least prompting and implementing **THE CHECKLIST TRAINING PROTOCOL.**

Activity 6.1 (Estimated time: 1–3 hours)
Most-to-Least Prompting Checklist

Tools: Most-to-least prompting checklist—Form 6.1

*Objective*s: Conducting most-to-least prompting

EXAMPLE:

TEACHER PROVIDES TARGET STIMULUS (CUE) WITH A PROMPT

Example: The teacher asks the student to use a napkin when food is on his face. Because this is the student's introduction to the task, the teacher provides a full physical prompt by providing hand-over–hand assistance to wipe the student's face.

When the student responds to this without resistance:
The teacher provides a partial physical prompt, by lightly guiding the student's hand to wipe the student's face.

When the student responds to this correctly (by cooperating with the teacher):
The teacher provides a gestural prompt by pointing to the napkin and/or areas of the face that need to be cleaned.

When the student responds to this correctly:
The teacher provides a shadow prompt by keeping her hands about 1–3 inches from the student's hands.

When the student responds to this correctly:
The teacher removes the prompts altogether.

Instructions:

Select a task lesson that uses most-to-least prompting with the student. Ideally, this would be a program that is in the beginning stages of acquisition, or a program with which the student is experiencing difficulty.

Activity 6.2. (Estimated time: 1–3 hours)
Most-to-Least Prompting Data Collection
(Note: This activity will be completed in conjunction with activity 6.2)

Tools: Form 6.2

Objective: Record data while teaching a task that utilizes a most-to-least prompting strategy.

After you have practiced using the most-to-least prompting technique while teaching a task, you will take data on the student responses. After taking the data, you will calculate the percentage of steps that the student performed independently.

Form 6.1

MOST-TO-LEAST PROMPTING CHECKLIST

Part 1: Oral Checklist

	+/-
1. Describes importance of implementing most-to-least prompting:	
Most-to-least prompting offers the student more opportunities for success during tasks with which they are experiencing particular difficulty, or those that have histories of repeated failure. In these situations, providing the student with as much support as needed, then gradually fading that support ensures higher degrees of success and reinforcement. Gradual fading is utilized because when an effective prompt is removed prematurely, the student often fails to respond to the discriminative stimulus (S^D).	
2. Describes how one might use most-to-least prompting to teach a skill, and includes:	
a) a description of the target instruction and controlling prompt stimulus;	
b) a description of the progression of a most-to-least sequence, that is, by providing lesser degrees of assistance when the student produces the correct response within a specified amount of time;	
c) an example of a specific sequence, such as moving from full physical, to partial physical, to gestural prompt categories based on one or more (depending on the student's skills and learning history) correct responses at each more intrusive prompt level.	
PERCENT CORRECT	

Supervisor scores appropriate box for each item. Part 1 of checklist is administered by direct questioning.

CRITERIA FOR PASSING: 100% CORRECT SUPERVISOR RE-ADMINISTERS CHECKLIST IF BELOW 100%

Part 2: Performance Checklist

Instructions:

Supervisor administers Part 2 of the checklist by watching a digital recording or a video of a teaching session, and observing the specified behaviors during the lesson. For each item involved in the observation, the supervisor scores a (+) if the behavior is implemented correctly, a (-) if the behavior is implemented incorrectly, and N/A if it is not necessary or applicable to perform the behavior. For observed behaviors, administer the checklist one time. If time allows, re-administer across three students.

Implements most-to-least procedure by:	+/-	+/-	+/-	+/-	+/-	+/-
a) delivering the S^D and providing the degree of assistance necessary for the student to respond correctly;						
b) providing lesser degrees of assistance when the student produces a correct response within the specified amount of time, and;						
c) slightly increasing greater degrees of assistance when the student makes 1–2 errors at a given prompt level.						
Totals						
PERCENT CORRECT						

CRITERIA FOR PASSING: 90% CORRECT SUPERVISOR RE-ADMINISTERS CHECKLIST IF BELOW 90%

	+	-	N/A
Consistently blocks incorrect responses			

CRITERIA FOR PASSING: 100% CORRECT SUPERVISOR RE-ADMINISTERS CHECKLIST IF BELOW 100%

Form 6.2

Your Name_____Date(s)_____Instructor_____

This activity will be completed in conjunction with Field Assignment 6.2. After you have run a program using most-to-least prompting, you will run it again while taking data. Complete the form below. If your program is run in a discrete trial format, use Data Form 1 (below). If the program is run in a task-analysis format, use Data Form 2.

Data Form #1: Discrete Trial Format

1. Collect trial-by-trial data for a total of 10–20 trials.

Trial	1	2	3	4	5	6	7	8	9	10
+/P										

Trial	11	12	13	14	15	16	17	18	19	20
+/P										

Final Score*:_____%
*Total Number of independent unprompted responses (+)/Total Number of Trials X 100 = Percent Unprompted Correct Trials

Data Form #2: Task Analysis Format.

List All Steps of the Task Analysis You Are Observing	Score *(see below*)*
1.	
2.	
3.	
4.	
5.	
6.	
7.	
8.	
9.	
10.	
Percent Correct Independent (see below)	

Percent correct is number of independent (I)/Total Steps X 100

* Correct Unprompted Independent (I), Full Physical (FP), Partial Physical (PP), Gestural (G), Model (M), Verbal (V), Faded Verbal (FV)

Unit 6 Discussion Topics

1. Under what circumstances do you think it would be especially helpful to use most-to-least prompting with students?
2. Provide a few original examples of situations in which you believe using most-to-least prompting would be ill advised?
3. What circumstances would signal an opportunity to fade the artificial prompt?
4. Would there ever be a circumstance in which increased prompting would be considered after prompts had been faded? Why or why not?
5. What considerations are there when deciding how to reinforce prompted trials?

Unit 7
Graduated Guidance

 Noticing Samuel watch longingly as other children zipped around the playground on their bikes, Jeb couldn't wait to teach him how to ride a two-wheel bike independently. While Samuel had become proficient with the training wheels, now it was time for the next big step. After loading Samuel up with protective helmet and pads, they were ready for their first session. Jeb steadied the back of the bike seat while Samuel hopped on. "Ready! Set! Ride!!" he exclaimed. Samuel began to pedal and as he started to gain his balance, Jeb loosened his grip until just his fingertips touched the seat. When Samuel began to wobble a bit, Jeb tightened his grip. He continued to adjust his grip as necessary until Samuel maintained his balance. Then he shadowed Sam with his hands about a foot away. At this point, Sam really took off, pedaling away on his own!

Sally, Jeb's field facilitator, said "Hey Jeb, that was a perfect execution of 'Graduated Guidance!' Probably you read about that in your ABA course. Now you've applied it to a real life situation!"

"Yo, Sally! Reading about it is one thing but actually seeing it work, now that's something else altogether. Gotta' think of other ways to use this with the kids in the gym and out here on the playground!"

Unit 7 Objective

By the end of this week, you should be able to provide the student(s) the opportunity to be successful in motor tasks by implementing prompt fading with graduated guidance. You will learn how to gradually fade the physical prompt so that your student responds to the targeted stimulus by conducting graduated guidance and implementing **THE CHECKLIST TRAINING PROTOCOL.**

Activity 7.1 (Estimated time: 1–3 hours)
Graduated Guidance Checklist

Tools: Graduated guidance checklist—Form 7.1

EXAMPLE:

TEACHER PROVIDES TARGET STIMULUS (CUE)
ALONG WITH PROMPT

Example: Teacher is providing a bike-riding lesson. The student is participating in the first session on a two-wheeled bike without the training wheels.

The teacher guides the student by firmly holding the back of the seat.

When the student starts to gain balance:
Teacher fades to a partial prompt, such as lightly holding the back of the seat.

When the student maintains balance:
The teacher fades to a shadowing prompt by keeping hand within 1 inch of student's seat.

If the student starts to lose his balance:
Teacher blocks response (by preventing his fall) and returns to physical prompting by firmly holding his seat.

When the student regains balance:
Teacher fades again to a partial physical prompt, such as lightly holding the seat.

When the student maintains balance:
Teacher fades to a shadowing prompt, such as keeping hand within 1 inch of seat.

When the student continues to maintain balance:
The teacher removes the prompts altogether, allowing the student to independently ride the bike.

Instructions:

Select a lesson that uses graduated guidance with the student. Programs where this strategy is used involve teaching a motor response in the beginning stages of learning.

Form 7.1

GRADUATED GUIDANCE CHECKLIST

Part 1: Oral Checklist

	Score +/-
1. Describes the importance of conducting graduated guidance:	
Sometimes simply reinforcing a few physically prompted trials is sufficient for students with ASD to then make movements on their own. For others, abrupt transfer from physical guidance to no physical guidance is too large a step. When the physical prompt is prematurely dropped, stimulus control does not transfer to the naturally existing stimuli. Therefore, additional prompt fading steps must be added.	
2. Describes how one might use graduated guidance to teach a physical skill, and includes:	
a) a description of the target instruction and controlling stimulus;	
b) a description of fading of a physical prompt based on the level of independent engagement;	
c) fading that involves starting at the level where the student responds to the controlling stimulus (e.g. hand over-hand, touch, hand near but not touching, hand one foot away, etc.)	
d) continually adjusting the level of prompt depending upon student responses, that is, increasing the level of prompting if the student starts to respond incorrectly, and decreasing when the student regains more independent engagement within the same response and/or across responses.	
PERCENT CORRECT	

Instructions: Supervisor scores appropriate box for each item. Part 1 of checklist is administered by direct questioning.

CRITERIA FOR PASSING: 100% CORRECT SUPERVISOR RE-ADMINISTERS CHECKLIST IF BELOW 100%

Part 2: Performance Checklist

Instructions:

Supervisor administers Part 2 of the checklist by watching a digital recording or a video tape of a teaching session, and observing the specified behaviors during the lesson. For each item involved in the observation, the supervisor scores a (+) if the behavior is implemented correctly, a (-) if the behavior is implemented incorrectly, and N/A if it is not necessary or applicable to perform the behavior. For observed behaviors, administer the checklist one time. If time allows, re-administer across three students.

Conducts graduated guidance by:	Score first 10 trials									
	+/-	+/-	+/-	+/-	+/-	+/-	+/-	+/-	+/-	+/-
a) delivering the S^D and providing the degree of assistance necessary for the student to respond correctly;										
b) adjusting the intensity of physical assistance based on the level of the student's independence (gradually loosening the intensity and locus of assistance when the student begins to respond independently and increasing assistance if the student fails to make the correct response).										
Totals										
PERCENT CORRECT	_____ %									

CRITERIA FOR PASSING: 90% CORRECT SUPERVISOR RE-ADMINISTERS CHECKLIST IF BELOW 90%

	+	-	N/A
Consistently blocks incorrect responses			

CRITERIA FOR PASSING: 100% CORRECT SUPERVISOR RE-ADMINISTERS CHECKLIST IF BELOW 100%

Unit 7 Discussion Topics

1. When do you think it would be helpful to use graduated guidance with students?
2. What would you do if your student resisted your physical prompt?
3. Would there ever be a circumstance where you increased prompting again after it was faded? Why or why not?
2. What considerations are there when deciding how to reinforce a student throughout a graduated guidance procedure?

Unit 8
Least-to-Most Prompting

Jeb felt a little nervous as he set off on his own with Samuel for the cafeteria. Navigating the lunchroom crowd, he worried that Samuel would not know what to do. Hoping to be helpful, Jeb jumped in to help Samuel open his lunch box and all of the boy's containers. Samuel's teacher, Ashland, thanked Jeb for his attempts, but asked Jeb to watch him with Samuel the next day at lunch. Jeb was surprised to see Samuel open his lunch box on his own along with all the containers except one. When Samuel was unable to open that last container, he presented it to Ashland and spoke the word "help." Ashland opened it partially and signaled him to open the rest.

Jeb exclaimed, "Wow, I didn't know he could do all that!"

Ashland explained that Samuel had originally learned all those steps, by means of most-to-least prompting of each step identified on the basis of a carefully crafted task analysis. "But now that he knows how to do it, we need to remind the teachers to remember to back off to give Samuel a chance at independence!"

Unit 8 Objective

By the end of this week, you should be able to use least-to-most prompting to offer the student the opportunity to respond in advance of more intrusive prompts on each trial. This will be accomplished by conducting least-to-most prompting and implementing **THE CHECKLIST TRAINING PROTOCOL.**

Activity 8.1 (Estimated time: 1–3 hours)
Least-to-Most Prompting Checklist

Instructions: Select a task-analysis lesson that uses least-to-most prompting with the student. Ideally, this would be a program that the student is already working on, such as a self-care, vocational, leisure, or functional community skill.

NOTE: If you do not have a readily available task analysis, you may use the sample task analysis for washing hands.

Tools: Hand washing task analysis (if needed). Form 8.1 and Least-to Most Prompting Checklist—Form 8.2

EXAMPLE:

TEACHER PROVIDES TARGET STIMULUS (CUE) WITHOUT PROMPT.

Example: The teacher asks the student to use a napkin when there is food on his face.

If the student does not respond to this within 3 seconds: The teacher provides a gestural prompt by pointing to the napkin.

If the student does not respond to this in 3 seconds: The teacher provides a partial physical prompt, by lightly guiding the student's hand in the direction of the napkin.

If the student does not respond to this within 3 seconds: The teacher provides a full physical prompt by providing hand-over–hand assistance to wipe the student's face.

Form 8.1

Handwashing Task Analysis

Your Name_____Date(s)_____Instructor_____

This activity will be completed in conjunction with Activity 8.1. After you have run a program using least-to-most prompting, you will run it again while taking data. Complete the form below. For each step of the task analysis, enter the code that represents the level of prompting the student requires to complete that step.

Program Name: Washed Hands

Prompting Hierarchy Least to Most
Sample CODE:
I: Independent
M: Model
G: Gestural
PP: Partial Physical
FP: Full Physical

List the Steps of the Task Analysis You Are Observing	Score
1. Turn on faucet	
2. Put hands under water	
3. Get soap on hands	
4. Rub hands together 3–5 seconds	
5. Put hands under water for 3–5 seconds	
6. Turn off water	
7. Walk to paper towel dispenser	
8. Get paper towel	
9. Rub paper towel between hands 3–5 seconds	
10. Throw paper towel in trash	
Percent Correct Independent (see below)	

Percent correct is Number of Independent (I)/Total steps X 100
Comments:

Form 8.2

LEAST-TO-MOST PROMPTING CHECKLIST

Part 1: Oral Checklist

	Score +/-
1. Describes importance of conducting least-to-most prompting:	
Least-to-most prompting offers the student the opportunity to respond in advance of more intrusive prompts on a trial-by-trial basis. This is accomplished by interposing a small period of time between the relevant instruction and the prompt that least intrusively sets the occasion for the response. More intrusive prompting is applied only if less intrusive prompts are unsuccessful, which reduces the chance of applying unnecessarily intrusive prompts.	
2. Describes how one might use least-to-most prompting to teach a skill, and includes:	
a) a description of the target instruction and controlling stimulus	
b) a description of the progression of a least-to-most sequence, by providing greater degrees of assistance when the student does not produce the correct response within a specified amount of time	
c) an example of a specific sequence, such as moving from verbal to gestural to physical prompt categories based on lack of correct responding to less intrusive prompts.	
PERCENT CORRECT	

Instructions:
Supervisor scores appropriate box for each item. Part 1 of checklist is administered by direct questioning.

CRITERIA FOR PASSING: 100% CORRECT SUPERVISOR RE-ADMINISTERS CHECKLIST IF BELOW 100%

Part 2: Performance Checklist

Instructions:
Supervisor administers Part 2 of the checklist by watching a digital recording or a video recording of a teaching session, and observing the specified behaviors during the lesson. For each item involved in the observation, the supervisor scores a (+) if the behavior is implemented correctly, a (-) if the behavior is implemented incorrectly, and N/A if it is not necessary or applicable to perform the behavior. For observed behaviors, administer the checklist one time. If time allows, re-administer across three students.

Conducts least-to-most prompting procedure by:	Score first 10 trials									
	+/-	+/-	+/-	+/-	+/-	+/-	+/-	+/-	+/-	+/-
a) delivering the S^D and giving the student the opportunity to perform the response on each trial										
b) providing greater degrees of assistance when the student does not produce a correct response within the specified amount of time.										
Totals										
PERCENT CORRECT	____%									

CRITERIA FOR PASSING: 90% CORRECT SUPERVISOR RE-ADMINISTERS CHECKLIST IF BELOW 90%

	+	-	N/A
Consistently blocks incorrect responses			

CRITERIA FOR PASSING: 100% CORRECT SUPERVISOR RE-ADMINISTERS CHECKLIST IF BELOW 100%

Activity 8.2 (Estimated time: 1–3 hours)
Least-to-Most Prompting Data Collection
(Note: This activity will be completed in conjunction with Activity 8.1)

After you have practiced using the least-to-most prompting technique while teaching a sequentially-based task, you will take data on the student responses. After taking the data, you will calculate the percentage of steps that the student performed independently.

Tools: Form 8.3 (if you are using a task analysis that has been already implemented at your field site. Form 8.1 if you need to use the handwashing task analysis.

Objective: Record data while teaching a sequence that utilizes a least-to-most prompting strategy.

Form 8.3

Your Name_____Date(s)_____Instructor_____

This activity will be completed in conjunction with Activity 8.1. After you have run a program using least-to-most prompting, you will run it again while taking data. Complete the form below. For each step of the task analysis, enter the code that represents the level of prompting the student requires to complete that step.

Program Name_____

Prompting Hierarchy Least to Most
Sample CODE:
I: Independent
M: Model
G: Gestural
PP: Partial Physical
FP: Full Physical

List the Steps of the Task Analysis You Are Observing	Score
1.	
2.	
3.	
4.	
5.	
6.	
7.	
8.	
9.	
10.	
Percent Correct Independent (see below)	

Percent correct is Number of Independent (I)/Total steps X 100
Comments:

Activity 8.3 (Estimated time: 15 minutes)
Interim Field Facilitator Assessment

Written Requirements: Form 8.4

Objectives: To demonstrate an acceptable level of professionalism, you will identify and engage in professional skills including, but not limited to, receptivity, flexibility, helpfulness, responsibility, reliability, rate of productivity and timeliness.

Instructions for Practicum Student

Please fill in the information requested in the heading. Then give the attached form to your field supervisor or facilitator to complete. If applicable, request that it be sent to your instructor before the end of the current week and ask for your own a copy of the completed form.

If you are a parent working with your own child at home, you may ask a member of your child's team or another family member to complete the form. If you are working alone, assess your own performance. When you submit the form, please attach an explanation of your circumstances.

Form 8.4 (p. 1 of 2) Assessment of Practicum Student's Professional Skills

Upper portion to be filled out by ABA Practicum Student

ABA Student's Name _____ Date_____
Field Facilitator's Name _____
Field Facilitator Contact Information:
Phone _____ Fax _____ email _____
ABA Instructor's Contact Information:
Phone _____ Fax _____ email _____

(ABA students working from a distance should provide the *field facilitator* with a stamped envelope addressed to the instructor. Overseas students should use OVERSEAS AIRMAIL stamps.)

Instructions for Field Facilitator

   Thank you for your willingness to facilitate our ABA student's participation in your program. We hope this relationship is proving to be productive. At this point, our ABA student has been participating in the field practicum for several weeks. To help guide his or her progress, we ask you to take just a few minutes to complete the form below. Toward the end of the sequence, we shall make a similar request to allow you, the student and the ABA instructor to assess the student's progress in the interim.

This portion to be filled out by the Field Supervisor or Field Facilitator

1) Please **complete** and **duplicate** the form. 2) Give one copy to the practicum student.
3) Send another to the ABA instructor by the end of the week. Keep the original for your own files.

ABA Practicum Student's Professional Skill	5	4	3	2	1	N/A
Is friendly (regularly looks directly at, smiles, greets people individually)						
Listens respectfully (waits while they talk; responds to the point)						
Responds to and gives positive and constructive feedback						
Is flexible (adjusts to new conditions)						
Is helpful in the program						
States plans and expectations clearly						
Undertakes responsibilities and plans time carefully						
Meets responsibilities s/he has undertaken						
Schedules time realistically						
Completes responsibilities on time						
Is prepared in advance of instructional sessions						
Strives for excellence in written and oral communication						
Is patient with his or her student						
Works productively with his/her student						
I would recommend hiring this student as a Behavior Analyst						

5 = consistently;   4 = most of the time;   3 = at an acceptable level;
2 = once in a while;   1 rarely or not at all;   N/A Not applicable

Unit 8 Discussion Topics

1. When do you think it would be helpful to use least-to-most prompting with students?

2. Share your experience with conducting least-to-most prompting:
    a) What were the specific prompts that you used?
    b) Were they effective?
    c) Did you think you should have used different prompts in your hierarchy, in terms of intensity or modality?

3. Compare and contrast situations where you might use most-to-least prompting vs. least-to-most prompting.

4. Of what value is your Field Facilitator's assessment of your professional performance? What other feedback might you have appreciated?

Unit 9
Take a Break![22]

Take a moment to skim through your progress chart and the packet of materials you have prepared to date. You will be impressed with the quantity of your accomplishments!

During a relatively, short amount of time you have conducted preference assessments and social responsiveness sessions, as well as begun to implement discrete trial and task-analyzed instruction. In addition, you have begun to take data and learn prompt fading strategies. Upon your return, you will continue to learn how to fade prompts, and begin to provide more naturalistic instruction through incidental teaching. Ultimately, you will be able to follow any instructional program designed to teach students with autism with these foundational teaching strategies.

Unit 9 Optional Discussion Topics

1. Share your reaction to your own review of your accomplishments to date.
2. Describe how you spent your break.
3. This breather may have allowed you to form some new perspectives. What are they?

---

[22] *Instructor*: Depending on your academic or program schedule, you may wish to place this break elsewhere or skip it altogether.

Unit 10
Time Delay Prompting

Jeb had been working with Sam for several months, and concluded that sometimes he should step back to see what Sam actually was capable of doing on his own.

One week, the school had a winter party, and they put some yummy treats on the table. Instead of anticipating what Sam wanted, Jeb decided to just wait and see, if, and what, Sam would request independently. Sam just sat there looking longingly at the food. Only after Jeb asked Sam what he wanted, did Sam say he wanted the popcorn.

Given that state of affairs, Jeb decided to try to promote Sam's spontaneity by using a new time-delay prompting strategy about which he had been reading. It worked like this:
Jeb held up a piece of popcorn and said "Say, 'I want popcorn!'" When Sam imitated Jeb, he gave Sam a piece of popcorn. The next time he displayed the popcorn he waited a few seconds, then modeled "I want popcorn!" Sam imitated him again. The third time, Jeb held up the popcorn and began to wait, Sam anticipated the prompt by spontaneously saying "I want popcorn!"

Jeb said, "Wow, that time delay strategy really works! I can't wait to try this with all sorts of things Sam wants! His life will be so much richer when he becomes capable of asking for things without waiting for people to ask him what he wants! This is gonna' be great!"

Unit 10 Objectives

By the end of this unit you should be able to implement the time delay prompting strategy, as well as observe time delay and other strategies used in group settings by:
1. conducting time delay strategies using the **CHECKLIST TRAINING PROTOCOL.**
2. observing situations where time delay and other prompting strategies are used to help transfer control from prompt stimuli to stimuli delivered from teachers or during functional routines in the natural setting.

Activity 10.1 (Estimated time 1–2 hours)
Time Delay Prompting Checklist

Tools: Time delay checklist—Form 10.1
Objective: Conducting time delay checklist using **CHECKLIST TRAINING PROTOCOL**

Step 1: CHOOSE A TASK
With the input of your field facilitator, choose 1–2 programs where you can conduct a time delay strategy. When selecting a response to use for this exercise, make sure that the response is already in your student's repertoire and under the control of a prompt stimulus.
Programs that this strategy can be used with include:
- Requesting
- Purchasing skills
- Assembly tasks
- Making beds
- Social play
- Independent travel
- Verbalizing affection

Step 2: DETERMINE THE DESIGNATED NATURAL STIMULUS

Task	Natural Stimulus
Requesting preferred item	Preferred item
Requesting help	Difficult task
Open door	Knock on door

Step 3: DETERMINE THE EFFECTIVE PROMPT
This would be the most unobtrusive prompt possible that is effective in reliably occasioning the response. These can be:
- a gesture
- a verbal model
- a full physical prompt
- a partial physical prompt
- a visual cue, such as
  - a word
  - a picture
  - a script
  - a symbol
  -

Natural Stimulus	Possible Prompt	Target Response
Preferred item [juice}	Say 'I want juice'"	"I want juice"
Difficult task	Say 'I need help'"	"I need help"
Knock on door	"Open the door"	Opens door

Step 4: DETERMINE THE LENGTH OF THE TIME DELAY AND INSERT IT BETWEEN THE NATURAL STIMULUS AND THE PROMPT

CONSTANT TIME DELAY: **Determine the length of time before prompting, such as 3 seconds, 5 seconds, or 10 seconds**

.

Example:

PRESENT NATURAL STIMULUS	DELAY PROMPT
Present juice	Wait 5 s"Say 'I want juice'"

PROGRESSIVE TIME DELAY:

Example:

PRESENT NATURAL STIMULUS	DELAY PROMPT
Present juice	Wait 0 s "Say 'I want juice'"
Present juice	Wait 2 s "Say 'I want juice'"
Present juice	Wait 4 s "Say 'I want juice'"
Present juice	Wait 6 s "Say 'I want juice'"

EXAMPLE OF TIME DELAY WITH A STUDENT WHO COMMUNICATES WITH 2–3 WORD SPEECH UTTERANCES

CONTEXT: The preference assessment shows that the student likes to bounce a ball.

Step 1: The teacher sits across from the student and allows him to bounce the ball for 5 to 10 seconds.

Step 2: The teacher says, "It's my turn!" and takes the ball and plays with it for 5 to 10 seconds. If the student does not request the ball back, the teacher implements the time delay strategy by:

   a) Holding up the ball and looking expectantly at her student for 5 seconds. If he does not request,

   b) Models "I want ball!"

   c) After the student imitates her she gives him the ball.

   d) She repeats this process, increasing the length of the time delay by 2 s on each opportunity, until the student requests in the presence of the ball.

EXAMPLE OF TIME DELAY WITH A STUDENT WHO COMMUNICATES WITH A VOICE OUTPUT SYSTEM

Context: Art table

Student: Starts to reach across another student to get a marker.

Teacher: Blocks access to the marker and looks at the student expectantly for 5 seconds

Student: Does not request, but rather just looks at teacher

Teacher: Points to the voice output system

Student: Activates the voice output system to say, "I want marker"

Teacher: Gives student the marker

Teacher: Positions other art materials out of reach so that the student has multiple natural opportunities to practice throughout the project.

Form 10.1

TIME DELAY CHECKLIST

Part 1: Oral Checklist

Supervisor scores appropriate box for each item. Part 1 of checklist is administered by direct questioning.

	Score +/-
1. Describes importance of implementing time delay:	
This is one method to ensure that the student will follow the targeted discriminative stimuli designated to evoke the behavior . The time delay induces transfer of control from the prompt stimuli (artificial) to the target S^D (natural) by introducing a pause between the S^D and the prompt.	
2. Describes why it is important to use time delay as an element of natural language training:	
Students often wait until they are spoken to before they communicate their wants and needs. The time delay procedure is a method used to increase the spontaneity of a student's communicative attempts by waiting for a request rather than automatically providing desired items or activities. After the brief period of waiting, a prompt is provided.	
2. Describes how one might use time delay, and includes:	
a) a description of the student's desired item and the prompt	
b) a description of the time delay procedure: displaying the targeted S^D, and waiting a specific brief period of time before providing the prompt, (after which, if the student responds appropriately, as by correctly saying, signing, using a voice-activated device or exchanging a picture) the reinforce is presented.	
PERCENT CORRECT	

CRITERIA FOR PASSING: 100% CORRECT SUPERVISOR RE-ADMINISTERS CHECKLIST IF BELOW 100%

Part 2: Performance Checklist

Instructions:
Supervisor administers Part 2 of the checklist by watching actual teaching session or a digital recording or a video tape of a teaching session, and observing the specified behaviors during the lesson. For each item involved in the observation, the supervisor scores a (+) if the behavior is implemented correctly, a (-) if the behavior is implemented incorrectly, and N/A if it is not necessary or applicable to perform the behavior. For observed behaviors, administer the checklist one time. If time allows, re-administer across three students.

Implements time delay procedure by:	Score first 10 trials									
	+/-	+/-	+/-	+/-	+/-	+/-	+/-	+/-	+/-	+/-
a) delivering the targeted discriminative stimulus (S^D)										
b) waiting for predetermined duration…5s, 10s, etc. (rather than immediately giving a prompt)										
c) waiting expectantly—using non-verbal cues (e.g. expectant facial expression, saliently Displaying materials)										
d) immediately reinforcing the student if the targeted response follows the S^D										
e) prompting the student to make the correct response after the time delay										
f) increasing the length of the time delay over successive teaching opportunities if using progressive time delay										
Totals										
PERCENT CORRECT	_____ %									

CRITERIA FOR PASSING: 90% CORRECT SUPERVISOR RE-ADMINISTERS CHECKLIST IF BELOW 90%

Activity 10.2 (Estimated time 1–2 hours)
Shadowing Observation

As you gain competence in prompting strategies, you will be observing highly competent instructors implementing prompting in more naturalistic situations. You will observe "shadowing," where an instructor delivers prompts for the purposes of transferring control from prompt stimuli to cues in the natural environment. Observe a student in a group receiving instruction, and a student responding cues during a functional routine, such as making a bed or washing dishes. You will then complete a guided observation form for this experience.

Tools: Form 10.2

Instructions:
- With the input of your Field Facilitator, choose at least 3 students and/or programs to observe shadow prompting. (If you do not have live examples, please view the programs on the Discrete Trial Training Module).
- Arrive at the scheduled time with Form 2.3, a pencil or pen, and a clipboard.
- Complete Form 10.2 by listing the program name during which you observed a specific type of lesson, and describe each component of shadowing seen.

Form 10.2

Guided Observation
Shadowing

Observe an experienced teacher running a lesson with a prompter (shadow) providing assistance as needed. The shadow will sit or stand behind the student and will use prompt fading and specific reinforcement strategies to guide appropriate responses while constantly working to shift stimulus control to the teacher or ongoing activity.

1. List the programs you are observing (this lesson can be a language or academic group, mealtime, vocational program, independent work, etc.).
    a.
    b.
    c.

2. The shadow is required to act unobtrusively. How was that done?

3. Did the shadow interrupt/redirect inappropriate behavior? How?

4. If prompting strategies were used to guide the student to respond cues from the teacher, list them here (e.g. time delay, other least-to-most hierarchies?)
.

5. If prompting strategies were used to guide the student to respond cues during functional routines (e.g. handwashing, arrival and departure routines), list them here (e.g. time delay, other least-to-most hierarchies?)

6. What was the student response to prompting strategies used?

7. Describe any peer interactions that occurred during the observation. Were there any prompts used to facilitate the behavior? Do you feel that least-to-most prompting was used? Why or Why not? What was the benefit to using least-to-most prompting? (*Time delay, gestural, partial physical full physical, etc.*)

8. Who administered reinforcement? How was it administered (at the end of the task, intermittently, differentially, etc.)?

Unit 10 Discussion Topics

1. When do you think it would be helpful to use time delay prompting with students?
2. Share your experience in using the time delay strategy:
   - Was it effective?
   - Were you able to fade it completely?
   - Do you think this is the best prompt-fading strategy to use with this student/task combination?
3. Share your observations of prompting in the natural environment. Do you think the strategies that you observed will be successful method in transferring control from the prompt stimulus to the natural cue?

Unit 11
Shadowing

One day Rosa was observing her first-grade student Bailey. Bailey was able to read, could answer some simple comprehension questions, and even displayed emerging writing skills. What he lacked, it seemed, was the ability to complete classroom routines.

Each day at 10:30, Bailey's teacher would ring the bell and say "Time for recess!" Invariably, Bailey would continue reading. He did not seem to notice that the other students were putting their books away, nor lining up at the door. The paraprofessional serving Bailey would often put the boy's books away for him, and then repeat the teacher's direction "Bailey! It's time for recess!" While Bailey remained absorbed by his book, she would add, "You need to line up at the door," physically guiding him to the line of children.

Bailey's teacher wondered if there was a way for Rosa to help Bailey participate more independently in this classroom routine.

Rosa consulted with Ginger, who gave her some practical advice about "shadowing." She explained that shadowing was a technique that an instructor could use to help a student to identify natural cues in the environment (in this case, the ringing of the bell, and the other students lining up), by moving from physical and verbal prompts to gestural or pictorial prompts. Ginger suggested delivering these less intrusive prompts from behind Bailey, so that he didn't rely on Rosa's visual presence to complete the routine.

They decided that tomorrow, when the recess bell rings, instead of putting Bailey's book away, Rosa would prompt Bailey to do it by himself. To direct Bailey's attention to them, Rosa would point to the other children, so eventually he might model their behavior; but she also would stand behind him, then gently place her hand over his, as a way of assisting Bailey to put his own book away.

Rosa tried this, and after a couple of days, she noticed that she did not have to use as much pressure to physically guide Bailey to complete the entire routine. In fact, once she got him started, he was able to do most of the routine on his own. Rosa stayed close by, just to make sure, and she was glad she did, because at times, Bailey would try to leave the book on the table next to, rather than on, the shelf. When this happened, Rosa would point to the shelf, and this gesture successfully prompted Bailey to complete the last step minus any further prompt.

After several days, Bailey was responding to her gestural prompt by directing his attention to the actions of his peers, at which point, using his peers as a model, he then completed the entire routine on his own.

Unit 11 Objectives

Assuming you have completed formal coursework in or otherwise mastered information about applied behavior analysis in autism educational practice, along with its principles, practices, and other key features, by the end of this week you should be able to carry out appropriate shadowing techniques to assist students to engage in functional and group activities by determining situations which would require shadowing and identifying natural cues, and prompts, and perform a shadowing session using the **CHECKLIST TRAINING PROTOCOL.**

Activity 11.1 (Estimated time 1–2 hours)
Identifying Opportunities for Shadow Support
Shadowing Checklist

Objective: Determining situations where a student would require shadowing, identifying natural cues, and describing shadowing support, and perform the **CHECKLIST TRAINING PROTOCOL**

Written Requirements: Forms 11.1 and 11.2

Instructions:

For this assignment, you will be observing a student(s) during the course of the normal school routine. You will learn to identify opportunities where shadowing support should be provided to a student. In addition, you will identify natural cues in the environment, and either list the shadow prompts you see occurring, or if no shadow prompts are occurring, suggest those that would be useful.

Step 1: Identify activities where student would require shadowing support. Shadowing support should be provided during any activity where you would like the student to ultimately function independently. This could include:

- self-help activities such as dressing, brushing teeth, or washing hands
- classroom routines, such as an arrival or departure routine where the child is expected to organize their personal items
- group activities, such as circle, physical education, and art activities
- leisure activities with peers which may include skills such as greetings, turn taking, or engaging in simple conversation

Step 2: Identify any natural cues that occur during the activities you listed that would signal to the student that an action needs to be performed, such as:

- an environmental cue, such as the dismissal bell being rung (natural cue to begin departure routine), or sticky hands (natural cue to wash hands)
- a verbal instruction from a teacher leading a group, such as telling the class to "line up" or "time to go outside"

Activity 11.2 (Estimated time 1–2 hours)
Shadowing Checklist

Tools: Form 11.2

Objective: Conducting shadowing.

Instructions:

For this assignment, using a situation that you identified in Activity 11.1, implement shadowing using the CHECKLIST TRAINING PROTOCOL.

Form 11.1

Your Name _____ Dates_____
Instructor _____
Indicate the day(s) _____ and times _____ you are attending
this location each week.

Observe a student during the normal course of the school day. Determine activities during which the student would benefit from shadowing support, so they could eventually respond independently. If possible, include functional and group activities.

List the activities, natural cues, and shadow prompt. If the child is *not* receiving a shadow prompt during an observed activity, suggest a type of shadow prompt that would help. Two examples have been added to each category to get you started.

Identifying Natural Cues during Functional Tasks

	Activity	Natural Cues	Shadow Prompt
1.	Handwashing	child stands in front of sink	staff stands behind child; points to faucet
2.	Lunch Time	zipped lunch box is on table	staff stands behind child; points to zipper
3.	Circle Time	teacher sings clapping song and models clapping	staff sits behind child and physically prompts clapping
4.			
5.			
6.			
7.			

Form 11.2

SHADOWING CHECKLIST

Part 1: Oral Checklist

Instructions: Supervisor scores appropriate box for each item. Oral checklist is administered by direct questioning.

	Score +/-
1. In response to the questions "What is Shadowing?" and "How does it operate?" states: Shadowing is a step used to fade from physical tofs other forms of guidance (e.g. spoken, written, pictorial, gestural). In shadowing, the teacher/trainer/aide uses his or her hands to follow the movement of the student without actually touching him/her.	
2. In response to the question "Why is it important to effectively *shadow* a student?": To ensure the s/he eventually will begin to respond appropriately to natural cues, or follow functional routines more independently in the natural setting.	
3. Describes student behaviors indicative of the need for shadowing support:	
a) engaging in inappropriate behavior or stereotypy	
b) failing to follow a teacher's instruction	
4. Identifies general circumstances in which providing shadowing support would be appropriate: Situations in which the goal is to enable the student to gain more independence, as in group activities, activities of daily living, self-care routines, independent seatwork, job skills or leisure activities.	
5. Describes under what circumstances and how shadowing should be faded: As the student responds with increasingly greater independence, the distance between the person conducting the shadowing and the locus of the student's movements can gradually be lengthened and ultimately dispensed with almost entirely.	
PERCENT CORRECT	

CRITERIA FOR PASSING: 100% CORRECT SUPERVISOR RE-ADMINISTERS CHECKLIST IF BELOW 100%

Part 2: Performance Checklist

Instructions:

Supervisor administers Part 2 of the checklist by watching an actual teaching session or a digital recording or a video tape of a teaching session, and observing the specified behaviors during the lesson. For each item involved in the observation, the supervisor scores a (+) if the behavior occurs, a (-) if the behavior does not occur. For observed behaviors, administer the checklist one time. If time allows, re-administer across three students.

Implements shadowing procedure by:	Score first 5 opportunities				
	+/-	+/-	+/-	+/-	+/-
1. acting unobtrusively: a) speaking quietly b) sitting or standing behind the student					
2. refraining from delivering an S^D					
3. implementing appropriate prompting procedures when the student does not respond to the teacher					
4. implementing least-to-most prompting procedures when a student requires assistance in following a classroom routine					
5. providing intermittent social reinforcement when appropriate and thinning reinforcement in a timely manner					
6. recording data appropriately					
Totals					
PERCENT CORRECT	_____%				

CRITERIA FOR PASSING: 90% CORRECT SUPERVISOR RE-ADMINISTERS CHECKLIST IF BELOW 90%

Unit 11 Discussion Topics

1. Did you run into any challenges when looking for situations where students are being shadowed? Explain your answer.
2. Did you find any situations where students may have benefited from shadowing, yet were not receiving supports? Explain your answer.
3. What do you think may inhibit a student from receiving adequate shadowing support?
4. How might you handle a situation where the teacher who is shadowing is providing too much assistance, or is otherwise inhibiting a student's independent functioning?

Unit 12
Incorporating Preference and Choice

During their lunch break, Allie complains to Jeb, "You know, I'm feeling a little frustrated."

"Yea? What's up?"

"Well, they asked me to try to teach Samuel how to count, but he doesn't seem the least bit interested. I did demonstrate mastery of the Discrete Trial Checklist, and feel that I know how to teach this skill. I also contracted for Samuel's preferred reinforcers, but he keeps looking at his fingers and gazing out the windows instead of doing the lesson. Honestly, I feel like I'm spending most of the time just trying to get Samuel to attend, and when I do get him to focus on the instruction, he takes forever to count out the chips! I don't think he's ever going to get this."

Ginger joins Jeb and Allie at the lunch table. "I couldn't help overhearing you describe your discouragement about Samuel's counting. I was having the same trouble with some of the other kids, until I tried giving them more choices and using teaching materials *they* liked. When I did that, they really perked up! Let's give it a try and see if it helps."

By displaying an array of possible items and letting Samuel choose from among them, Ginger shows Allie how to discover what stimulus materials interest Samuel at the moment. "Now, you try it," Ginger suggests.

So, Allie gathers cars from a toy train, some blocks, and a bowl of popcorn. She asks Samuel to choose the one he wants. Samuel immediately reaches for the trains. Now Allie tells Samuel to count out three cars. When he does, she lets him put them together and push them around the track. Samuel has really perked up!

Allie then continues to ask him to count out more cars, each time adding the number to those he previously counted correctly. The session is enjoyable, as Samuel appears to remain absorbed and happy. Most of all, the scores of his counting skills have shot up in just that single session! Allie has been enjoying herself so much that she is surprised when the dismissal bell rings.

During her drive home, Allie muses, "Letting Samuel choose his learning tools worked so well, I am going to rethink all the tasks I have been teaching, and figure out a way to give Samuel (and our other students) more choices. I'll try to identify instructional materials they find interesting. A little up-front planning obviously can go a long way toward making teaching not only more fun, but ultimately more effective!"

As she rounds into her driveway, another thought strikes her: "Hmm, I wonder whether letting Samuel choose the *order* of his assigned instructional activities on his activity schedule might be a good idea too! Might be worth a try!"

_____

Unit 12 Objectives

By the end of this week, you should be able to integrate preference and choice into your teaching sessions by:

1. providing choices of tasks, reinforcers, materials and sequences of activities.
2. using preferred stimuli as reinforcers, task materials, and activities.

Activity 12.1 (Estimated time 2 hours)
Preferred Activity and Choice Checklist

Now that you have learned how to conduct preference assessments and social responsiveness sessions, you will be learning how to integrate choice and preference into your teaching. Permitting choice gives students shared control over the teaching sessions and prepares them better to negotiate to attain their preferred objects and activities during other activities of daily living.

Tools: Form 12.1 Preferred activity and choice checklist

Objective: Integrate choice and preference in your teaching sessions and implementing **THE CHECK-LIST TRAINING PROTOCOL.**

Preparation:

Part 1-Oral Checklist: Before working with your student, describe to your supervisor the rationale and the procedure for implementing choice and preference into your teaching sessions.

Your supervisor then will administer the oral portion of the checklist by means of direct questioning. Correct responses will be acknowledged while any incorrect responses will be followed immediately with corrective verbal feedback. Your supervisor will re-administer the oral portion of the checklist until you can orally describe the competency at acceptable criterion levels.

Integrating preference into your session

- Conduct a preference assessment
- Provide an adequate supply of preferred items and activities available for the session
- Plan ways to integrate preferred items and activities into the session by:
  o Using preferred items as reinforcers
  o Using preferred items as task materials
- Intersperse preferred activities within program trials

Example
> You are conducting a counting activity. Suppose your student likes trains. Ask the student to count the number of train cars as you put them together. Then join him in playing with the trains for a few minutes before conducting the next counting trial.

Integrating choice with your session

Before you start teaching, consider ways to incorporate choice-making into your session. Possibilities include:

- Choice of *materials*. Examples:
  o "Do you want the blue marker or the red marker?"
  o "Do you want the bike or the scooter?"

- Choice of *tasks*. Examples:
  - "Do you want to do spelling or math?"
  - "Do you want to play with the blocks or the dolls?"
  - "Look at your choice board. Pick one." (The choice board contains pictures of activity options from which the student can choose.)

- Choice of *reinforcers*. Examples:
  - Ask, "Do you want to work to use the computer or to go to the book center?"
  - Permit access to a bin with preferred toys and activities
  - Provide a choice board or activities
  - Provide a school store in which they exchange tokens for choices of activities

- Choice of *sequences* of tasks
  - Provide choice between work tasks—such as counting or addition
  - Provide choices in a visual display, such as a choice board with pictures of tasks or a shelf with clearly labels bins of tasks
  - If the student can read and write, allow her to write her own schedule at the beginning of the session with spaces for options of tasks during work time

Hint: Offering clear options (as above) works better than asking an open-ended question like "What do you want to work for?" or a yes/no question like "Do you want juice?"

REMEMBER! When giving choices, provide the options in a form you know the student is able to understand. Choice modalities include:

- pictures
- symbols
- written words
- sign language
- gestures
- vocal speech
- actual objects

Some students, even those possessing vocal speech, may not understand what you are saying. Often they will repeat (echo) the last thing you say. For example, if you say "Do you want milk or juice?" they might answer "Juice"; but if you say "Do you want juice or milk?" they might answer "Milk." If this is the case, try offering choices by holding up objects or pictures and orally naming the choice the student makes: "Milk."

After your student chooses the object or activity, make sure that s/he actually engages in that activity. Then you can be assured that their indicated choices and what they truly want correspond.

Form 12.1

PREFERRED ACTIVITY AND CHOICE CHECKLIST
Part 1: Oral Checklist

Instructions: Supervisor scores appropriate box for each item. Part 1 of checklist is administered by direct questioning.

	+/-
1. Student describes why it is important to use preferred activities and choices in teaching sessions:	
Enabling preference choice enhances the reinforcing function of objects or events, as well as reduces Escape-motivated behavior.	
2. Student describes how to provide choice and preference in a teaching session by:	
a) providing choices of tasks	
b) providing choices of materials	
c) providing choices or reinforcers	
d) providing choices of the sequence of activities	
e) providing choices in a modality that the student understands	
3. Student describes how to integrate preferred stimuli into the session by:	
a) using preferred stimuli as reinforcers	
b) using preferred stimuli as task materials	
c) interspersing preferred activities between teaching trials	
d) varying preferred items	
e) making preferred items visible and within 5 ft. of student	
PERCENT CORRECT	

CRITERIA FOR PASSING: 100% CORRECT SUPERVISOR RE-ADMINISTERS CHECKLIST IF BELOW 100%

Part 2: Performance Checklist

Supervisor administers Part 2 of the checklist by observing an actual teaching session, a digital recording or a video tape of a teaching session, and observing the specified behaviors for the first ten trials of the lesson. For each item involved in the observation, the supervisor scores a (+) if the behavior occurs, a (-) if the behavior does not occur. For observed behaviors, administer the checklist one time. If time allows, re-administer across three students.

Preparation Step:	Score +/-
Staff conducts preference assessment	

SCORE 5 SESSIONS

	+/-	+/-	+/-	+/-	+/-
Staff uses preference and choice in session (a teaching session of at least 10 trials) by:					
a) providing choice of task and/or task materials at least once					
b) providing choice of reinforcers at least once					
c) using preferred item(s) as part of activity					
d) using preferred item(s) each time consequences were given for appropriate behavior					
e) varies preferred item(s) as consequences for appropriate behavior					
f) interspersing program trials with preferred activities (trial on each side of preference)					
g) making preferred item(s) visible and within 5 feet of the student					
PERCENT CORRECT		%			

CRITERIA FOR PASSING: 90% CORRECT SUPERVISOR RE-ADMINISTERS CHECKLIST IF BELOW 100%

Unit 12 Discussion Topics

1. Do you think it is important to incorporate a student's choices and preferences in a teaching program? Why or why not?

2. Share your experience in using preference with your student:
   What were the students' preferred items?
   How did you incorporate preference into the session?
   Was it effective?

3. The literature states that a student is more responsive when preferred items are used. Was that your experience? How do you think the session would have gone if you had not used preference and choice?

4. Were some items too "preferred?" That is, did the student's desire for the item distract the student from the session? If so, what did you do about it?

Unit 13
Incidental Teaching

Jeb made his first visit to a new home program, where Tony, a toddler diagnosed with ASD, was receiving behavioral intervention. He had expected to see Tony at a little table with a therapist, learning through discrete trial intervention. When he got to the house, Tony's mother Wanda came to the front door with a huge smile on her face. She was also dripping wet in a bathing suit! She said. "Oh, excuse my appearance, we are working with Tony in the pool!" Jeb was a bit puzzled, mumbling to himself, "Working in the pool?"

Wanda led Jeb into the back yard and jumped into the swimming pool. Tony was on the deck with Sarah, his ABA therapist. Tony happily ran to the side of the pool and smiled at his mom, who had outstretched arms. Sarah held Tony's hand, and modeled, "Say 'Want jump!'" When Tony imitated Sarah's model, they jumped in and landed with a SPLASH! Wanda caught Tony and gave him a big kiss! Tony laughed with delight, and climbed out of the pool to play the jumping game again. The next time he approached the side of the pool, Sarah held his hand. He said "Want Jump!" on his own, and they jumped in the pool again! Afterward, the team dried off moved over to the trampoline. They played the same game "Want jump!" Tony saw a huge leaf pile, ran to it and said, "Want jump" to his mom. She let him jump into the pile one time before returning to rinse off in the pool and starting the game over.

Later, they had the team meeting. Jeb asked why they were not doing therapy at the little table in the basement, similar to what he saw in other intervention programs. The team responded that Tony to learn to request, they had to capitalize on HIS interests, and he liked nothing more than jumping in the pool. The team was initially worried, thinking that he would not be able to focus given the distraction of the water. They were surprised that not only was he more focused, but he was easier to prompt, happier, and he learned to request much faster than when he was at the table. They followed his lead and played the jumping game in different places so that he would be exposed to multiple exemplars for generalization purposes. And they had Mom join them, so that he would learn to talk to her as well as the therapist.

Jeb said, "Wow, this incidental teaching sure looks fun! Next time I will bring my swim trunks too!"

Unit 13 Objectives

This week, you will be learning how to design natural opportunities to enhance learning of specific, predetermined objectives for your students. You will learn to design teaching opportunities by:

1. setting up the environment to set the occasion for natural learning; and
2. capitalizing on a student's ongoing interest by embedding teaching opportunities in the context of preferred activities.

Activity 13.1 Incidental Teaching Checklist
(Estimated time 1–2 hours)

Objective: To design teaching opportunities by setting up environment to:
1. set the occasion for natural learning; and
2. capitalize on your student's ongoing interests by embedding teaching opportunities within the context of preferred activities.

Tools: Form 13.1
The **CHECKLIST TRAINING PROTOCOL** will encompass these objectives.

Instructions:

Sometimes the student initiates a communicative response which requires further sophistication or elaboration. The youngster may utter the word "truck," but fail to indicate the function that word is to perform. Is it to serve as a request (mand) or as a description (intraverbal)? When this happens, the student can be prompted to elaborate communication in a more functional way: "I want (a) truck," or "I see a truck," or "There is a truck!" At other times, the response is more restricted than the student's actual capabilities. For example, while a student may be able to say "I want banana," she simply says, "Banana." When this happens, you can prompt the student to elaborate her communication in a more functional way: "I want (a) banana!" The *incidental teaching strategy* serves effectively to accomplish this goal. To apply this strategy, utilize the following steps:

Step 1: Observe to recognize the apparent intent of your student's communicative initiations. These initiations may be vocal (e.g. "banana") or non-vocal (e.g., reaching for the banana) or gestural (e.g. (pointing to it without reaching). The appropriate spoken label would be something like "Look—banana!" especially if it were hanging from the ceiling or on the teacher's head.

Step 2: Block physical or visual access to the desired object or activity.

Step 3: Model an elaborated response for the student.

Step 4: In the case of manding, give the student the item or access to the activity after the student correctly elaborates the response. In the case of apparent intraverbal responding (points to or laughs at) calling for social attention, present known social reinforcers such as "Yes. Funny!" (laughing), or saying "How silly. The banana is hanging from the ceiling (… on my head)!"

SET THE OCCASION FOR LEARNING!

To set the occasion for natural teaching opportunities, first you need to familiarize yourself with your student's verbal repertoire (in what manner; at what level, s/he is capable of communicating.) Then you need to determine your student's preferences:

You have already learned to conduct a Preference Assessment (see Unit 3). When using incidental teaching, you'll need to identify the student's preferred items or activities at the time you plan to make use of incidental teaching. And remember! Your student's preferences may change from one moment to the next, so it is important to watch for cues suggesting that an item or event remains effective as a reinforcing stimulus or if it is no longer preferred. If a student appears to become disinterested with an item, activity, or non-responsive to social interactions, discontinue using them as a teaching tool for the time being. If a student shows an interest in a new stimulus, even if you are doing something at the time, try to seize it as a teaching opportunity! Continually watch the student's behavior to see what s/he attempts to do or obtain.

Then:

- Set the context where preferred items and activities are available. Suggestions include:
  o play centers
  o art tables
  o "sensory bins" with items such as water play, sand play, or other interesting tactile stimuli
  o providing frequent play breaks with preferred materials during more structured training
  o playgrounds and gymnasiums
  o snacks and lunches
  o school stores
  o directed play, game, dance or music sessions

CAPITALIZING ON YOUR STUDENT'S ONGOING INTERESTS BY EMBEDDING TEACHING OPPORTUNITIES IN THE CONTEXT OF PREFERRED ACTIVITIES. Examples include:

- arranging and allowing the student to engage in a repetitive and predictable activity; then interrupting the activity for a set time delay. Examples include:
  o stopping the swing while the individual is swinging on a swing set
  o taking turns with a preferred toy; then delaying the child's turn
  o giving a few pieces of preferred food, and when the student is finished, providing more food. Then when the student finishes the second time, withhold the food until an appropriate verbal response is emitted
  o make obvious preparations to pour a favorite drink and then stop
  o use a paintbrush to paint a preferred picture and then allow the paint on the brush to run out
  o provide choices from a set of a few preferred items or activities

Some further examples of incidental teaching include:

CONTEXT: On the playground, the teacher has been pulling a student in a wagon. The teacher stops.

STUDENT: Looks at the teacher and rocks his body to try to get the wagon going again.

TEACHER: Looks at the student expectantly.

STUDENT: Student looks at teacher and does not respond.

TEACHER: Models the sign *go.*

STUDENT: Imitates the sign *go.*

TEACHER: Pulls wagon for 5 seconds.

TEACHER: Stops wagon and looks at the student expectantly.

STUDENT: Signs *go.*

OTHER IDEAS!

- PREPOSITIONS
  - Put a preferred item in a funny location, like on top of a toy bear. When the student asks for the item, ask "Where is it?" Then, if necessary, prompt as minimally as possible: ("on t"; "taa"; "on top of" "on top of bear.")

- POLITE LANGUAGE
  - When a student requests an item, prompt him to ask again, while modeling "Please" at the end of the request

- COMMENTING
  - Read a story with pop up pages. When a page pops out and the student looks at it with interest, prompt him to label it (e.g. "A ghost!)

- REQUESTING ATTENTION
  - Take turns with a preferred item, and then hold the item and turn away. When the student starts to reach for you, prompt him to say "Excuse me!"

- ADJECTIVES
  - A student asks for juice. Hold up two kinds of juices, and say, for example "Do you want *apple* juice or *orange* juice?"

Form 13.1

INCIDENTAL TEACHING CHECKLIST

Part 1: Oral Checklist

Supervisor scores appropriate box for each item. Part 1 of checklist is administered by direct questioning.

	+/-
1. Describes importance of conducting incidental teaching:	
When teaching specific objectives in natural contexts, you increase students' motivation by capitalizing on their interests and providing them access to multiple exemplars. This method helps students generalize learned skills to a greater extent than if they were taught via more formalized drills.	
2. Describes how one might use incidental teaching by setting up the environment to set the occasion for natural learning, and includes:	
a) a description of how to 'seed' the environment with preferred activities	
b) a description of how to create opportunities for incidental teaching by either: <ul><li>taking turns with a preferred item</li><li>interrupting a predictable activity sequence</li><li>presenting a preferred item just out of the student's reach</li></ul>	
c) a description of how to use least-to-most prompting if the student does not respond to the targeted S^D	
d) a description of the targeted correct response	
3. Describes how one might use incidental teaching, capitalizing on the student's ongoing interests, and includes:	
a) a description of the student's communicative initiation	
b) a description of the targeted S^D and targeted correct response	
c) a description of how to block access to the desired item	
d) a description of how to prompt the student response	
PERCENT CORRECT	

CRITERIA FOR PASSING: 100% CORRECT SUPERVISOR RE-ADMINISTERS CHECKLIST IF BELOW 100%

Part 2: Performance Checklist

Instructions:
Supervisor administers Part 2 of the checklist by watching an actual teaching session, or a digital recording or a tape of a teaching session, and observing the specified behaviors during the lesson. For each item involved in the observation, the supervisor scores a (+) if the behavior is implemented correctly, a (-) if the behavior is implemented incorrectly, and N/A if it is not necessary or applicable to perform the behavior. For observed behaviors, administer the checklist one time. If time allows, re-administer across three students.

	Score first 5 trials				
Performs incidental teaching procedure by:	+/-	+/-	+/-	+/-	+/-
a) recognizing student initiation					
b) deciding whether to comply and follow through.					
If deciding to comply and follow through:					
c) withholding access to desired object					
d) prompting elaborated response using model or time delay procedure					
e) reinforcing correct response by providing access item/activity					
f) elaborating target response					
Totals					
PERCENT CORRECT	_____%				

CRITERIA FOR PASSING: 90% CORRECT SUPERVISOR RE-ADMINISTERS CHECKLIST IF BELOW 90%

Unit 13 Discussion Topics

1. Did you find situations where the student initiated communication, but it was not up to his or her potential? Describe.
2. What strategies did you use to prompt more elaborate communication?
3. Describe the communicative behavior of your student during the incidental teaching interaction.
4. Was the incidental teaching procedure effective in elaborating your student's communication?
5. How could you set up opportunities to use incidental teaching opportunities during your student's day to facilitate elaborated communication?
6. How might you take data on the use of these procedures throughout the day?
7. How might you generalize the use of procedures to:
    *   other staff?
    *   family members?
    *   peers?

Unit 14
Running a Program

Rosa was so pleased with the success at using Discrete Trial Teaching methods to enable little Abby to discriminate and label the names of a range of colors! She had accomplished that by isolating and having her student, Abby, name stimuli of specific colors, while adding distracter stimuli little by little. Now, Abby was able both to identify and to name many colors, and, she had learned them so quickly! So, having read about how Marckel, Neef and Ferreri (2006)* were able to successfully teach children to combine color and shape names to request particular items (round + white = marshmallow; round + brown = cookie), Rosa now decided to try a similar method to teach Abby the names of certain shapes.*

She began with a square in isolation; and in very short order was able to teach Abby to choose and say, "square" in the presence of a distracter shape—a circle. But, unfortunately, Rosa was going to be out of school for a few days and would have to decide whether or not to postpone teaching Abby about circles and triangles. Feeling a little frustrated, she went to Ginger, her field facilitator, and related her dilemma to her. "What should I do, Ginger? I really think Abby's catching on by using the specific procedures and materials I've been applying."

"Well, Rosa, it's probably not as serious a dilemma as you might think."

"I don't know, Ginger," Rosa complained. "Every time I saw someone trying to teach her about her colors, they used different colors, different directions and even responded differently to her when she was wrong! She seemed to be awfully confused!"

"Hmmm," Ginger queried. "Why don't you explain your procedures to the staff and suggest materials they can use with Abby?"

"That's a great idea, but there's so much that goes into it, I'm afraid they'll forget some of the parts and really confuse Abby," Rosa groaned.

"Well, Rosa, you're probably right, because I've noticed that when different people attempt to copy a procedure without access to clear guidelines, they do tend to return to teaching in ways familiar to themselves. So, each person approaches the task differently. Talk about confusing! That's why here at Walden, we write lesson plans for each skill."

"Makes sense. So, how do Walden teachers go about writing lesson plans?"

"Well, a lesson plan is supposed to outline everything involved in teaching a skill, including the materials, specific teaching procedures, including any prompts you're going to use, the delivery schedule for reinforcers that have worked successfully in the past, and plans for generalization and maintenance. When everything is clearly designed and written out, the lesson becomes easier for others to reproduce. So the lesson plans provide for more consistency in teaching, thereby helping avoid students' becoming confused. They also allow the teacher to better evaluate a student's true abilities, by ruling out discrepancies in programming."

"Oh, I feel so much better," Rosa sighed. "I'm going to sit right down and prepare a set of lesson plans for Abby. That way all of us will be consistent in how we handle her lessons."

---

*Marckel, J.M., Neef, N.A., & Ferreri, J. (2006). A preliminary analysis of teaching improvisation with the Picture Exchange Communication System to Children with Autism. *Journal of Applied Behavior Analysis, 39*, 109–115.

Unit 14 Objectives

By the end of this week, you should be able to set up an appropriate training environment, summarize the data recorded during the session, carry out a teaching session (run a program), and familiarize yourself with training techniques used in group or independent work situations. You will:

1. utilize a student's daily data sheet, program lesson plan, and set list to set up the training environment by gathering and appropriately arranging materials, reinforcers, data sheets and seating.
2. record accuracy data while observing programs being run and summarize the data at the end of the session. You should include at least one program that targets a functional skill using a task analysis protocol.
3. run a program following **The CHECKLIST TRAINING PROTOCOL.**

Activity 14.1 (Estimated time: 1–2 Hours)
(Note: This activity will be completed in conjunction with Activity 14.2.)

Setting up the Environment

Now, it's time to use the tools you've learned in previous weeks to begin running programs that will help to ensure your student's educational success! You have seen that before beginning any program with a student, the learning environment needs to be set up according to a well thought-out plan developed by the educational team. The plan gives you the 'nuts and bolts' of the program you are going to run. This activity will give you the opportunity to use a specific plan to set up the learning environment for your student.

Written Requirements: Form 14.1

Objective: Utilize a student's daily data sheets, program lesson plan, and set list to set up the training environment by gathering and appropriately arranging materials, reinforcers, data sheets and seating.

Instructions:

With the input of your Field Facilitator, choose three programs for a particular student. These programs should have comprehensive lesson plans available to review, and require trial-by-trial accuracy data.

Schedule 1–2 hours to complete this activity (along with Activity 14.2). Arrive at the scheduled time with:

- Form 14.1
- A pencil or pen
- A clipboard

Complete Form 14.1 including the steps listed below:

- With guidance from the lesson plan provided for each program, list the objective, the steps of the teaching guide, and the criterion for mastery.
- After reviewing the set list provided for each program, list the S^D, materials required, reinforcement schedule, prompt procedures, current set, and description of a correct response.
- Design the learning environment including the materials, established reinforcers, data sheets, and proper workspace arrangements (clear workspace, seating, etc.).
- Gather all materials listed in the lesson plan and set list that will be utilized when running the specified program.
- Arrange the environment to allow for successful implementation of the program by the instructor.

Form 14.1
(To be completed in conjunction with Activities 14.1)

Your Name_____Date(s)_____Instructor_____
Indicate the day(s)_____ and time(s)_____ you are attending this location each week.

Choose three instructional programs for a particular student or student(s). Refer to the lesson plan and the set list for each program. Complete the form below for each program. Observe the instructor implementing the program.

1. Identify the objective listed in the lesson plan. Write the objective here.

2. List the steps of the teaching guide here. (Always begin a program by establishing a viable reinforcer, a positive rapport with the student and attending behaviors.)

Step 1: Run preference assessment/social approach.
Step 2: Establish attending behaviors.

3. List the criterion for mastery here. This will give you information as to when the student has mastered a particular set/program.

4. Review the set list to answer the following questions:

a. What is the S^D for the current set?

b. What materials are required to run this program—list work materials, visuals (timers, token boards, etc.), reinforcers, adaptive equipment, etc.

c. What is the reinforcement schedule for this program? (FR1, FR2, VR2, VR3?) Is a token economy system going be used?

d. Describe the current set. (The specific step to be mastered.)

e. Define the correct student response. Define an incorrect response (if applicable).

f. How much assistance will the student be provided throughout the learning session? Errorless learning? Corrective feedback? And, if so, are specific procedures outlined?

5. Graphically design the learning environment. Include materials, placement of reinforcers, data sheets, program boo and seating arrangements.

6. Gather all materials listed above and arrange the learning environment to allow for successful implementation of th program by the instructor.

Activity 14.2 (Estimated time 1–2 hours)
Collecting and Calculating Data
(Note: This activity will be completed in conjunction with Activity 14.1.)

Are you ready for some math homework?

After you have appropriately set up the previous three programs, you will observe the programs while they are being run by the instructor. You will collect data on each skill, and you will use the data to determine whether or not the student has mastered the skill.

Written Requirements: Form 14.2

Objective: Record data while observing programs being run and summarize the data at the end of the session.

Instructions:

- After completing all steps of Activity 5.1, observe the student working on the programs listed in that activity.
- Be sure to have with you Form 5.2, a pencil or pen, and a clipboard.
- Complete Form 5.2. You will be collecting data, calculating for percent correct, and summarizing the data to decide whether it reflects mastery criterion. Using this information, you will make statements as to the direction the program will take.

Form 14.2

Your Name_____Date(s)_____Instructor_____

This activity will be completed in conjunction with Activity 14.1. After you have completed setting up the environment to allow for successful program implementation, you will observe the instructor run a program, and you will record trial-by-trial data for at least ten trials. Complete the form below.

Program #1_____

1. Collect trial-by-trial data for a total of ten trials.

Trial	1	2	3	4	5	6	7	8	9	10
+/-/P										

2. Compare your data with the instructor. Are your data points similar?

3. Calculate a percentage 'correct' for the data collected (correct/incorrect x 100).

4. How does the data reflect the *mastery criterion* (refer to question 3 in Activity 14.1)?
   Does the student need more practice? Can the lesson progress to the next set? Explain your answers.

Program #2_____

1. Collect trial-by-trial data for a total of ten trials.

Trial	1	2	3	4	5	6	7	8	9	10
+/-/P										

2. Compare your data with the instructor. Are your data points similar?

3. Calculate a percentage 'correct' for the data collected. (correct/incorrect x 100).

4. How does the data reflect the *mastery criterion* (refer to question 3 in Activity 14.1)?
   Does the student need more practice? Can the lesson progress to the next set? Explain your answers.

Program #3_____

1. Collect Task Analysis Data

List All Steps of the Task Analysis You Are Observing	Score(see below*)
1.	
2.	
3.	
4.	
5.	
6.	
7.	
8.	
9.	
10.	
Percent Correct Independent (see below**)	

*Correct Unprompted Independent (I) Full Physical (FP), Partial Physical (PP), Gestural (G), Model (M), Verbal (V), Faded Verbal (FV)

2. Compare your data with the instructor. Are your data points similar?

3. Calculate a percentage 'correct' for the data collected.
 (**Independent/total steps x 100)

4. How does the data reflect the *mastery criterion* (refer to question 3 in Activity 14.1)?
    Does the student need more practice? Can the lesson progress to the next set? Explain your answers.

Activity 14.3 (Estimated time 1–2 hours)
Running a Program Checklist

You have already practiced running discrete trial training sessions with students in the classroom. Now, you will be setting up the program, implementing the lesson, collecting data and summarizing the data at the completion of the lesson.

Objective: Run a program following the **CHECKLIST TRAINING PROTOCOL.**

Written Requirements: Running A Program Checklist (Form 14.3), and data collection sheets

Preparation:
- Schedule a 10–15 minute appointment with your supervisor to choose a student with whom you can practice running a program. List three programs that you will be implementing with a student. Include one that follows a task analysis format.
- Set up the training environment prior to calling the student (task materials, reinforcers, data sheet and appropriate seating).
- Obtain a DVD or digital recording device to record yourself running three programs you have chosen.

Form 14.3

RUNNING A PROGRAM CHECKLIST

Part 1: Oral Checklist

Supervisor scores appropriate box for each item. Part 1 of checklist is administered by direct questioning.

	Score +/-
Describes two benefits of running a program according to a specific lesson plan:	
a) Allows for consistency across different members	
b) Controls for reliability and validity in analysis of student progress	
PERCENT CORRECT	

CRITERIA FOR PASSING: 100% CORRECT SUPERVISOR RE-ADMINISTERS CHECKLIST IF BELOW 100%

Part 2: Performance Checklist

Instructions:
Supervisor administers Part 2 of the checklist by watching an actual teaching session, or digital recording or a video tape of a teaching session, and observing the specified behaviors during the lesson. For each item involved in the observation, the supervisor scores a (+) if the behavior occurs, a (-) if the behavior does not occur. For observed behaviors, administer the checklist one time. If time allows, re-administer across three students.

Preparation Step: Sets up training environment prior to calling the student by:	Score +/-
a) gathering materials: work materials, reinforcers, data sheets, token economy (if applicable)	
b) displaying appropriate reinforcers	
c) arranging the environment appropriately: work materials, reinforcers, seating, etc.	
PERCENT CORRECT	

CRITERIA FOR PASSING: 100% CORRECT SUPERVISOR RE-ADMINISTERS CHECKLIST IF BELOW 100%

Implements teaching procedure by:	Score first 10 trials									
	+/-	+/-	+/-	+/-	+/-	+/-	+/-	+/-	+/-	+/-
a) delivering the specified stimuli according to step.										
b) delivering appropriate prompts, if necessary										
c) delivering appropriate consequences										
d) waiting the appropriate time between trials										
e) alternating trials of acquired skills with difficult trials										
Totals										
PERCENT CORRECT	____ /50 x 100 = ____ %									

CRITERIA FOR PASSING: 90% CORRECT SUPERVISOR RE-ADMINISTERS CHECKLIST IF BELOW 90%

Data Collection: Demonstrates ability to collect data appropriately by:	Score +/-
a) matching own data with that of the experienced instructor	

CRITERIA FOR PASSING: 100% CORRECT SUPERVISOR RE-ADMINISTERS CHECKLIST IF BELOW 100%

Unit 14 Discussion Topics

1. Why would it be important for all components of the student's programs to be written down?

2. What is the importance of writing down specific student responses in the set lists?

3. Why would it be important for each therapist to run the programs the same way? What would be the detrimental effects to the student if the programs weren't run consistently?

4. What are some factors that may contribute to therapists running the programs incorrectly?

5. How can a supervisor ensure that the programs are being run as specified?

6. What is the importance of taking so much data? How does data collection affect student performance?

Unit 15
Evaluating Performance

Activity 15.1 (Estimated time: 30 minutes)
Final Field Facilitator Assessment

Written Requirements: Form 15.1

Objectives: To demonstrate an acceptable level of professionalism, request that your field supervisor or facilitator review your professional demeanor in the practicum setting. The information they provide should enable you and your supervisor to identify specific professional skills you will want to preserve and those you probably will want to refine.

Instructions

1. Please fill in the information requested in the attached form.

2. Prepare as many copies as you will need.

3. Early in the week, give the form to your *field facilitator* and/or field supervisor and any others from whom you would appreciate receiving feedback, along with stamped envelopes addressed to your instructor. Ask them to
   - complete the form
   - make a copy
   - mail the original to your instructor, if applicable
   - give you a duplicate copy

4. If you wish, schedule a meeting with the Field Facilitator and/or Field Supervisor to discuss any of the ratings, especially the positive ones. This should help reinforce your constructive efforts as well as to identify opportunities for improvement.

5. Do the same with any others who have completed the form.

6. Send your instructor a short paragraph describing your plan to maintain and improve your professional skills.

7. *... and this is critical:* Write and distribute notes of thanks to everyone in your setting who has assisted you in any way. Be sure to recognize how much time they spent and provide examples of ways they invested it in helping you to do a good job. Send copies to your instructor.

Form 15.1 (p. 1 of 2)
Assessment of Practicum Student's Professional Skills

Upper portion to be filled out by ABA Practicum Student

ABA Student's Name _____ Date_____ Field Facilitator's Name _____

Field Facilitator Contact Information:
Phone _____ Fax _____ email _____

ABA Instructor's Contact Information:
Phone _____ Fax _____ email _____

(If working from a distance, ABA student should provide the Field Facilitator with a stamped envelope addressed to the instructor. Overseas students should use OVERSEAS AIRMAIL stamps.)

For Field Supervisor or Facilitator:

We thank you for your willingness to facilitate our ABA student's participation in your program and hope this relationship has proven to be productive.

This portion to be filled out by the Field Supervisor or Facilitator

1) Please **complete** and **duplicate** the form. 2) Give one copy to the practicum student, and another to the ABA instructor within the week. Keep the original for your own files.

ABA Practicum Student's Professional Skill	5	4	3	2	1	NA
Is friendly (regularly looks directly at, smiles, greets people individually)						
Listens respectfully (waits while they talk; responds to the point)						
Responds to and gives positive and constructive feedback						
Is flexible (adjusts to new conditions)						
Is helpful in the program						
States plans and expectations clearly						
Undertakes responsibilities and plans time carefully						
Meets responsibilities s/he has undertaken						
Schedules time realistically						
Completes responsibilities on time						
Is prepared in advance of instructional sessions						
Strives for excellence in written and oral communication						
Is patient with his or her student						
Works productively with his or her student						

5 = consistently   4 = most of the time   3 = at an acceptable level
2 = once in a while   1 = rarely or not at all   NA = not applicable

Form 15.1 (p. 2 of 2)

ABA Student's Name _____ Date_____
Field Facilitator's Name _____

Please comment on the best aspect(s) of the ABA student's performance.

_____
_____
_____
_____
_____
_____
_____
_____
_____
_____
_____
_____
_____
_____
_____
_____

Please add any further comments on here.

_____
_____
_____
_____
_____
_____
_____
_____
_____
_____
_____
_____
_____
_____
_____
_____
_____
_____
_____

Activity 15.2 (Less than 1 hour)
Student Evaluation of Your Field Experience

Written Requirements: Assessments to be administered by your instructor or field supervisor

Objectives: To produce an evaluation, you will complete an assessment form prepared by your university, training program, instructor or supervisor.

Instructions

1. At the end of this portion of the course your instructor, supervisor or assessment team should supply you with one or more forms for you to complete.
2. Follow the instructions accompanying the assessment(s).
3. Notify your instructor or supervisor that you have submitted those forms, as requested.

Unit 15
Discussion Topics

1. Reflect on this practicum experience.
    a) What aspects would you definitely retain? Why?
    b) What aspects would you adjust—in what way, and why?

2. Did your previous coursework prepare you for this practicum?
    a) What aspects were most helpful in preparing you? Why?
    b) What aspects were least helpful? Why?
    c) Describe how and why would you alter the latter.

3. Comment on any other aspects of your ABA experience that you wish to.

CONGRATULATIONS!
YOU FINISHED PART 1!

References

Cohen, H., Amerine-Dickens, M., Smith, T. (2006). Early Intensive Behavioral Treatment: Replication of the UCLA Model in a Community Setting. *Journal of Developmental & Behavioral Pediatrics, 27*(2), 145–155.

Dyer, K., Williams, L., and Luce, S. C. (1991). Training teachers to use naturalistic communication strategies in classrooms for students with autism and other severe handicaps. *Language, Speech and Hearing Services in the Schools, 22,* 313–321.

Dyer, K, and Kohland, K. (1991). Communication training at the May Center's integrated preschool: Assessment, structured teaching and naturalistic generalization strategies. In E. Cipani (ed.). *A guide for developing language competence in preschool children with severe and moderate handicaps.* Springfield, IL: Charles C. Thomas.

Dyer, K., Martino, G., and Parvenski, T. (2006). The River Street Autism Program: A Case Study of a Regional Service Center Behavioral Intervention Program. *Behavior Modification, 30*(6), 925–943.

Koegel, R. L., & Koegel, L. K. (2006). *Pivotal response treatments for autism: communication, social, and academic development.* Baltimore, MD: Brookes Publishing.

Lovaas, O. I. (1987). Behavioral treatment and normal educational and intellectual functioning in young autistic children. *Journal of Consulting and Clinical Psychology, 55,* 3–9.

Luce, S. C., & Dyer, K. (1995). Providing effective transitional programming to individuals with developmental disabilities. Invited paper, *Behavioral Disorders, 21*(1), 36–52.

EVIDENCE BASE FOR COMPETENCY-BASED CHECKLISTS

Choice and Preference

Ahern, W. H., Clark, K.M., DeBar, R., & Florentino, C. (2005). On the role of preference in reponse competition. *Journal of Applied Behavior Analysis, 38* (2), 247–240.

Dyer, K. (1987). The competition of autistic stereotyped behavior with usual and specially assessed reinforcers. *Research in Developmental Disabilities, 8,* 606–626.

Dyer, K. (1989). The effects of preference on spontaneous verbal requests in individuals with autism. *The Journal of the Association for Persons with Severe Handicaps, 15,* 184–189.

Dyer, K., Dunlap, G., and Winterling, V. (1990). The effects of choice making on the problem behaviors of students with severe handicaps. *Journal of Applied Behavior Analysis, 23,* 515–524.

Foster-Johnson, L., Ferro, J., & Dunlap, G. (1994). Preferred curricular activities and reduced problem behaviors in students with intellectual disabilities. *Journal of Applied Behavior Analysis, 27,* 493–504.

Pace, G. M., Ivancic, M. T., Edwards, G. L., Iwata, B. A., & Page, T. J. (1985). Assessment of stimulus preference and reinforcer value with profoundly retarded individuals. *Journal of Applied Behavior Analysis, 19,* 381–389.

Peck, C. A. (1985). Increasing opportunities for social control by children with autism and severe handicaps: Effects on student behavior and perceived classroom climate. *Journal of the Association for Persons with Severe Handicaps, 10*(4), 183–193.

Social Responsiveness

Baker, M. J., Koegel, R. L., & Koegel, L. K. (1998). Increasing the social behavior of young children with autism using their obsessive behaviors. *The Journal of The Association of Persons with Severe Handicaps, 23,* 300–308.

Gaylord-Ross, R. J., Haring, T. G., Breen, C., & Pitts-Conway, V. (1984). The training and generalization of social interaction skills with autistic youth. *Journal of Applied Behavior Analysis, 17,* 229–247.

Koegel, R. L., Dyer, K., & Bell, L. K. (1987). The influence of child preferred activities on autistic children's social behavior. *Journal of Applied Behavior Analysis, 20,* 243–252.

Vismara, L. A., & Lyons, G. L. (2007). Using perseverative interests to elicit joint attention behaviors in young children with autism: Theoretical and clinical implications for understanding motivation. *Journal of Postive Behavior Interventions, 9*(4), 214–228.

Discrete Trial

Dib, N., & Sturmey, P. (2007). Reducing stereotypy by improving teachers' implementation of discrete-trial teaching. *Journal of Applied Behavior Analysis, 40*(2), 339–343.

Dunlap, G., Dyer, K., & Koegel, R. L. (1983). Autistic self-stimulation and intertrial interval duration. *American Journal of Mental Deficiency, 88,* 194–202.

Koegel, R. L., Dunlap, G., & Dyer, K. (1980). Intertrial interval duration and learning in autistic children. *Journal of Applied Behavior Analysis, 13,* 91–99.

Koegel, R. L., Glahn, T. J., & Nieminen, G. A. (1978). Generalization of parent training results, *Journal of Applied Behavior Analysis, 11,* 95–109.

Koegel, R. L., Russo, D. C., & Rincover, A. (1977). Assessing and training teachers in the generalized use of behavior modification with autistic children. *Journal of Applied Behavior Analysis, 10,* 197–205.

Sarokoff, R. A. & Sturmey, P. (2007). The effects of instructions, rehearsal, modeling, and feedback on acquisition and generalization of staff use of discrete trial teaching and student correct responses. *Research in Autism Spectrum Disorders, 2*(1), 125–136.

Most-to-Least Prompting

Anglesea, M. M., Hoch, H., & Taylor, B. A. (2008*).* Reducing rapid eating in teenagers with autism: Use of a pager prompt. *Journal of Applied Behavior Analysis, 41,* 107–111.

Betz, A., Higbee, T., & Reagon, K. A. (2008). Using joint activity schedules to promote peer engagement in preschoolers with autism. *Journal of Applied Behavior Analysis, 41,* 237–241.

Krantz, P. J., & McClannahan, L. E. (1993). Teaching children with autism to initiate to peers: Effects of a script-fading procedure. *Journal of Applied Behavior Analysis*, *26,* 121–132.

Graduated Guidance

MacDuff, G. S., Krantz, P. J., & McClannahan, L. E. (1993). Teaching children with autism to use photographic activity schedules: Maintenance and generalization of complex response chains. *Journal of Applied Behavior Analysis, 26,* 89–97.

Singh, N. N., & Millichamp, C. J. (1987). Independent and social play among profoundly mentally retarded adults: Training, maintenance, generalization, and long-term follow-up. *Journal of Applied Behavior Analysis, 20,* 23–34.

Wacker, D. P., Steege, M. W., Northup, J., Sasso, G., Berg, W., Reimers, T., Cooper, L., Cigrand, K., & Donn, L. (1990). A component analysis of functional communication training across three topographies of severe behavior problems. *Journal of Applied Behavior Analysis, 23,* 417–429.

Least-to-Most Prompting

Correa, V. I., Poulson, C. L., & Salzberg, C. L. (1984). Training and generalization of reach-grasp behavior in blind, retarded young children. *Journal of Applied Behavior Analysis, 17,* 57–69.

Heckaman, K. A., Alber, S. R., Hooper, S., & Heward, W. L. (1998). A comparison least-to-most prompts and progressive time delay on the disruptive behavior of students with autism. *Journal of Behavior Education, 8,* 171–201.

Tarbox, R. S. F., Wallace, M.D., Penrod, B., & Tarbox. J. (2007). Effects of three-step prompting on compliance with caregiver requests. *Journal of Applied Behavior Analysis, 40,* 703–706.

Time Delay

Charlop, M. H., Schreibman, L., & Thibodeau, M. G. (1985). Increasing spontaneous verbal responding using a time delay procedure. *Journal of Applied Behavior Analysis, 18,* 155–166.

Halle, J. W., Marshall, A. M., & Spradlin. J. E. (1979). Time delay: A technique to increase language use and facilitate generalization in retarded children. *Journal of Applied Behavior Analysis, 12,* 431–439.

Ingenmey, R., & Van Houton, R. (1991). Using time delay to promote spontaneous speech in an autistic child. *Journal of Applied Behavior Analysis, 24,* 591–596.

Shadowing

Koegel, R. L., Russo, D. C., & Rincover, A. (1977). Assessing and training teachers in the generalized use of behavior modification with autistic children. *Journal of Applied Behavior Analysis, 10,* 197–205.

Lattimore, L. P., Parsons, M. B., & Reid, D. H. (2008). Simulation training of community job skills for adults with autism: A further analysis. *Behavior Analysis in Practice, 1*(1), 24–29.

Pelios, L. V., Macduff, G. S., & Axelrod, S. (2003). The effects of a treatment package in establishing independent academic work skills in children with autism. *Education & Treatment of Children,* (26), 1–21.

Incidental Teaching

McGee, G. G., Krantz, P. J., & McClannahan, L. E. (1985). The facilitative effects of incidental teaching on preposition use by autistic children. *Journal of Applied Behavior Analysis, 18,* 17–31.

Hart, B., & Risley, T. R. (1975). Incidental teaching of language in the preschool. *Journal of Applied Behavior Analysis, 8,* 411–420.

McGee, G. G., Almeida, M. C., Sulzer-Azaroff, B., & Feldman, R. S. (1992). Promoting reciprocal interactions via peer incidental teaching. *Journal of Applied Behavior Analysis, 25,* 117–126.

Treatment Integrity

DiGennaro, F, D,, Martens, B. K., & Kleinman, A. E. (2007). A comparison of performance feedback procedures on teachers' treatment implementation integrity and students' inappropriate behaviors in special education classrooms. *Journal of Applied Behavior Analysis, 40,* 447–461.

Koegel, R. L., Russo, D. C., & Rincover, A. Assessing and training teachers in the generalized use of behavior modification with autistic children. *Journal of Applied Behavior Analysis, 10,* 197–205.

Wilder, D. A., Atwell, J., & Wine, B. (2006.) The effects of varying levels of treatment integrity on child compliance during treatment with a three-step prompting procedure. *Journal of Applied Behavior Analysis, 39,* 369–373.

PART 2
DESIGNING, IMPLEMENTING, AND FUNCTIONALLY ANALYZING THE EFFECT OF A BEHAVIORAL INTERVENTION

Responsibly Undertaking Independent Action

"Oh. There they are." Lucy and Hal, wave to another couple over to their table.

"Dawn? Art? Where did you go? We all left the presentation about the same time. We were starting to worry."

Art pushes the hair off his brow, where it rapidly re-settles itself. Taking his wife by the arm, he guides and seats her at the table.

"Any specials on the menu today?" he asks.

"The fish sounds great, if you like striped bass."

Dawn brightens. "You bet. Claude's Seafood Bistro does a terrific job with it—really fresh; poached with white wine, onion, leeks, carrots and their other magic ingredients; and it's good for my diet. I've got to find a way to shed these extra 15 pounds."

"Oh stop fussing about your weight, Dawn. You look just fine," Lucy observes.

"And so squeezable." Art gives his wife a gentle hug. "Anyway, you're *my* favorite woman."

"Sure, you can say that, Lucy. Look at you. If you tried on your old cheerleader outfit, I bet it would fit like it did when we were back in school."

"Speaking of hair, I just found another gray one in mine this morning," Lucy replies. "Time sure is marching on."

"Okay, Okay ladies. Enough of that complaining about getting older. We're all doing that. I'm sure you've noticed how my hairline keeps receding. Do *I* keep harping about that?"

"All the time!" the other three respond in unison.

"Not to change the topic, but what did you guys think of the travelogue?" Hal asks.

"Those pictures of rivers and mountains, the canyons, the coast, the desert in bloom; our national treasures. I want to see them all," sighs Dawn.

"Me too," Lucy sighs, "But, who are we kidding? It seems like every time the four of us get together we talk about doing something like that—buying a nice comfortable RV, and just taking off to really explore the country; then before long another year has passed."

Hal reminisces about how back even before they were old married folks, they'd sit around and fantasize on the same theme. But then the identical old arguments kept cropping up: so many arrangements to make; the time and money it would take….

"And now that we're well into our thirties," he adds, "our careers are taking off. Before long it will be too late. We'll never want to interrupt them. It seems the further we put it off, the less likely it is to happen."

"So what do you say we just bite the bullet and do it?" Art announces.

Over the meal, the two couples continue talking about the trip they have dreamed of taking for years. But now it is time to commit, and each still harbors concerns. With the big conference coming up in a few months, Lucy worries about missing out on important contacts she was hoping to make with publishers of travel guides. Art  doesn't know if he can afford to take an indefinite leave from his position as a senior photographer for *Architectural Digest,* and Hal wonders if his bosses were really serious when they offered to let him freelance over the Internet.

Dawn is due for a sabbatical and is fairly certain that her teaching position or one like it will be waiting when she returns. Her big issue is how her garden will survive.

Tugging his beard, Art concludes, "Okay, guys, every time we discuss this, we come up with all kinds of reasons to delay. Last year it was the convention. The year before, money. Let's be honest. If we really mean it, we'll stop making excuses and just go!"

"Speaking of money, we've thought of a way we might be able to save: by splitting the costs five ways and, in the bargain getting the services of a really good cook. We're thinking maybe we can talk my sister Ginger into joining us, at least for part of the time. You guys know her. What do you say?"

"Good idea, Lucy," Dawn concurs. "One thing in her favor is how good-natured she is. You said she's hoping to take a break while we'd be gone, so she can finish writing up her thesis. Maybe she'll decide she can do that just as well in the RV. I think we should invite her."

The others nod their agreement.

"So let's ask her. But either way, what's our decision? Do we or don't we go?"

The four exchange glances with their spouses, nod, join hands and raise their arms over their heads.

"Yes!!"

******

We too are embarking together on a journey of sorts. We have considered the challenges and agreed to invest our resources toward honing our skills as behavior analytic *practitioners*. While we have yet to decide how to get underway, and our final destination is a mystery, we do know our purpose: *to actually start applying in the field the scientifically supported behavior analytic methods we have been learning about in our coursework and design our own programs.* Unless we are working at home with a child in our own family, most of us will have identified a host educational or treatment program, familiarized ourselves with its clientele, staff, and operation, and learned foundational intervention skills in Part 1. In Part 2 we will actually design an instructional program and begin to teach it to one or more students on the autism spectrum. If some of us are already affiliated with a program we may be able to dispense with some of the suggested activities in Units 1 and 2 in Part 1 and move right along to the next activities in the sequence.

Final Project Report

Your *Final Project* will consist of a written report that thoroughly describes the essential phases of your own original teaching program. Relevant instructions and guidelines are provided in Part 2 in Units 26 through 28. Briefly you will be asked to prepare the format for your completed *Final Project* according to the current guidelines of the *American Psychological Association (APA) Publication Manual* and will include:

- The functional rationale for your selection of client skills and teaching methods, including the current and future conditions essential to support lasting change.
- A concise review of the research literature to support your choice of teaching methods.
- Your clearly stated teaching objective(s).
- Operational definitions of target behavior(s) and/or skills taught.
- A description of your measurement system, including inter-observer agreement data.
- A clear and thorough description of the teaching methods you used.
- A description of the method you used to demonstrate the *integrity* or *fidelity* of your *treatment* (i.e., that the method you described is what you actually did).
- Graphs depicting the client's progress, plus a written description of your results.
- A thoughtful, analytic discussion of successes and failures experienced: how those events might relate to contemporary evidence on the subject, plus suggestions for ways to improve upon your program, in practice and through research.
- An accurate bibliography.

You will find preparing your final report less daunting than you might imagine at this point. Why? Because each week you will be assembling parts smoothly into a coherent final product—just like combining the pieces of a jigsaw puzzle—until the total picture emerges.

So welcome aboard again! Join us on this field practice adventure in designing our own programs. Regardless of your ultimate destination, we promise that as you conscientiously pursue these activities, you will become progressively more skillful in applying behavior analysis.

Instructions: If you are in a new practicum setting, please duplicate the first two Units of Part 1.

The Unit-by-Unit assignments (Table 16.1) lists the suggested activities for Part 2. As in Part 1, you need to complete each set of activities and have your supervisor/instructor review them and provide feedback. You will allot about an hour a week for team discussion if others are participating in this field experience.

If you use Table II.1 *alt* to propose an alternative schedule, we recommend you discuss this with your instructor or supervisor. This adjustment can be reflected in the individual contract form (Please use Form 1.3 from Part 1). Also, similar to Part 1 will be your progress reporting. Please use Table II.2 (or II.2 *alt)* for this purpose.

Table II.1 Unit by Unit Assignments: Activities and Forms PART 2

(Also budget at least 1 hour per week for *discussions;* from 1-4 hours for *tutorials.*)

Activity #	Abbreviated Title of Activity	Form	Abbreviated Title of Form	Time Estimate (in hrs.)
16.1	Support & Student Assignment	16.1	Meeting w. Student's Program Coordinator	1-2
16.2	Observing and Narrating	16.2	Narrative cover sheet	2
16.3	A-B-C Analyses	16.3	Alberto	1
17.1	Original A-B-C Analysis	17.1	ABC Analysis	½ to 1
17.2	Getting to Know Your Student	17.2	Summary ABC	1-4
17.3	Finalizing Student; Future Directions	17.3	Individual child; ABC Analysis	1-4
18.1	Ongoing Instruction	18.1	Field Assignment	2
18.2	Assisting Teachers, Parents	18.2	Assistance	TBA
18.3	Recent Research	18.3	Journal List	4-6
18. 4	Recording and Submitting DVD	18.4–18.6	Parent, Admin. video consents, Cover sheet	2-4
19.1	Applying Pre-designed Teach/Train Pkg.	19.1	Pre-designed Teaching/Training	3-6
19.2	Revised Objective	19.2	Revised objective & contract	0-1
19.2	Designing Measurement System	19.3	Measurement system	1/2 -2
19.3	Summarizing a Journal Article	19.4, .5	Journal article report, Conceptual article	1-3
19.4	Baseline Performance DVD	19.6	DVD cover sheet	2.4
20.1	Testing Recording	20.1	Testing recording	1 to 5
20.2	Article: Measurement, Graphing	20.2	Journal article report	1 to 3
20.3	Graphing Data	20.3	Graphing you own data	1-2
20.4	DVD Recording	20.4	DVD cover sheet	1
21.1	Collecting, Plotting, Baseline Data	21.1	Collecting data	1
21.2	Rethinking Instructional Objective	21.2	Revised objective(optional)	0-2
21.3	Programming for Learning	21.3	Teaching plan (W's & H)	2-3
21.4	Testing the Waters	21.4	Testing waters	1-3
21.5	Field Facilitator Assessment	21.5	Facilitator's assessment	¼
23.1	Ongoing Teaching	23.1	Ongoing teaching	2
23.2	DVD Recording	23.2	DVD cover sheet	2-4
23.3	Summarizing Journal Article	23.3	Journal report	1-2
24.1	Progress Report	24.1	Progress report	1-2
24.2	Article Generaliz. and/or Mainten.	24..2	Generalization article	1-2
25.1	Modified Progress Report	25.1	Progress report (modified)	1-4
25.2	Summary of a Journal Article	25.2	Journal report	1-3
26.1	Detailed Outline for Final Report	26.1	Outline of final report	3-6
26.2	DVD Recording	26.2	DVD cover sheet	1
27.1	Preparing Final Graph(s)	None	No form	2-5
27.2	Writing Introduction to Final Report	None	No form	1-2
27.3	Writing Abstract	None	No form	1
28.1	Completing Your Final Report	None	No form	4-6
28.2	Final Field Facilitator Assessment	28.1	Field Facilitator evaluation	½
28.3	Final DVD	28.2	Final DVD recording	1
28.4	Student Evaluation of Experience			< 1 hr.

Alternate Table II.1 alt . *Optional Pacing Adjustments. (Estimated time 0–1 hours)*

Indicate your Unit by Unit Assignments. Also budget at least 1 hour per unit for *discussions;* from 1–4 hours for *tutorials.*

Activity #	Abbreviated Title of Activity	Form	Abbreviated Title of Form	Time Estimate lin hours

Table II.2. Progress Chart for Completion of Standard Weekly Assignments PART 2

Directions: Put an X in the box next to each assignment and above the date when completed. Allow enough time to read/study tutorials, and for discussions (record across bottom row).

Form	Item												
28.4	Evaluation of experience												
28.3	Final DVD recording												
28.2	Field Facilitator Evaluation												
28.1	Final Report –No form												
	Abstract—No form												
	Introduction—No form												
	Final graph(s), No form												
26.2	DVD cover sheet												
26.1	Outline of final report												
25.2	Journal report												
25.1	Progress report (modified)												
24.2	Generalization article												
24.1	Weekly progress report												
23.3	Journal report												
23.2	DVD recording												
23.1	Ongoing teaching												
21.5	Facilitator's assessment												
21.4	Testing waters												
21.3	Teaching plan (Ws & H)												
21.2	Revised objective(optional)												
21.1	Collecting data												
20.4	DVD cover sheet												
20.3	Graphing No form												
20.2	Journal article report												
20.1	Testing recording												
19.6	Baseline DVD recording												
19.4, .5	Journal report												
19.3	Meas. system												
19.2	Revised obj. & contract												
19.1	Teaching/Training packages												
18.3	Journal list												
18.2	Assistance												
18.1	Field Arrangements												
17.3	Individual child												
17.2	Summary ABC												
17.1	ABC Analysis												
16.3	ABC—Alberto												
16.2	Narrative cover sheet												
16.1	Mtg w. Program Coord.												
	Unit Discussions												
	UNIT	16	17	18	19	20	21	22	23	24	25	26	27	28

Table II.2 alt. Progress Chart for Completion of Individually Contracted Unit Assignments

Directions: List *Forms* and *Items* you plan to do. Highlight due date boxes. Put an X in the box on the line and above the week when you actually did complete each assignment.

Form	Item													
	_____													
	UNIT	16	17	18	19	20	21	22	23	24	25	26	27	28

Unit 16
Planning the Journey
Assessing Environment and Student Performance

"Hey Lucy, would you pass me that pile of brochures about the Maritimes? The ones about B & B's and those *The Maritime Area's Greatest Eateries* and *Matchless Breakfast Fares?*"

"I think it's clear that your focus is on filling your stomach, Hal!"

"Maybe, but I also want to take a look at the local maps and highway guides."

"Umm. What is that glorious aroma?"

Art elbows his way through a swinging door, hauling a heavily laden wooden tray.

"Could one of you make room for your coffee mugs and these pecan-cinnamon rolls? Another of Ginger's great recipes. And quick, please grab the napkins before I drop them."

Hal helps himself to a steaming bun. "Sure hope she decides to join us. But back to business. Let me tell you what I discovered by reading this publication on local fairs and celebrations."

"Let me guess, Hal… they have GREAT food booths!" teases Lucy.

Our group of travelers has set aside this morning to plan their journey. They hope to structure their route loosely enough to be able to capitalize on the unexpected. Today they want to clarify what territory they want to be sure to cover. A relaxed Sunday morning is the perfect time to share their hopes and dreams for the adventure.

★★★★★

Assisted by your instructor, this is your unit to begin planning your own special journey; one that will start you on the road to a successful ABA teaching practice. Your ongoing association with your instructor and any fellow practicum students with whom you might be lucky enough to be connected should heighten your own reinforcement. The biggest reinforcer of all, though, will be in the form of *your* students' improved skills and abilities. The better acquainted you are with your students and their challenges, their peer groups, environments, and other influences, the more successful that outcome will be.

Unit 16 Objectives

Assuming you have completed formal coursework in or otherwise mastered information about behavioral assessment, including observing, recording and functionally assessing behavior, along with how to identify relationships among antecedents, behaviors and consequences of student behavior, by the end of this unit you should demonstrate your ability to observe children in a chosen location and use behavior analytic terminology to:

1. complete a practice example.
2. conduct an environmental assessment interview with your Field Facilitator that covers the instructional setting, reinforcers, staff dynamics, resources and general environmental culture or practices.
3. select a specific setting in which you will fulfill your practicum requirement.
4. schedule several hours of observation there this unit.
5. with the input of your Field Facilitator, identify the student you will be teaching.
6. observe the student under ongoing conditions.
7. record a narration of the way you see the student interacting within his or her environment to enable you to:
    - identify possible skills you could teach that meet the requirements of both this practicum and the child's needs
    - list antecedents, behavioral responses and consequences as they are presented in a simulated example
    - evaluate consequences by their likelihood for increasing or interfering with given behaviors

Several activities, including a practice analysis of a sample narration plus an actual observation, narrative recording, and A-B-C analysis, will prepare you for your own real journey into the world of behavior analytic applications in autism education. You begin by designing your teaching program.

What do we mean by a "teaching program?"

We mean *a set of carefully crafted lessons*—a sequence of steps you will follow in guiding the child toward achieving a particular learning goal or skill. That target outcome should be consonant with the student's *individualized educational program* or *family service plan*. When we talk about a learning goal or *skill,* we mean it in a broad sense.

- Yes, it could be *academic,* as in learning to read a list of words or stories, to master some arithmetic facts or solve some problems, to identify places on a map or explain the jobs of community helpers.
- Or it could be *social,* as in gaining entry to a play group, participating in a game or conversation, joining a peer or adult in playing with a particular toy, or joining in a group activity such as cooking, crafts, board game or other project.
- Maybe the goal you choose will be in the *communicative* realm, such as teaching the student to use of a set of spoken or written words, display pictures or signs to request (*mand*) particular reinforcers or to describe (*tact*) special events; altering vocal tones (*prosody*), telling jokes or asking riddles, or conversing with others.
- *Self-management* is another possible area: teaching adherence to an activity schedule, practicing relaxation, making productive choices, or staying safe.
- Related are *self-care routines,* like showering or bathing, dressing, choosing appropriate clothing to match weather conditions and/or social appropriateness.

The list of possibilities is endless, and it is a bit premature for us to consider at this point. Now you need to focus on gaining information about your site and sharing it with your instructor. Only after you identify a child and a teaching goal that will be *meaningful* and *interesting* for all involved will you be able to apply your newly acquired knowledge of teaching skills; to offer constructive interventions that will benefit the child with whom you've chosen to work and the staff and family responsible for their well being.

> **Note:** In this initial field experience we are committed to teaching you to use an *all-positive approach*. We do not include direct punitive methods for reducing unwanted behaviors. If a contextually inappropriate behavior (CIB) has been functionally assessed by a qualified individual (i.e., a board-certified behavior analyst) and replacement behaviors have been identified, you might choose to work toward promoting those positive alternatives.

Now we move on to the assigned activities. Depending on your particular situation, the amount of time you invest this unit will vary considerably. We urge you to read the material in advance, to allow you sensibly to (whoops)

PLAN AHEAD!

Activity 16.1 (Estimated time: 1–2 hours)
Obtaining Support and Student Assignment

> **Note.** If yours is a home-based program, omit non-relevant items, and record an N/A where appropriate. If possible, try to involve some peers or family members in conducting a few of the observations.

Prior to carrying out your field assignments, you must obtain the support of a key person at your site. Typically, this is the individual coordinating the student's individual plan or program and/or the parent(s). In addition, you must identify personnel/parent reinforcers, personnel or family dynamics, resources, and the general environmental culture to determine the most promising circumstances for supporting the continuation of your work after your practicum has ended. This activity guides you through the process.

Written Requirements: Form 16.1

Objective: To become better informed about the environment of your host organization (the place where you will be teaching) and the student(s) to be assigned to you. Included are the physical characteristics of the setting, the material and social reinforcers available, human resources, general staff practices and values (their reinforcers), plus a description of the organization's general "culture"—its values and habitual practices.

Instructions

Request an appointment for early in the unit to talk with your field facilitator, or, if the program is home-based, to the child's parent. To prepare yourself for that meeting, note the important points you will cover under each of the items on Form 16.1. Cover those and other relevant features of the program during the conversation. If you are unsure, share these in advance with your instructor. Then summarize each key point on the form and submit it to your instructor.

Form 16.1
Meeting with Coordinator of Student's Program

Your Name _____ Date _____ Instructor's name _____

Name (with permission) or Pseudonym of Program _____

1. The long-term goals, vision, and/or purpose of your host organization.

_____
_____
_____
_____

2. Your involvement in this behavioral field practicum course.

_____
_____

3. The nature of your participation as a field-practicum trainee and what you are expected to do at your host program.

_____
_____

4. What you hope to accomplish for yourself and for your host organization by the end of the semester.

_____
_____

5. From whom and how you have been and will continue to receive your supervision.

_____
_____

6. What you anticipate contributing to your host organization's goals and objectives.

_____
_____

7. What you are hoping that person will be able to do to assist you in the process.

_____
_____

8. What your participation should be able to contribute toward the mission, vision or long-term goals of the program.

_____
_____
_____
_____

9. Now offer to answer any questions. If uncertain about anything, say how and by when you plan to get back with the requested information. When in the slightest doubt, be sure to run the question by your instructor. Admitting you do not know all the answers is better than to mislead.

10. Say what you feel you gained from this experience.

_____
_____
_____
_____
_____

Activity 16.2 (Estimated time: 2 hours)
Observing and Narrating a Child's Behavior

The best place for you to begin your journey is by watching students in their natural surroundings. Careful observation is your key to deciding *who* to teach, *what* skills to address and *how to be most effective*.

Written requirements: Form 16.2

Objectives: To enable you to conduct a student observation, you will:

1. finalize the setting in which you will fulfill your practicum requirements and schedule several hours of observation this unit.
2. with the input of your Field Facilitator, identify the student you probably will be teaching.
3. observe the student under regularly ongoing conditions.
4. record a narration of the way you see the student interacting within his or her environment.
5. identify possible skills you could teach that both meet the requirements of this practicum and the child's needs.

Preparation

1. Schedule several hours to observe one or more students in an actual site.
2. Observe the student interacting with staff and peers during regularly scheduled activities.
3. Talk with your field facilitator about your mutual interests (e.g., communication, self-help, social skills, recreation, academic skills etc.) and concerns.
4. With the guidance of your field facilitator, focus in on one student.
5. Schedule one or more formal observations. You will need to set aside several blocks of time during which you anticipate seeing the student engaging in the behavior of interest.
6. Arrive at the scheduled time equipped with:
   - several sheets of paper and a clipboard, notebook or laptop
   - a pencil with an eraser
   - several copies of *Form 16.2* to use as a cover sheet
   - a speedy hand

Instructions

Narrate a Student's Behavior.

1. To start you off, we offer an example of a narration. Here we are interested in the student Alberto's social skills; that is, how he interacts with others in a free-play situation with other children. The observer has recorded the description displayed in *Figure 16.1.*

Figure 16.1 Written Narrative

> *Time: 1:10*
>
> *Classroom common area; then play zones: block area, dress-up center; trucks, cars; arts and crafts*
> *One lead teacher; two assistant teachers (one male); one intern (all others female)*
>
> *The children, ages 3–4 (eight boys, three girls) have been lying down for their after-lunch rest. Now the teacher plays a chord on her guitar and says, "Okay, you have rested so well, you can get up and play. Don't forget to put your mat in your cubby."*
>
> *Most of the children stretch and get up. So does Alberto. He wants ~~to runs~~ over to the toy car area. The teacher says "Alberto, mat," and points to the boy's mat and then to his cubby. Alberto continues to approach the toy car area. The teacher goes to him and gently guides him back to his mat, points to it and waits. Alberto stops and kicks the mat. The teacher takes Alberto's hands and guides him to pick up the mat. Together they walk to the cubby; Alberto puts the mat away by himself. The teacher praises him; says "Great going, Alberto," and gives him a "high-five."*
>
> *Alberto turns and runs to the car area, seizes a car and pushes it back and forth. No other children are present. He continues pushing the car in this way for the next two minutes, back and forth, back and forth. Now one of the other children, Sarah (?) comes along. She takes a dump truck, pushes it toward Alberto and says, "Let's play trucks." Alberto continues pushing the car back and forth. He does not look at Sarah or say anything. Sarah puts some blocks in the truck and pushes it toward Alberto, saying "Do you want a turn?"*
>
> *Alberto keeps pushing his car back and forth. Sarah moves off to join another little girl who is putting on a long-skirted gown in the 'dress-up' corner. Alberto continues pushing the car back and forth for three more minutes.*

2. Now it is your turn.[24]

    a.   Fill out the Narrative Recording Cover Sheet (Form 16.2. It includes the general conditions in effect (*the context*):
- the location
- others present
- time of day
- weather conditions
- scheduled and unscheduled ongoing activities and events

    b.   For about ten minutes, observe and script everything you see happening with the student. Pay careful attention to details, including interactions with other people in the room, distractions that might not be noticed, and especially attempts the student may be making to communicate, which may be overlooked or misunderstood. Write it all down.

In other words, as if you were a DVD camera, write down a description of what you would have recorded, including:
- any teacher prompts and/or instructions
- actions of other children affecting the student you are watching
- what the child is doing
- what happens as a result right away and afterward
- and any other clearly relevant events

Rule 1 for narrative recording is: ***Write down only what you can detect objectively***; what you directly see, hear, smell, touch, taste. Do not include your guesses or inferences, your assumptions about what is going on within the child's head, or the intentions of others. Remember, the behavioral approach limits itself to what we can objectively observe, measure and record. Inferences can be distracting, misleading and may be downright wrong.

We never really know what a person is thinking. Even if we ask, the person's thoughts can be distorted. Or suppose we even were able to measure brain activity. All we would discover is that certain groups of neurons are firing, and little more. Notice in Figure 16.1 how the observer changed her wording, eliminating '*wants to*,' because she realized that *wants* is an inference about Alberto that cannot be directly seen.

---

[24] ***Instructor***: You may need to assist students who encounter difficulty locating a field site. In very special cases, you may opt to allow these students an extension on this assignment.

Form 16.2: Narrative Cover Sheet (Attach narrations)

We suggest you retain this form as a master and prepare copies for your personal use.

Narrative Recording

Your Name _____ Date _____ Initials of person observed _____

Instructor's Name _____

Context:

Time of Day _____

Weather conditions (circle the condition):

Others present _____

Ongoing activity _____

Previous activity _____

Last time food eaten _____ (Describe) _____

Last time fluids consumed _____ (Describe) _____

Accessible materials and supplies

_____

_____

Other surrounding physical and social conditions: _____

_____

_____

_____

Narrative (Attach additional pages as needed, headed by your and your instructor's name and the date.)

_____

_____

_____

_____

_____

_____

_____

_____

_____

_____

_____

_____

_____

_____

_____

_____

Mini-Tutorial on Narrative Recordings and A-B-C Analyses

 Narrative recordings enable you to begin to analyze conditions (context, antecedents and consequences) that may be related to the behavior(s) of interest. Over days, a series of A-B-C analyses can help you begin identifying functional antecedents and consequences. If you conducted the narrative recording correctly and thoroughly, you will have recorded information about the following events:

Behaviors

These, as you surely recall, are the person's *actions*, not necessarily *mis*behaviors; just what the person does—good, bad or indifferent. In an A-B-C analysis, we pay close attention to these behaviors, and how they relate to the events that proceed or accompany them—the *antecedents* (and broader context)—and to the events that follow them—the *consequences*.

Antecedents

You recognize, too, that specific *antecedent* event(s) may occur right before the behavior(s) of interest to *trigger* or *set the occasion for* that behavior.[25] For instance, did the teacher give an instruction, display or distribute a material? Did a bell ring? Did another child approach, or a parent enter? What else was happening? Because any single one or combination of these events can influence the behavior(s) of interest, recording *all* of them is very important.

Consequences

Keen observers usually detect particular events occurring immediately following the behavior(s) of interest—the consequences of the behavior(s).[26] These can be quite *obvious* (such as the teacher's praise or reprimand). Or they can be *subtle* (a raised eyebrow, a tightening of the lips, a shrug or distinctive vocal tone). Yet any or the full set may exert a minor or major influence on those behavior(s), especially as the contextual events and direct antecedents vary. *So be sure to make note of these.*

While conducting an A-B-C analysis, we begin to speculate about the influence of each consequence, by scoring it as *positive* (the student works for it or seems to "want" it), *neutral* (the student seems "indifferent" to it) or *negative* (the student works to avoid it or "doesn't seem to want it"). We can only "speculate," as it is difficult to be certain of the stimulus function during initial observations. Our purpose is to develop a sound hypothesis, which we will attempt to confirm once we begin measuring, recording and analyzing our data. Sometimes you will find yourself unable to decide what the function of a particular consequence might be. In those cases, just check *neutral* or leave the boxes empty.

Let us see how the A-B-C technique plays out by starting to analyze the earlier brief scenario about Alberto.

First we review the context:

Alberto has rested with other children and most likely is ready to go. He has eaten recently and probably is not hungry. His teacher's presence apparently does make a difference to some extent, in that he complies with her guidance without protest. The toy car seems to exert quite a powerful influence, whereas Sarah's and the other children's presence ....

Next we note the student's *behaviors*: e.g., rising from the mat; running to the car area etc. Yes, record each behavior first, and then immediately fill in its antecedents and consequences.

---

[25] In your early work in experimental or applied behavior analysis, you may have learned to call these *discriminative stimuli or S^ds*.

[26] Do you recognize these as S^+s or S^Rs or S^rs for reinforcers; S^Ps or S^-s for punishers or aversive stimuli?

The *antecedents* are the events that appear to trigger the behavior:
Alberto rises when the musical chord sounds. That clearly is an effective antecedent. So, possibly, is seeing the other children get up. His teacher's instructions and gestures to pick up the mat and put it in his cubby do not lead to compliance, but her guidance does.

And, insofar as the *consequences* are concerned, the first one for not putting away the mat is the teacher's pointing and instructing. Another consequence is not being able to access the toy cars. The combined guiding and pointing are followed by his compliance. At that time we see another set of consequences: praise and a "high five," followed by access to the toy cars. There is a set of potential reinforcers to try in the future.

Is it an Is it a
Antecedent? Consequence?

Sometimes observers notice that a given *consequence* also seems to *trigger* the next response. Yes, the very same event sometimes can function both as a consequence of one behavior and an antecedent for the next.

For instance, the teacher shows a picture. The student labels it incorrectly. The teacher corrects the error by supplying the right name. That act can serve as an antecedent to the next response: the correct label. In A-B-C analyses we list the same event, the teacher's reaction, twice: as both a consequence for the error and an antecedent for the next (correct) response.

Maybe it is
Both

Soon, you will complete the full A-B-C analysis.[27] Meanwhile, have you noticed anything else this scenario may be telling us? How about Alberto's possible *strengths*: His responsiveness to the musical signal and the teacher's presence and guidance? What about his possible *weaknesses* in the communication and social areas? Repeated A-B-C analyses would allow us to explore these and related matters more closely.

---

[27] A-B-C analyses often are used during *functional assessments*, designed to begin the process of assessing the function of destructive or self-abusive behavior. Assuming this is an initial experience for you, though, we advise you against targeting the reduction of maladaptive behaviors. Instead we ask you to use this A-B-C analysis simply to try identifying some of the items or events that can serve as a student's reinforcers while learning new skills.

Activity 16.3 (Estimated time: 1 hour)
The Relation between Environmental Conditions and Behavior: A-B-C Analyses

Written Requirements: Form 16.3

Objectives: To identify relationships among antecedents, behaviors and consequences in a practice example, you will:

1. list antecedents, behavioral responses and consequences as they are presented in a simulated example
2. evaluate consequences by their likelihood for increasing or interfering with presented behaviors

After completing the behavioral narrative, you begin to examine what conditions (context, antecedents and consequences) appear to be related to the behavior of interest. A series of A-B-C analyses can allow you to begin to identify antecedents and consequences that function to heighten or possibly interfere with particular behaviors. Once these are recognized, you may be able to use the information to support suitable behavioral objectives and to avoid improper conduct.

Instructions

1. Review the narration (Figure 16.1) describing Alberto's actions after rest time.
2. Then view the sample portion of an A-B-C analysis based on that product (Figure 16.2).
3. Complete the A-B-C analysis for Alberto (Form 16.3).
4. Now look over that completed A-B-C analysis for Alberto and add your comments on:
    a. his possible strengths and weaknesses
    b. some potential reinforcers for him

Did you notice how much the toy car seemed to matter to him? He could move there quickly and directly and play alone for extended time periods. What other strengths did you detect? Did you see his possible weaknesses in the social and communication areas?

As we review *potential reinforcers* it is obvious that access to the car area is important to him, as he rapidly approaches it. Other reinforcers seem valuable as well: apple juice, music, and praise from the teacher. But it is conjecture. It is too soon to be certain. Decisions about reinforcer choice should be based on information supplied by people who know the student well, and confirmed by reinforcer assessments.

5. Submit the competed form to your instructor.[28]

---

[28] ***Instructors*** should make every effort to return this submission rapidly to students. While not essential, having your feedback might ease their preparation of the next activity.

Figure 16.2: A-B-C Analysis

Your Name ___Mona K.___ Date ___10/18___ Name (pseudonym) of person being observed ___Alberto___

Context

Time of Day ___1:10 P.M.___ Weather conditions (underline the condition):  Others present ___Whole group (eight boys, three girls) Keiko is absent___

Ongoing activity ___Up from rest; zones___ Previous activity ___Rest___

Last time food eaten ___11:30 A.M.___ (Describe) ___Alberto ate about a half cup of rice and beans.___

Last time fluids consumed ___11:30___ (Describe) ___drank ½ cup o.j.___

Accessible materials and supplies ___Dress up zone; blocks; trucks and cars; arts and crafts table___.

Other surrounding physical and social conditions ___I am present. Children seem to be getting used to my being there___

Antecedent	Behavior	Immediate Consequences	Positive	Neutral	Negative
Teacher plays chord on guitar; tells children they can get up and play; reminds them to put mats in cubbies	Gets up; runs to toy car area	Teacher says, "Alberto, mat"; points to cubbie			
"Alberto, mat." Points to mat. Waits.	Approached toy cars	Teacher guides back to mat; points to mat			Probably
Teacher points to mat and waits	Kicks mat	Teacher guides him		Can't tell (not struggling)	
At cubby	Puts mat in cubby by himself	"Great going, Alberto." Gives him a "high five"		Maybe, but not certain.	

Sulzer-Azaroff & Associates, *Applying Behavior Analysis Across the Autism Spectrum: A Field Guide for Practitioners*

Form 16.3

Continuation of A-B-C Analysis for Alberto

Your Name _____ Date _____

Antecedent	Behavior	Immediate Consequences	Positive	Neutral	Negative

What hypotheses can you start to make about Alberto's behavior in terms of:

- his response to verbal instructions
- his play preferences

In a sentence or two, summarize what you learned about Alberto from this A-B-C analysis.

Unit 16 Discussion Topics

Note. Reminder: In a face-to-face class, you only need to think about these topics in advance and jot down some notes for yourself. Your instructors then can coordinate the discussion.

In a distance course, you should choose **at least two** of these topics and post your response on the group's discussion board *or* add your own new topic.

1. Now that you have visited your practicum site, without mentioning any names or identifiers (except with explicit permission of the site manager) tell us about it.

Include information about:
   - why you approached this program
   - whether it is a home or community program
   - if it is public or private
   - urban, suburban or rural
   - the number and composition of the staff
   - number and age range of children served
   - proportion of typically-developing to children with special needs
   - other salient features

2. In your own words, tell the others in your group about the episode(s) you narrated in writing.
   - How did the experience match your expectations?
   - What surprises were there?

3. Conducting A-B-C analysis can be *challenging* but very *informative*. Say in what way you did or did not find that to be the case.

4. Let's talk about your own investment of resources this unit:
   - How effectively did you manage your time this unit?
   - Are you keeping a record of how long each activity takes you, preparation included?
   - Are you recording your progress? If so, how does that affect you?
   - How closely did it match the printed time estimate?

5. Probably you are curious about the experiences of the other members of your group. What questions would you like to ask them?

Your assignments for the next unit will be fairly time-consuming, but stimulating and fun. Take a look at those and see exactly what you will be expected to cover. Assuming you feel fairly confident, have about one to two available hours remaining in the unit, and your instructor approves, you are well advised to complete *Activities 17.1* and *17.2* ahead of time.

Unit 17
Charting Your Course:
Choosing Student Learning Objectives

Today Ginger bounces in, her green eyes sparkling. After mulling over the invitation, she has agreed to join the group, at least for a few months.

"So, I understand we're supposed to make some plans today?" she inquires.

"I guess so. In a way, though, don't you wish we could just climb aboard right now and go absolutely anywhere the spirit takes us without any forethought?" Dawn muses.

"Mmmn! Remember the good old days, Luce," Hal reminisces, "when we were young and happy-go-lucky; just took off on the spur of the moment?"

"That trip during senior year—the lobster shack? Best seafood I ever tasted."

"Absolutely! And watching the sunset from Cadillac Mountain. What a vista! Fantastic sunset! Good thing we took the blanket along!" A mischievous look passes between them.

"And then the lake in the woods, the one where we saw that great blue heron up in the tree feeding its baby."

"And the dead end, when we needed to double back," she adds wryly.

"I remember your telling us about that. Wasn't that the time you ran out of gas?" Ginger reminds them.

"It was. Those are the kinds of experiences that taught us that, as appealing as spontaneity sounds, we're better off planning ahead. So what do you say we get to it?"

★★★★★

Probably most of us have memories to share of times of greater freedom and fewer responsibilities. Today, though, having matured, we probably are in a different place. We take our responsibilities seriously. Although we may not know exactly where our own particular ABA journey will end, we certainly recognize the direction we want to take, and are sure to invest what it takes to plan accordingly. Time is too precious to squander by indulging our impulses. Now, just as we would check to be certain our vehicle is in good condition and has sufficient fuel before departing on a trip, we educators of students with autism recognize the importance of setting a very precise course of action from the very start.

Our focus for this unit will lead you to an understanding of the purpose and direction of your personal area of study. The questions you ask will enable you to chart an efficient course. So plan with care. See to it that all the essentials are in place. Your reward will be the gains your students make.

Unit 17 Objectives

Assuming you have completed formal coursework in, or otherwise mastered information about specifying instructional objectives and based on information gleaned from interviews, behavioral observational and archival data, by the end of this unit you should be able to choose appropriate learning objectives for your student by:

1. identifying and evaluating the relationships between your student's specific behaviors and the consequences and antecedents affecting them (A-B-C relationships).
2. generating a report summarizing your A-B-C analysis.
3. analyzing archival data.
4. proposing teaching objectives and defining preliminary target behaviors and measurement procedures for *your* student, by:
   - classifying antecedents, behavioral responses and consequences as presented in your narrative (see Activity 16.2, Unit 16)
   - evaluating consequences by their effect; that is, by the extent to which they increase or interfere with presented behaviors
   - generating a report of your A-B-C analysis that includes, but is not limited to, a description of how the context appeared to affect conditions and responses and an explanation of your choice of reinforcers
   - based on your child's school records, identifying prior teaching objectives and needed skill domains
   - conducting an additional A-B-C analysis related to the skill area you have chosen
   - for the child, identifying and defining possible
     - teaching objectives
     - related target skills
     - reinforcing items or events
     - teaching procedures

Note. **For this unit's set of exercises:**

If you currently are *employed* in a program, we suggest you set objectives jointly with your job supervisor. In case you are participating in a *home program*, you will want the input about instructional objectives from the parent(s) and, if relevant, the family service program coordinator.

Activity 17.1 (Estimated time: 30 minutes–1 hour)
Conducting an Original A-B-C Analysis

For the last unit you used the A-B-C method to analyze a narrative recording for a fictitious student, Alberto. You also observed an actual student and narrated his or her ongoing activities. You also may have analyzed it using the same A-B-C method.

Written Requirements: Complete A-B-C Form

Objectives: To identify and evaluate A-B-C relationships affecting the behavior of *your* student, you will:

1. classify antecedents, behavioral responses and consequences as they are presented in your narrative (see Activity 16.2, Unit 16).
2. evaluate consequences by their likelihood to increase or interfere with presented behaviors.
3. Then, after completing this activity and receiving your instructor's feedback, you will become more proficient in conducting A-B-C analyses.

Instructions:

1. Return to the original narrative you recorded last unit for Activity 16.2.
2. Use a *copy* of Form 17.1 to conduct your A-B-C analysis.
3. Note down:
   - each thing you saw your student *do* that is, the *behavior (B)*
   - the full set of immediate *antecedent* events (*A*s), such as receiving new directions, instructions, signs, sounds, specific materials, or perhaps actions of others; and
   - *all* the immediate social and other environmental consequences (*C's*) to the behavior that you observe

Note. Remember that:

1. Items under the *Behavior* column need to be limited to what you observe the selected student doing. Actions of others affecting the student do *not* belong in the *behavior* column; those are *antecedents* or *consequences*.

2. More than one single antecedent and/or consequence may occur or be present at a single moment, as in the case of the teacher saying, "Good work," smiling, and patting the child on the shoulder. Yes, because we cannot know which is having what effect at this point, include the whole set. Eventually, clear patterns should begin to emerge.

3. A consequence also may double as the antecedent for a subsequent behavior.

4. *Examine consequences.* Now examine the nature of every consequence of each behavior you noted. For clearly obvious ones, say whether the consequence appeared to be a *positive reinforcer* (that would function to *increase* the future rate of the act it followed), *neutral* (lacking any function) or *negative* (that would function to *reduce* the future rate of that act). You can usually infer that an event is positive when the child approaches or reaches for it, smiles or consumes it, says "thank you" in an enthusiastic voice and so on; or that it is "apparently negative" when the child rejects—pushes away, cries, turns, or moves away from that consequence. If you cannot tell, either just check *neutral* or leave the boxes empty. Or if you feel you must speculate, jot down your guesses.

5. Speculate in general about the influence of the context, antecedents and consequences.

6. Submit the pages to your instructor.

Form 17.1 (p. 1 of 2)

A-B-C Analysis[29]

Your Name _____ Date _____ Initials of person observed _____ Instructor's Name _____

Context

Time of Day _____ Weather conditions (underline the condition):

Others present _____

Ongoing activity _____

Previous activity _____

Last time food eaten _____ (Describe) _____

Last time fluids consumed _____ (Describe) _____

Accessible materials and supplies _____

Other surrounding physical and social conditions _____

Antecedent	Behavior	Immediate Consequences		
		Positive	Neutral	Negative

[29] Dyer, K. (2011). A-B-C- analysis. In F. Volkmer (ed.) *Encyclopedia of Autism Spectrum Disorders*. New York:Springer; Mayer, R. G., Sulzer-Azaroff, B., & Wallace, M. *Behavior Analysis for Lasting Change*, 2nd ed. New York: Sloan Publishing.

Sulzer-Azaroff & Associates, *Applying Behavior Analysis Across the Autism Spectrum: A Field Guide for Practitioners*

Form 17.1 (p. 2 of 2)

Your Name _____ (Pseudo) Name of Person Being Observed _____ Date _____

Antecedent	Behavior	Immediate Consequences	Positive	Neutral	Negative

What **contexts** do you think would be most supportive of this student's learning?

Based on the above, speculate about some effective **reinforcers** for this student.

What **antecedents** appear to function most powerfully?

Activity 17.2 (Estimated time: 1–4 hours)
Getting to Know Your Student

Note: If *you still need a student to teach*, make an appointment with your field facilitator. After describing that program's needs and your own goals and interests, discuss:

1) Your own role and responsibilities as a student in this practicum course.
2) What your participation will contribute to their program.
3) The roles and responsibilities of your instructor and the Field Facilitator.
4) Ask the field facilitator to suggest students who would be available and appropriate to your area of study.
5) Once a student has been identified, determine toward what objectives you will work with this student.

Written Requirements: Form 17.2

Objectives: To generate a report summarizing your A-B-C analysis, you will include:

- a description of how the context appeared to affect conditions and responses, and;
- an explanation for your choice of reinforcers

Instructions

1. Observe your student on several occasions over one or more days and under a variety of situations, such as during formal instruction, unstructured "free-time," lunch period, group activities and so on. Focus on a breadth of behaviors, especially including adaptive ones. If necessary, you can do this on the same day, though separate observations are preferable.
2. Record a narrative for each observation.
3. Analyze each behavior sample, using the A-B-C format.
4. After examining your materials closely, try to detect any patterns in your student's behavior. Then complete the form below (*Summary of A-B-C Analysis*) for **at least one** set that you feel is especially *relevant for your student* and submit the whole packet to your instructor.

Form 17.2 (p. 1 of 2)

Summary of A-B-C Analysis

Your Name _____ Instructor's Name _____ Date _____

Objective

This activity should provide you with some useful tools for encouraging and reinforcing your student's progress toward achieving his or her instructional objectives.

Instructions

1. Tell us briefly about your student, along with *the main objectives* included in his/her individual educational or family service program.

_____
_____
_____
_____
_____
_____

2. Review the A-B-C analyses you conducted to look for patterns in your student's behavior.
   a) List the behavior(s) of interest.

_____
_____
_____
_____
_____
_____
_____

   b) Explain your specific interest in those behaviors.

_____
_____
_____
_____
_____
_____

   c) Describe how the *context* appeared to affect the child's responses to antecedents and/or consequences.

_____
_____
_____
_____

   d) Say why you have drawn those conclusions.

_____
_____
_____
_____
_____

Form 17.2 (p. 2 of 2)

Your Name _____ Instructor's Name _____ Date _____

    e) Identify the conditions that seem to be functioning as *antecedents* of each of the behaviors you listed above.

_____
_____
_____
_____
_____
_____

    f) Identify the *consequences* of the behavior(s) you listed.

_____
_____
_____
_____
_____
_____

    g) Say which of those seemed to be positive (+), negative (-), or neutral (0), by placing the corresponding symbol next to each item above.

    h) Say which consequences you might be able to use as reinforcers when you teach this person. Defend your choice(s).

_____
_____
_____

    i) Say which antecedents you might be able to use as prompts when you teach this person.

_____
_____
_____

3. In a sentence or two, summarize *in general* what you learned by conducting these A-B-C analyses, including any patterns that seem to be emerging.

_____
_____
_____
_____
_____
_____
_____
_____

4. What was the *most* important thing you learned from this exercise?

_____
_____
_____
_____

5. Add any further comments or questions for your instructor here:

_____
_____
_____

Activity 17.3 (Estimated time: 1–4 hours)
Finalizing Your Student Selection and Planning Future Directions

Written Requirements: Forms 17.3 and 17.4

Objectives: To conduct an archival data analysis, propose teaching objectives,[30] (including the behavior of interest, conditions under which it should and/or should not occur, and standards by which its accomplishment will be determined as having been achieved) and then define preliminary target behaviors and measurement procedures for *your* student:

1. identify prior teaching objectives and needed skill domains from your child's school records
2. generate an additional A-B-C analysis related to the skill area you have chosen
3. identify and define possible target behaviors
4. generate possible teaching objectives for your child
5. generate preliminary teaching procedures

Instructions

In activity 17.2 you should have become better acquainted with your student. You are now ready to collaborate with your instructor and field facilitator to begin to decide *what* to teach. The attached form asks you to:

1. Talk to your Field Facilitator and finalize the specific area of skill development in which you will be working. (Remember, at this stage, to focus only on *constructive* skills—those you hope to increase or teach, *not* to reduce.)
2. With your host's permission, and under conditions of confidentiality, read your student's records. Review any objectives included in the student's *Individual Educational Program* (IEP) or *Individual Family Service Plan* (IFSP) and consider these when deciding what to teach your student.
3. Conduct another narration and A-B-C analysis of your student during an activity specifically related to the skill area you have chosen (Form 17.4).
4. Based on that, generate and justify a few potential teaching objectives.[31] To help you define those objectives in the most functional way, read the mini-tutorial on specifying target responses, complete the exercise, and, if you and your instructor or supervisor agrees, turn it in for feedback.
5. If feasible, contact or visit the student's parent(s) to introduce yourself, discuss your plans and gain and incorporate their input.
6. Turn in the Activity 17.2 Form, narrative recording, Form 17.3, and A-B-C Form 17.4 to your instructor and wait for feedback before proceeding.
7. Meanwhile, continue observing your anticipated student and find out how you can be helpful at the site. Probably, among others, teachers or parents will appreciate your
   - collecting data
   - preparing and organizing materials
   - cleaning up afterwards
   - carrying out training trials in ongoing programs, for generalization purposes.

… Now begin to think about some promising ways to teach your student.

---

[30] Refer to pages 67–70 in Mayer, Sulzer-Azaroff & Wallace (2012), *Behavior Analysis for Lasting Change, 2nd Ed.* Cornwall-on-Hudson, NY: Sloan Publishing.

[31] **Instructor:** Working on a single instructional objective is appropriate for students attending their sites for about nine hours a week. Those of you committing to additional hours should plan to have your ABA student develop additional teaching objectives accordingly (e.g., 2 objectives for 18–20 hours a week etc.)

Preparing Behavior-Change Objectives: a Tutorial

"You know," Rosa comments to Allie and Jeb, "I'm beginning to feel much more at home here at Walden—more comfortable with the students, teachers and professional staff. And now that we've completed all the check-lists, I'm really anxious to begin designing my own programs."

"Now that's a fact," Jeb agrees. "I've been thinking about how I could use what we've been learning and practicing, to try out some of my own ideas. One I have is to find a way to teach two or more kids to play together; you know, like tossing bean-bags or balls back and forth, pushing each other on the swings, pulling one another in the wagon instead of me having to do it all."

"You too?" Allie interjects. "Just yesterday, Carson seemed about to lose it completely. Thank goodness, I realized, just in the nick of time, he wanted to sharpen his pencil so he could finish his arithmetic paper. One tantrum averted! So last night, it came to me: I could teach him how to ask for that by teaching him to combine some of his pictures: He already knows to get help with his "help" icon and uses the picture of the pencil to get a pencil. Maybe he could learn to combine the two: help plus pencil. I'm going to talk to Ginger about that before she leaves on that trip she's been talking about."

"Did I hear mention of my name?" Ginger has slipped quietly into the room.

"Right. The three of us were talking about how we're itching to begin designing our own behavior-change programs; getting some ideas about what we'd like to do. I've been watching the kids at lunch and the way they sometimes try to grab food from one another. My sister is having the same problem with my niece, so they don't dare go to restaurants with her. I'd love to find a way to teach her to ask instead of grabbing. Being able to get out for a meal once in a while sure would improve their family life!"

"You guys are awesome," Ginger replies. "I agree, Rosa, now that you've demonstrated the check-listed skills, the three of you are ready to move on to the next level: designing your own programs."

"But wait a sec. How about that rumor—about your taking a break?" Jeb questions. "I feel ready enough, but not to go the whole way alone."

"Not to worry. You'll have Herb here to help you; he'll be joining us for our weekly meetings and stay on with you while I'm gone; and these days various Internet programs allow us to view ourselves and our clients in action from a distance. Between Herb, me, and modern technology, you'll have lots of support—and by the way, he's planning on joining our meeting today."

"Phew. That's cool. I was beginnin' to worry."

"So speaking of designing new programs, where do you think we should begin?" Ginger asks.

"That's an easy one. As Prof banged into our heads, by specifying our behavioral objectives."

All nod in agreement.

*"Ah. Great minds think alike. And, speak of the devil, here comes Herb with some materials you're probably going to appreciate, on specifying behavioral objectives. Shall we take a look? With their permission, I've extracted and modified a section from Mayer, Sulzer-Azaroff and Wallace's **Behavior Analysis for Lasting Change, 2nd ed. (2012)."[32]***

******

---

[32] See pages 67–70 in Mayer, Sulzer-Azaroff & Wallace (2012) for a more complete discussion of this topic.

Preparing Behavioral Objectives: A Tutorial

- *What is a behavioral objective?* A statement of what the student is to do at the end of an intervention.

- *How do we choose really meaningful objectives?* By becoming very well acquainted with our students/clients; discovering their missing skills, particular those of a pivotal nature, or those of their behaviors that interfere with their own progress or that of others.

- *When do we begin to specify our behavioral objectives?* After we have decided what high-priority goals we hope to pursue; such as functioning more successfully on work assignments, within social groupings, and out in the community.

- *What are the main components of a behavioral objective?*
  1. the objectively stated *goal behavior*: in general, what *reasonably achievable* behavior we are hoping in the future to observe the person doing.
  2. the clearly-specified conditions and/or context within which the behavior is to occur, including the setting, furnishings, materials, personnel, and so on.
  3. the criteria, or standards for determining when the objective has been accomplished (Mager,1962; 1972; 1997b).

To determine how well prepared they are, Herb asks the group to mention some goal behaviors.

Rosa offers: "How about 'Sally will join the family for a meal in a restaurant, sit quietly and eat only from her own plate?'"

"I'd pick: 'Two kids will interactively play together, using gym or playground equipment."

"Neat, Jeb. And you, Allie?"

"Mine would be teaching one or two students to connect two different signs, symbols or words together to permit them to communicate and thereby get what they want at the time."

Now, you, our reader, having already seen various examples here and previously, we ask you to offer two or three such statements for students or clients of your own.

_____
_____
_____
_____
_____
_____
_____
_____

"Aha! Now we know what they are to be doing. I've got a sneaking suspicion you guys are ahead of me. So where do we go next?"

Rosa nods: "The conditions. I think I've already alluded to mine: 'With the family, in a restaurant."

All nod their agreement.

"Mine would be something like 'When he doesn't have a way to express what he wants with a single word, gesture or icon' or something like that. Have to think about it a little more."

"Maybe add 'having the ability to combine and communicate the components of the concept'—you know, like the parts of the whole new idea?" Jeb offers.

Allie flashes him a thumbs-up.

"...and, as for my own, I think I've already done that by talking about the gym or playground; though maybe I'd better say something about which kids, what equipment and such. Let me think about that a little more."

Rosa now looks a little troubled. "But suppose they're out in the neighborhood playground. We don't want your guys going over and trying to share equipment belonging to strange kids, do we?"

"Now that you mention it, let me think about how to say it—maybe add something like 'with permission of his parents, or supervisors, care-givers, whatever... maybe the other kids!"

Now, reader, it's your turn to specify the environmental *conditions* under which you would want to see the behavior you just listed occur, now and in the future, along with *the conditions* under which you definitely *would not* want to see (or hear etc.)—the *restrictions or limitations*—on its happening.

_____
_____
_____
_____
_____
_____

Herb proposes. "You also might want to add the materials the student would have access to? You've got your gym and playground equipment, Jeb. How about the rest of you?"

As Rosa and Allie are pondering the *materials* they would need, join them by listing those you would require in order to enable your student to achieve the objective you are considering:

_____
_____
_____
_____
_____
_____

"Gosh, I just thought of something. How am I going to know when enough is enough and move on to some other objective? We could keep going forever with restaurant manners."

"Mine too. How many kids does my student need to play with? For how long? How many pieces of equipment would they need to use... I'd want to know when we've achieved the objective."

Allie slowly nods her concern with the issue at hand. "I'd better put a limit on the two word-combinations I hope to teach, too, or else I might be spending the next ten years working with Carson on two-word combos."

Now it is time for you to step in with the *conditions and limitations (the circumstances under which the behavior should and should not occur)*, and *general criteria (fluency, rate, number/frequency &/or percentage correct per time block etc.)* you would use to conclude that your student(s) reached the specific instructional objective you are planning on pursuing. Be certain to include such considerations (frequency or number, rate, consistency, acceleration, fluency, percentage, quality standards, achieved over a particular unit of time) before you shift over to a maintenance mode by thinning out reinforcer density):

- Particular aspects of the performance
- Conditions (errors, times, places, social context, etc.), limitations or restrictions (how, which, where, when with whom, under which conditions the behavior should or should not occur)
- Durability of the change, in terms of time, resistance to unraveling and so on:

_____

_____

_____

_____

_____

_____

One thing more. You are going to want to specify a numerical basis for determining when your student has achieved the objective; that is, the standards or criteria you will use to judge its attainment. Generally, observing the objectified behavior performed just once would be unconvincing. You want to see it happen consistently, whenever conditions are appropriate. Ask yourself what would convince you (and others concerned with the outcome) how frequently and consistently the designated behavior should be repeated. How many times in a row should the specific behavioral objective occur as designated and over how long a period of time? For instance, Jeb probably would like to see his students interact during physical activities for at least five minutes *several times in a row—say three days in a row for each of two weeks*.

Now here is an opportunity for you to practice this point. Using one of the examples from this text or another of relevance to your own circumstances, propose a behavioral objective that incorporates each of the features described above. (See, for instance, table 17.1 from Mayer, Sulzer-Azaroff & Wallace, 2012). After you have prepared that objective, show it to someone naïve on the topic of designing behavioral objectives. Then ask "Would you be convinced the objective had been achieved if each of the elements of the objective were met?" Write their response below.

_____

_____

_____

TABLE 17.1 Measure of Proficiency Levels[33]

Dimension	Measure	Definition	Examples
Level of Proficiency	frequency	The number of times a response occurs	Paula will complete 4 reports. Shakisha will provide at least 1 answer and 1 question when conversing with peers. The team will accumulate 20 days without a lost-time injury.
	percentage	Proportion or number of times achieved or correct, divided by total possible times multiplied by 100	Ramon will complete 90% of his assignments each week. 80% of the work teams will have a quality assurance plan in place by the end of the fiscal year.
	duration	The length of time that passes from the onset to the offset of a behavior	Shakisha will converse audibly for at least 30 seconds. Henri will brush his teeth for a full 2 minutes. Betsy will exercise for a full hour.
	rate	The number of times a response occurs within a given period of time or per opportunity	Bruno will practice an hour a day. Betsy will exercise 5 days per week. Betsy will do 25 push-ups within 3 minutes. The team will assemble 30 engines per day.

How did you do? Do you feel you need to modify the objective any further? Why? And if so, say how you would re-state it.

_____

_____

_____

"When I read about behavioral objectives last year I wondered why we needed to be so, you know, picky," Jeb comments. "But now that we're out here in the real world, I'm beginning to see how taking the time to define what we are hoping and trying to achieve can really pay off –by making sure we take the most direct and promising path to the goal, without wandering off into dead ends."

"I agree," Rosa adds, "time is limited and these kids need to progress toward more mainstream society as well and as fast as possible. When we pause to spell out our objectives very carefully, we avoid digressing up blind alleys."

"I'm convinced too. Although I feel as if I'm ready to rush in and begin shaping behavior on my own—like yesterday, I'm going to give my objectives another going-over so the ones I come up with promise to give everyone the biggest bang for the buck.

---

[33] From Mayer, Sulzer-Azaroff & Wallace (2012). *Behavior Analysis for Lasting Change, 2nd Ed.* (p. 68) with permission.

Now it's your turn, again. Ponder the behavioral objective(s) you currently are considering pursuing. Convince your audience that the utility/value, practicality, achievability, clarity, and other advantages are sufficient to justify their pursuit.

_____

_____

_____

_____

_____

_____

_____

_____

_____

Form 17.3 (p. 1 of 6)

Your Name _____ Date _____ Instructor _____

Focusing on an Individual Student

1. Name (with permission) or pseudonym of program or family _____

2. Name of field facilitator _____ Phone number _____

   Email address _____

3. Initials or pseudonym of student you will be teaching _____

4. Area in which you will be working. Check the relevant box or fill in the portion under "Other."

Pivotal skills[34]
☐ imitating   ☐ following directions   ☐ joint attention

other (specify) _____

Functional communication
☐ requesting   ☐ describing   ☐ elaborating   ☐ complying with instructions

other (specify) _____

Engagement in
☐ academic skills   ☐ activities of daily living   ☐ physical/motor skills

☐ recreational, leisure skills   ☐ self-help skills   ☐ social skills

Other (describe) _____

5. History

   a) In a few sentences, summarize what you have learned by reviewing the student's records. Limit your comments to what others have *observed* about the youngster; not their subjective interpretations. Try to cover *developmental level, skills or deficits* in the communication, academic, physical/motor, self-help, social or other relevant domains, but concentrate most heavily on the area you identified above under #4.

_____
_____
_____
_____
_____
_____
_____
_____
_____

---

[34]*Pivotal behaviors* are those central to wide ranges of functioning. See Koegel, R. L. & Kogel, L. K. (1995). *Teaching Students with Autism.* Baltimore, MD: Paul H. Brookes, Publishing. See also Whalen, C. & Schreibman, L. (2003). Joint attention for children with autism using behavior modification procedures. *Journal of Child Psychology and Psychiatry, 44*:3, pp. 456–468.

Form 17.3 (p. 2 of 6)

Your Name _____ Date _____ Instructor _____

    b) If you have read the child's Individual Educational Plan, say how the area on which you are proposing to work relates to that plan.

_____

_____

6. Narrate your student's actions during an activity related to the area on which you are proposing to focus and analyze what you observed by using the attached *A-B-C Recording Form.* Attach the narration and A-B-C- forms.

7. Now propose two or three objectives you think would be appropriate for you to pursue with the student. Be sure to include the *behavior* (what the student will be doing), the *contextual arrangement* (with what materials, under what other conditions—time, place, physical arrangements), following what specific antecedents (if appropriate). Also include a *standard* for judging when the objective will have been mastered. The latter might include level of correctness (accuracy), number of times correct in a row (frequency), number of times correct in a row within a given time period (rate) or other important details that will enable all to agree when the youngster has mastered the objective.

Objective 1:

Given (context and direct antecedents or "discriminative stimuli") _____

_____

the student will (the behavior or "target response") _____

_____

(the standards or criteria) _____

_____

_____

Objective 2:

Given (context and direct antecedents or "discriminative stimuli") _____

_____

the student will (the behavior or "target response") _____

_____

(the standards or criteria) _____

_____

_____

Objective 3:

Given (context and direct antecedents or "discriminative stimuli") _____

_____

the student will (the behavior or "target response") _____

_____

(the standards or criteria) _____

_____

Form 17.3 (p. 3 of 6)

8. After meeting with the child's teacher and/or parent,
    a) say which objective you have elected to pursue; or indicate an alternative objective you have found mutually acceptable. Write it here:_____

Given (context and direct antecedents or "discriminative stimuli") _____
_____
_____

the student will (the behavior) _____
(the standards or criteria) _____
_____
_____

    b) Add anything else you learned from the meeting_____
_____
_____

9. If feasible and you have not done so already, try to meet the student's family in their own or the program setting. Add any information you have gained in that experience that you feel will impact on your success with the objective(s) you are hoping to pursue.
_____
_____
_____
_____

10. Consider the factors below that may affect the success of your intended teaching program:
- Scheduling your time with the student for regular accessibility.
- Note those times and days of the week here _____
- Identify the location in which you will be able to teach _____
- Say how this location will favorably support for what you want to teach _____
_____
- Will an array of effective reinforcer choices be available for you to use? _____
- What other human resources and materials will be available at the chosen time and place?
_____
_____

Given all the above, are you sure you really want to proceed toward that objective?

☐ Yes definitely ☐ Probably ☐ A bit apprehensive ☐ Really unsure

☐ I think I'd better think it over once again. Comments? Questions?
_____
_____
_____
_____
_____
_____

11. If you have started to think about a method for promoting your selected objective, summarize it here._____
_____
_____
_____

Sulzer-Azaroff & Associates, *Applying Behavior Analysis Across the Autism Spectrum: A Field Guide for Practitioners*

Form 17.4 (p. 1 of 2)
A-B-C Analysis

Your Name _____ Date _____ Name (pseudonym) of person being observed _____

Context

Time of Day _____ Weather conditions (underline the condition):

Ongoing activity _____ Previous activity _____ Others present _____

Last time food eaten _____ (Describe) _____ Last time fluids consumed _____ (Describe) _____

Accessible materials and supplies _____

Other surrounding physical and social conditions _____

Antecedent	Behavior	Immediate Consequences	Positive	Neutral	Negative

Form 17.4 (p. 2 of 2)
Your Name _____ (Pseudo) Name of Person Being Observed _____ Date _____

Antecedent	Behavior	Immediate Consequences	Positive	Neutral	Negative

What **contexts** do you think would be most supportive of this student's learning?

Based on the above, speculate about some effective **reinforcers** for this student:

What **antecedents** appear to function most powerfully?

***Note* to fast-paced students**[35]: Some participants in this practicum are just becoming acquainted with their field settings, while others are thoroughly familiar with the site, the pupils and their learning needs. Perhaps you are in the latter category and have a clear sense of your student and the instructional objective(s) you will address. In that case you may want to begin learning more in depth about what the research has to say on the subject of your interest. Just move on early to Activity 18.1 in Unit 18.

An important feature of this practicum is your instructor's observvation of you and your student engaged in teaching interactions by seeing video records of you both in action. So, another get-ahead option is for you to take the initial steps involved in preparing those film recordings (Activity 18.2).

Unit 17 Discussion Topics

(You may be talking back and forth several times. Anticipate spending a minimum of an hour.)

1. Comment on any or all of the following:
   a. How your anticipated learning as a result of spending time in an actual educational program now compares with your present discoveries.
   b. What you found most appealing about your particular objective and the objectives some of your classmates hope to pursue.
   c. The steps you are considering following in teaching the objective.
   d. How confident you feel about taking the route you are proposing.
2. Describe an example of something from your earlier readings that you now have actually seen. Discuss any changes in your perspectives as a result.
3. What information/feedback would you appreciate from your instructor and/or your classmates?
4. Add any other topics of relevance to this Unit's assignments.

Please remember to remain positive and supportive and to respect confidentiality.

---

[35] A number of participants in our field trials expressed a preference for "getting into the literature" as soon as possible.

Unit 18
Gearing Up
Assessing the Learning Environment and Defining Your Role

Dawn is rushing out of the office, trying to make it home in enough time to manage a few loads of laundry. Suddenly, her cell phone chimes an old-time Beatles' tune.

"Hi Lucy."

"How'd you know it was me?"

" '*Hard Days Night*'. That means you."

"Awesome!"

"So, what's up?"

"Well, I was wondering what you're planning on packing for our trip? Are you taking any rain gear? Heavy sweaters? A skirt, just in case?"

"All of them, I suppose. And thanks for reminding me about the rain gear. I can just see us dying to go hiking, but stuck inside 'cause we don't want to get wet. Are you bringing the first aid kit?"

"Will do. And I wanted to let you guys know I spent hours on the Internet researching our route. You know—motels, restaurants, and points of interest. Even saw some streaming videos. Some of those places seem really attractive."

"Great minds apparently think alike! I just returned from the library with an armload of books and magazines. Hope to spend the next week going through the pile to see what to follow up on."

*****

Suppose you were planning a trip to a tropical island. You wonder what the sleeping and dining facilities are like. Can snorkel equipment, golf clubs, and fishing gear be rented? Will there be a shop selling suntan lotion and sundries? Or suppose it's a business trip. Typical concerns might be whether the hotel has Internet hookups, projectors and the rest. Those are the sorts of questions you'd probably want answered.

Similarly, in our present situation, before launching into your own teaching, unless the site is very familiar to you at this point, you probably will need to examine in fine detail the surroundings and its resources: its rooms and functions, furnishings, materials, program activities, teaching methods, available assistance and so on. A*nd* you surely want to know what the latest research has to say about the methods you are considering applying. This week, by asking you to be both an observer and a participant, we give you a chance to do that.

Week 18 Objectives

Assuming you have completed formal coursework in or otherwise become skillful in locating and reading fundamental texts and experimental journal reports in the ABA field, by the end of this week you should be able to begin to identify research reports related to your chosen area of interest and produce a video in your student's instructional setting by:

1. reviewing empirical articles related to your chosen skill domain and identify teaching strategies employed and other key components
2. obtaining administrative, teacher and parental consent for video participation (If you have previously recorded videos in Part 1, you can skip this objective. If this is the first time recording, please USE FORMS 2.7 & 2.8 FROM PART 1)
3. recording a video of teaching interactions within your student's instructional setting.

Note to fast-paced students: Assuming you have already begun to locate the sources of promising papers, this is a good time to begin reading and summarizing at least one. Use the form included in next week's assignments under Activity 19.3.

Activity 18.1 (Estimated time: 4–6 hours)
Informing Yourself about Recent Behavior Analytic Research in Your Probable Teaching Domain

Objectives: You will be able to familiarize yourself with behavior analytic research in the area of your likely teaching domain by reviewing empirical articles related to your chosen skill domain

Written Requirements: Form 18.1
Instructions

To date, your learning might have been largely verbal. In your prior coursework, you have mastered numerous concepts and principles of behavior and learned *about* how to apply them effectively when teaching youngsters with autism. You recognize that behavior analysis prides itself on being an evidence-based approach to intervention. Fortunately, the knowledge base continues to grow in this area, as researchers and practitioners design, test and report on how new methods work out. One of your jobs as a responsible practitioner in this field is to know the well-established results and keep abreast of new developments. To do that you need to continue to study relevant scientific media—the printed and online journals reporting controlled research findings.

1. Given your growing familiarity with the setting, probably you are beginning to learn more about the students and their needs. Check some of the areas of particular focus in the setting.

   ☐ academic skills
   ☐ activities of daily living
   ☐ communication (spoken, sign or pictures)
   ☐ community participation
   ☐ engagement in general

   ☐ occupational skills
   ☐ physical/motor skills
   ☐ recreational, leisure skills
   ☐ self-help skills
   ☐ social skills
   ☐ Other (describe)

   _____

   _____

2. At this point, certainly you want to find out what has been achieved lately in autism education in areas of particular relevance to your anticipated work in this practicum placement. Schedule several hours in an actual or virtual library.[36]

3. Locate as many journals as you can that publish papers on education by means of behavior analytic interventions. Some, such as the *Journal of Applied Behavior Analysis,* are limited exclusively to behavior analytic papers, while others publish both scientific and conceptual papers.

4. Below is a list of journals that have published reports of research done in the area of behavior analysis applied to education in autism and other developmental disabilities. Titles in **bold** contain the heaviest concentration of these papers. A few (in parentheses) contain only occasional papers on this topic. A few others may no longer be in print or their titles may have changed, but they still can be obtained from some University Libraries directly or through their inter-library loan services. And new ones regularly come along. Watch for those!

---

[36] If you are using this Field Manual as a resource for an on-line course, probably the organization delivering the course will be affiliated with an on-line library. Otherwise many journals publish papers on their own websites, which you can either access freely or for a fee.

• American Journal on Mental Retardation	• **Journal of Applied Behavior Analysis**
• Analysis and Intervention in Developmental Disabilities	• Journal for the Division of Early Childhood
• Applied Research in Mental Retardation	• Journal of Child Psychology and Psychiatry and Allied Disciplines
• Autism: The International Journal of Research & Practice	• Journal of Communication Disorders
• Behavior Change	• (Journal of Consulting and Clinical Psychology)
• Behavior Modification	• (Journal of Developmental and Physical Disabilities)
• Behavioral Interventions	• **Journal of Early Intervention**
• (Child Development)	• **Journal of Positive Behavioral Interventions**
• Child and Family Behavior Therapy	• (Psychological Bulletin)
• Developmental and Behavioral Pediatrics	• Research in Developmental Disabilities
• Education and Treatment of Children	• Teaching Exceptional Children
• **Focus on Autism and Other Developmental Disabilities**	• (The Analysis of Verbal Behavior)
• **Journal of Autism and Developmental Disorders**	• (The Psychological Record)
• Journal of Autism and Child Schizophrenia	• Topics in Early Childhood Special Education
• (Journal of Abnormal Child Psychology)	
• Journal of the Association for Persons with Severe Handicaps	

5. The World Wide Web is an excellent source as well. Use a search engine to locate "journal articles–behavioral interventions in autism." Many journals display complete papers or abstracts over the Internet.

6. Browse through those journals and note the titles of papers. These can lead you to identify specific papers you may wish to read in full in the future. Some, such as the *Journal of Applied Behavior Analysis*, also furnish indexes at the end of each year. These can help you locate specific papers you may wish to read later on.

For purposes of this course, we ask you to limit your coverage to those that are scientific in the sense that papers include:
- a *justification* for doing the study
- a clear *experimental question* or hypothesis
- a precise *description of the methods* employed, including details about participants, setting, validity and reliability of behavioral measures, instructional or other behavior change procedures, and scientifically sound analytic methods
- a clear display and interpretation of *result*
- and a *discussion* and *conclusions* that flow logically from the above

7. Now report your discoveries by completing Form 18.1.

8. Form 18.1: Journal Listings

Your name_____ Date _____ Instructor's Name _____

1. List or abbreviate the journal title, year, issue, authors, and titles of *three* to *five* relevant articles you have located.

Journal Title	Year	Issue #	Author(s)	Title	Pages

2. After reading the abstracts, choose one you find especially interesting. (If it sufficiently fascinates you, read the whole article. You then will be able to complete the *Journal Summary Form* assignment for next week and be ahead of schedule.) For now, to get started, answer the following:

a) Why did you choose this particular abstract? _____
_____

b) What main area does it address?_____

c) Who were the participants or subjects?
_____

d) What did the investigators do? Assuming the abstract includes the *independent variable* (typically *the intervention* in ABA) list it here._____
_____

e) What were the dependent variables (measures of the behaviors that were changed)?
_____

f) What were their main findings? _____

g) What additional points were made in the abstract? _____
_____

h) Do you plan to read the full paper? YES/NO (Circle one). Why or why not?
_____

i) Write your questions or comments here _____
_____

Activity 18.2 (Estimated time: 2–4 hours)
Recording and Submitting a Video[37] of Ongoing Teaching at Your Practicum Site

Well-designed practicum courses designed to teach and support the correct use of behavioral procedures typically include observation and feedback from qualified instructors or trainers. Video-recorded observations have several added advantages: Both student and instructor can view, rewind and review any segment of interest. Practicum students can observe their own recent teaching interactions more objectively than while they were concentrating on teaching. Instructors can supply very precise feedback, guidance and reinforcement by indicating exactly the moment to which they are referring. And, when courses are offered from a distance, video images in action permit direct supervisory observations across the miles.

There are six video-recording assignments spread throughout the second segment of your field practicum. We recommend the schedule suggested in Table 18.1, although students and instructors may negotiate an alternative timetable.

Written Requirements: Forms 18.2 and see Forms 2.7 & 2.8 in Part 1
Objectives: To execute a video production in your student's instructional setting, you will:

1. obtain administrative, teacher and parental consent for video participation (see activity 2.4 in Part 1)
2. carry out a video recording of teaching interactions within your student's instructional setting; and
3. state teaching strategies and student responses as presented in your video production.

> **Note:** Please check with your instructor in advance regarding the compatibility of your equipment. For instance, as the technology for producing and streaming video images over the internet becomes simpler and more economical, you may have the opportunity to use that medium instead; but be certain your instructor can receive it.

---

[37] Streaming video may (preferably) be used to permit instructors to provide rapid feedback. Nevertheless, if feasible, the session also should be recorded for more precise feedback and future reference.

Table 18.1: Video Schedule

Unit	Description of Assignment	Student Responsibility
18	1. Obtain consents. 2. Complete an initial 2–3 minute "trial run" video capturing the teacher's or parent's typical teaching interactions with the child. 3. Have teacher or parent film you while teaching for 3–5 more minutes.	1. Read and follow these guidelines. 2. Obtain consents.[38] 3. Film parent/teacher briefly. 4. Have parent/teacher film you for 2–3 minutes 5. Give or transmit video and video form to instructor.[39]
19	Record a 3-minute segment that captures your student's baseline performance	1. Check again to see if everyone is still agreeable to video-recording. 2. Fully organize arrangements and supplies for your teaching session. 3. Prepare to video-record. 4. Give, or transmit video and video form to instructor
20	Film a 3–5 minute segment that captures the full set of teaching procedures represented in your current teaching program	1. Fully organize arrangements and supplies for your teaching session. 2. Prepare to video-record. 3. Have the parent/teacher record you for 3–5 minutes. 4. Give, or transmit video and video form to instructor.
23	Film another 3–5 minute segment capturing the full set of teaching procedures, including those you and your instructor have pinpointed for improvement.	1. Fully organize arrangements and supplies for your teaching session. 2. Prepare to video-record. 3. Have the parent/teacher film you for 3–5 min. 4. Give, or transmit video and video form to instructor.
26	Film another 3–5 minute segment capturing the full set of teaching procedures, including those you and your instructor have pinpointed for improvement.	1. Fully organize arrangements and supplies for your teaching session. 2. Prepare to video-record. 3. Have the parent/teacher film you for 3–5 min. 4. Give, or transmit and send video and video form to instructor.
285	Film a final 3–5 minute segment that shows the entire teaching procedure and allows for comparison with earlier records.	1. Arrange your teaching session. 2. Prepare to video-record. 3. Have the parent/teacher film you for 3–5 min. 4. Give, or transmit video and video form to instructor.

---

[38] Students may request permission of parents and/or teachers to show the video during practicum team meetings. In that case, the audience should be counseled to provide specific merited and positive feedback only.

[39] *Instructors/supervisors:* As always, feedback should be given as soon as possible, very specific, constructive and reinforcing. We suggests you use the Running a Program Checklist from Unit 15 to evaluate the teaching segments for this purpose.

Instructions[40]

If you have already obtained consent in Part 1, you need not repeat the process. If you have not obtained consent for your student(s), please refer to Activity 2.4 in Part 1.

1. Copy the form entitled *Form 18.2: Instructional Setting Video Recording.* Fill in the upper portion of the form before recording your video. Because this assignment is a recording of your student's instructional setting, Form 18.2 is a slightly different version than the cover sheets you will be using to describe *your own* teaching sessions.

2. Follow the attached guidelines to produce a three-to-five minute video record of an educational interaction between your assigned student and his or her parent or teacher. This will provide you with practice using the equipment, including positioning, sound and closeness adjustments. This first recording also will acquaint your instructor with the look and feel of the site and teaching situation.

3. View the recording and fill in the rest of the form to provide the details of the episode.

4. Prepare a separate *Video Cover Sheet* for your own teaching.

5. Now, exchange places with the teacher or parent. At this time *you* should assume the role of the teacher, instructing the same or a similar lesson.

6. Ask your associate to record your teaching for three-to-five minutes.

7. View that segment, filling out the remainder of this second form.

8. Give or send the recording and cover sheets to your instructor.

---

[40] Richard Fleming, Ph.D., composed these guidelines on video-recording consent and methods.

Form 18.2 (p. 1 of 3)
Instructional Setting Video Recording

DVD Cover Sheet

Your Name_____ Instructor's Name _____

Date__/__/___ Location of recording site_____

Time recording started _____ Stopped _____

Initials or pseudonym of student _____

1. Check roles of people present:

☐ Parent ☐ Regular classroom teacher ☐ Aide or assistant

☐ Other personnel (specify)

2. Provide any special instructions for your instructor related to playing this video-recording.

Explain_____
_____

3. Describe how the environment is arranged to support the activity, (e.g., time of day, arrangement of furniture, materials, other resources, number of children present, what they are doing, the ratio of adults to children) and any other aspects of the learning environment.
_____
_____
_____
_____

4. What are the objectives of the ongoing lesson or activity?
_____
_____
_____

5. State the skills, or target responses, being taught (see Mini-Tutorial for review).
_____
_____

6. Give a behavioral definition of the target responses being taught, including all key features.
_____
_____

7. Describe the procedures used to teach the skills, or target responses (e.g., what shaping procedures were employed?)
_____
_____
_____
_____

Form 18.2 (p. 2 of 3)

8. What reinforcers were used and how did the children respond to them? Please describe.

_____

_____

_____

9. Explain other pertinent ongoing activities that may have affected learning conditions (e.g., lunch was currently being prepared on the other side of the room).

_____

_____

_____

10. On the attached page, please identify the specific time and number on the disk counter or footage number and write a brief phrase to indicate what is happening during the video recording.

11. Add any further comments or questions you may have for your instructor.

_____

_____

_____

_____

_____

Form 18.2 (p.3 of 3)

Tape counter or footage number		Person teaching	Briefly describe what is happening (include a key word, action or object that will help your instructor find the right passage)	Comments
Started	Stopped			

Unit 18 Discussion Topics

Please select one or more of these topics to discuss with your fellow class members:

1. Discuss the importance of becoming familiar with the results of research in the area you have chosen to address. How prepared do you feel at this point to be able to understand these reports?

2. Tell the others about some of the exciting discoveries you have made by browsing through and/or reading journal articles.

3. What value can you see in recording and submitting video-recordings for:
   - your student
   - yourself
   - your instructor
   - your student's family
   - others

4. What practical advice can you offer to your fellow students about successful videotaping?

5. Talk about other original topics of relevance to this week's set of assignments... *and remember to respond to what your classmates have to say.*

Unit 19
Gearing Up
Refining Your Instructional and Measurement Plan

Hal studies the image on his computer screen—an art museum in Bilbao, Spain, designed by Gehry. The soaring planes and curves of metal excite his imagination.

"Hey, Lucy. Take a look here. What I wouldn't give to be able to photograph buildings like this, at different times of the day and in different lights and seasons."

Standing behind to view the screen, she rubs his shoulders, "Looks like you're into that 'Monet with a camera' fantasy again— being able to transform the image entirely by capturing variations of light and shadow from one time to the next. And now," she brightens, "we're about to go on our trip and you'll have your chance. Interesting possibilities are all over the place."

Hal voices his concerns. "That's definitely one of my goals for this trip. But I'm worried. With five of us traveling together, it may be hard to accommodate everyone's unique preferences. I make my living as a photographer, and have a good idea about the stops I would choose. The others probably have different priorities. You know me. It can take me hours or days to set up and capture things on film. Art probably will be way more interested in spending time in Florida to catch spring training."

"You're right. We could all have different agendas. But if we want to share this experience, we'll have to find a way to coordinate our needs. Think about Ginger. She is interested in meeting and interviewing people for her thesis on public attitudes toward special education. We'll all have to bend to her priorities as well."

"True. And even though we have the camping equipment, knowing you, Love, once in a while you'll want to stop at a motel for hot baths and other creature comforts. We'll have to make some reservations."

"Looks like we need another one of our planning sessions, don't you think?"

The next time the group assembles, Hal protests that he had been looking forward to a loose itinerary that would allow everyone to "do their thing." The others finally manage to convince him, though, that despite their ultimate destination remaining unknown, no one's goals are apt to be realized without further careful planning.

*****

Just as savvy travelers organize before taking a long trip, planning is essential for us as well. Having invested the time becoming acquainted with your setting and student, you should be ready to begin in earnest. At this point you need to experience participating as a teacher or change agent, then think about your own point of departure—*what* you are going to teach for your first teaching objective, and *how* you will track your student's progress and adhere to your intended teaching protocol. Defining these processes now will save you time and disappointment later.

198

Unit 19 Objectives

Assuming you have affiliated with a program, been tentatively assigned a student, completed formal coursework in or otherwise mastered information about valid and reliable observational measurement and have access to DVD-recording equipment and to relevant peer-reviewed journals in the field, by the end of this unit you should finalize your student's instructional objective, your measurement design and teaching contract, critique a research article or synthesize a theoretical review, and make a video record of your student's baseline performance, by:

1. observing and participating in teaching a particular lesson or program, while assessing the fidelity of your practices.
2. preparing a teaching objective including a defined target response, your reason(s) for selecting it, the procedure you will use to teach that objective, and your method for evaluating performance.
3. obtaining teacher and parental consent to your selected teaching objective.
4. generating a measurement design that includes data collection procedures and criteria and graphing methods to display and evaluate your student's performance.
5. identifying and demonstrating comprehension of a research article's major components and sections, and/or
6. generating a report synthesizing the main premises, questions and issues as presented in a theoretical review.
7. generating a DVD recording of your student's baseline performance. (Note at your supervisor's discretion, you can fulfill this requirement by conducting all of Activity 19.1.)

Activity 19.1 (Estimated time: 3-6 hours)
Observing and Participating in an Ongoing Program

Written Requirements: Form 19.1

Objectives: To observe and experience participating in an ongoing instructional or behavior change program you will:

1. identify a particular ABA instructional or behavior-change program being applied with a student.
2. observe the program being conducted.
3. participate in conducting the program.
4. assess the fidelity with which you are carrying out your treatment.

Instructions

1. Meet with your Field Facilitator or supervisor to identify an ongoing teaching or change program for your (probable) student.
2. Talk to the change agent about the purposes and methods of the program.
3. Follow the instructions on Form 19.1. Then submit them to your supervisor/instructor.

Form 19.1 p. 1 of 3

Your Name _____   Date_____

Applying Pre-designed Teaching or Behavior Change Programs

1. After conferring with the teacher and reading the student's individual educational or family service plan, volunteer to participate in teaching a specific pre-designed program or lesson for a minimum of two units, under the teacher's guidance. Examples might be a particular *incidental teaching activity, discrete trial instruction, Picture Exchange Communication System (PECS)* step, or a lesson individually tailored to meet the needs of the particular student. Label or describe the program or lesson and what it is designed to teach.

_____
_____
_____
_____

2. Learn as much as you can about this program or lesson by:
• *reading* about it from a general source.
Summarize what you learned in a sentence or two.

_____
_____
_____
_____
_____

• *reading* any peer reviewed, published literature on the method, looking especially for evidence of its success as a teaching method with students on the autism spectrum.
a) Cite the sources

_____
_____
_____
_____

b) Describe the findings briefly.

_____
_____
_____
_____

• *reviewing* any data taken on student progress.

a) Write a sentence describing the data:

_____
_____
_____

• *Watching* or *recording* the program being delivered. If a data system is in place, record student performance data. Describe the procedure and any results.

_____
_____
_____
_____

Form 19.1 p. 2 of 3

Your Name _____   Date_____

b) and/or *narrating* the lesson as it progresses.

_____
_____
_____
_____
_____
_____
_____
_____
_____
_____
_____
_____
_____
_____
_____
_____
_____
_____

c) Summarize the results and say in words what progress (if any) occurred during the session.

_____
_____
_____
_____
_____
_____
_____
_____
_____

3. Identify or design a procedural fidelity checklist. Attach it to this set of worksheets. You may find the "Running a Program" checklist from Unit 15 useful for this purpose.

4. Find a friend or associate to play the role of the student. Present the program to that individual while DVD-recording yourself.

a) Analyze and discuss your skills by:
• checking the procedural fidelity checklist.
• noting those aspects you performed especially well, according to the protocol.
• identifying those areas needing further shaping.

b) Continue practicing the procedure in simulation, until you and your associate note the fidelity of your application of the procedure is acceptable (e.g., > 85%).

4. When you and the teacher feel you are ready,
a) if appropriate, interact with the student informally at work or play until you both appear to feel comfortable in one another's presence. Describe the experience.

_____
_____
_____

Form 19.1 p. 3 of 3

Your Name _____   Date_____

b) begin to conduct the teaching/instructional or behavior change program you practiced. When you feel you are teaching according to plan, DVD-record yourself while conducting the program.

c) use the treatment fidelity checklist to assess the quality of your skills. Attach the form.

d) go over that or another recording with the teacher/trainer/manager to identify the items you succeeding in performing to standard. At your discretion, request the teacher's suggestions for future efforts.

e) repeat d) (above) until your treatment fidelity data convince you that your teaching performance is acceptable and being sustained.

d) graph the fidelity of your teaching.

100
95
90
85
80
75
70
65
60
55
50
45
40
35
30
25
20
15
10
5
0

e) Comment on the experience.

_____
_____
_____
_____
_____
_____
_____

Activity 19.2 (Estimated time: 0–1 hour)
Revised Final Teaching Objective (Optional)

Written Requirements: Form 19.2

Objectives: To independently generate your student's final instructional objective, you will:

1. propose a teaching objective, including a defined target response, rationale for selection, and a corresponding teaching procedure by which performance will be evaluated.
2. obtain teacher and parental consent to your working toward the selected teaching objective.

Instructions

During Unit 4 you proposed several instructional objectives and a tentative, final objective for your assigned student. Since then, you have spent time researching your student's history and becoming more familiar with the child's school and/or home environments. After observing your student and talking with teachers and/or parents, you may want to propose a revision to your preferred objective. If so, you will need to be certain that it supports the child's IEP or IFSP, and that you have the "go-ahead" to teach that revised objective. The attached form is to be completed whether or not you wish to alter your original objective. We ask you to explain the reasons for any changes and briefly describe the new teaching procedures you plan to use. If your objective has not changed, simply re-state your objective and descriptions.

Please remember that objectives should be constructive and not designed to reduce rates of behavior directly. You may, however, choose a constructive objective that is incompatible with an unwanted behavior, such as using words, signs, or pictures to get or do something in particular or requesting a break instead of throwing a tantrum.

Form 19.2 (p. 1 of 3)
Revised Instructional Objective

Your Name _____ Date _____ Instructor _____

1. Name (with permission) or pseudonym of program or family _____

2. Name of Field Facilitator _____ Phone number _____

and/or email address _____

3. Initials or pseudonym of student you will be teaching _____

4. Area in which you will be working. Check the relevant box or fill in the portion under "Other".

communication	☐	recreational, leisure skills	☐
academic skills	☐	self-help skills	☐
activities of daily living	☐	social skills	☐
physical/motor skills	☐	engagement in general	☐

Other (describe) _____

_____

5. If applicable, state your new objective(s), including the new behavior(s), the conditions under which they should occur, and the standards for concluding they have been achieved. Be sure to include the *behavior* (what the student will be doing), the *contextual arrangement* (with what materials, under what other conditions—time, place, physical arrangements etc.—following what specific antecedents, if appropriate). Also include a *standard* for judging when the objective will have been mastered.[41]

_____
_____
_____

6. If applicable, give your reasons for revising the objective. (You may conduct and attach another narrative recording to justify the change. Include what you learned from this new recording.)

_____
_____
_____
_____

7. Say how this objective relates to the child's individual plan.

_____
_____
_____

---

[41] Refer to Week 3 to review details.

Form 19.2 (p. 2 of 3)

Your Name _____ Date _____ Instructor _____

8. Print the objective on *a copy* of the attached "Final Teaching Contract."

9. After reading the measurement material to follow, describe the procedures you will follow to measure change _____
_____
_____

10. Then schedule appointments with the teacher and parent. Explain what you hope to teach and the reasons for this plan. In addition, consider the risks and benefits of teaching the skill you hope to teach and share this information with them. Obtain the necessary signatures of agreement. (If you are teaching the child in the home, the parent's signature will be sufficient.)

11. Explain what you hope to learn or gain from addressing your chosen objective(s).
_____

12. Give this form to your instructor[42] and await the go-ahead.

13. On receiving your instructor's agreement, prepare, sign and obtain signatures on the attached contract.

14. Give, fax or mail the signed contract to your instructor.

Instructor feedback:

☐   Go ahead as planned
☐   Try a different objective because
_____
_____

☐   I suggest the following revised version:
_____
_____
_____
_____
_____

---

[42] ***Instructors:*** Objective(s) should be pedagogically sound and appear reasonably achievable within the span of this practicum. Please return your feedback to the students within 24–48 hours, if possible, to permit them to continue progressing smoothly.

Form 19.2 (p. 3 of 3)

Final Teaching Contract

As a student of *Behavioral Interventions in Autism* I, (your name) _____, have been assigned to work with _____ (student pseudonym). His or her teacher (and/or parent) and I have conferred about an appropriate instructional objective for me to try to teach this child. We have agreed that under my instructor's supervision, the objective of this teaching is as follows:

_____
_____
_____
_____

Teaching this instructional objective will occur _____ (give time and days) and be located at _____ (student pseudonym) will be taught the skill of _____, using the following teaching procedure:

_____
_____
_____

Our reasons for selecting this objective are:

_____
_____
_____

I plan to measure _____'s progress toward reaching this objective and report the results weekly to my course instructor. From time to time, I also plan to send DVD recordings of our teaching interactions to my instructor for review. These and any other identifying information will be kept confidential, except in the case of the parent(s)' and teacher's future written agreement to share them with specifically designated others.

You as parent or guardian consent to the above objective, intervention, potential benefits, risks or discomforts, and understand grievance procedures. You are aware you may withdraw consent at any time, and teaching the objective will immediately be discontinued.

Parent _____ _____ _____
           Print name   Signature   Date

Teacher _____ _____ _____
           Print name   Signature   Date

Practicum student _____ _____ _____
                Print name   Signature   Date

Mini Tutorial on Validity, Reliability and Treatment Fidelity

Nick stands on the platform, his newly purchased sports jacket bulging up at the back.

Sam, the tailor, squints at his client and holds his thumb and forefinger out parallel to one another. "I'd say, about this much. Come back next week and I'll have it ready for you."

"Ya sure ya don't wanna measure it?"

"Nah. I been in this business a hundred years. Got an eye. Got an eye." Sam juts out his chin with an emphatic nod.

A week later, Nick returns.

"That jacket ready yet, Sam? It'd better be. The boys and I have a big meeting tonight and I wanna look my sharpest."

"Not a problem; not a problem. Here."

Sam slips the jacket on Nick and helps him button it.

Nick tries to peer around to the back, as Sam "smoothes" it down, surreptitiously bunching up a bit of the fabric in his hand.

"See, perfect fit!"

As Nick enters the meeting that evening, one of the guys turns to the others, pops his thumb toward Nick, and raises an eyebrow. "Who's your tailor? Must be Sam; the guy who never needs to measure!" and the rest of the gang stamp and hoot in merriment.

What do you think? I think Sam had better take a long vacation—right away.

Measure precisely to detect changes in student performance

Yes, being casual about measuring a jacket or even planning an adventure is one thing, but lack of precision in assessing what a human being, especially a child with autism, is another. Although it is not uncommon for experienced teachers to estimate student progress reasonably well, subjective assessments do not offer the essential accuracy. *Precise measurement* is becoming a requirement in all areas of education today. Educational policy makers are beginning to insist on solid *evidence* of success. They are beginning to understand what behavior analysts have known for a long time. Each of the behavioral procedures we have introduced has been put to scientific scrutiny, which entails use of precise measurement methods. The ABA field has developed refined measurement methods to assess validity and reliability of measurement, thus insuring their precision.

Validity and Reliability of Measurement

Sam the tailor took the quick and easy way to measure; not an uncommon practice everywhere. After all, taking time to do a thing the right way costs what? More money? So it is important for us as educators to scrutinize the reliability of our own methods.

Goaded by his girlfriend, Venus, Hercules, a slightly oversized hunk of a guy, decides to try the latest fad diet (the *treatment*).

"How are you going to know if the diet is working?" asks Venus.

"I'll know by how my clothes fit."

"No, no, no, no! That's not a *valid* way. The size of your clothes varies all over the place. You'd better use your bathroom scale (the *measurement instrument*) to monitor change, but also, be sure it is *reliable*."

Hercules agrees. He weighs himself several times in a row on his own and on his doctor's carefully calibrated scale. Noting their exact match, he concludes his scale is *reliable*.

Perhaps you are wondering what this might have to do with using behavioral interventions with children with autism? Here is an example.

In an effort to increase Drew's expressive communication, his teacher decides to try a *natural learning* strategy described at an in-service lecture. The intervention requires considerable planning, organizing and staff vigilance. The teacher and aide get together daily to ask each other how they think the system is working. "I can't see much of a difference. Can you?" "Me either." A week later, they abandon the effort.

What the pair missed was that Drew was beginning to couple sounds with his communication attempts. Had the two used a more objective, precise and sensitive method to observe and record, such as including a checklist for sounds and gestures approximating communicative utterances, they would have seen that Drew was taking some initial steps toward spoken communication. Eventually he might have begun to talk.

Measure to assess the stability or *reliability* of your instruments

Suppose you had been using a particular teaching method with a student. Your data showed though he had been showing signs of progress, recently he had slowed. Before abandoning your program, it would be prudent to review the specifics of your measurement procedures. Was the measurement system reliable? Were the measures consistent over time? Had your scoring changed—maybe gotten more rigid? If you had been assessing reliability regularly you would know.

To review, we often assess reliability in ABA by having two trained observers independently score the same behavior. We then compare scores, item by item, using the formula: number of agreements divided by number of agreements plus disagreements. Multiplying that figure by 100 yields a *percentage of agreement*. Agreement indices of over 80% generally are considered acceptable. Scores failing to meet that level suggest a need to refine the process.

Quality Assurance through Measurement

Reliable measurement also is crucial to *assuring quality* of products and services, requiring consistency of ingredients, as well as how they are combined. When we purchase a specific brand of cookie, camera, detergent, caviar, or heart medication, we want to be certain the ingredients are consistent with the manufacturer's description. It is not just a case of buyer satisfaction, but may impact consumer health, and certainly reflects on the ethics of the manufacturer or packager. When it comes to *the way we teach,* we need the same kinds of assurances.

Measure to assure *treatment fidelity*; that procedures are implemented as intended.

Maybe for a while Hercules' weight had been decreasing, but then began to plateau. After rechecking the scale's reliability, the obvious question would be "Is he sticking to his diet?" This is a question of *treatment fidelity or the integrity of the intervention.* A reliable method of verifying the accuracy of Hercules' reporting—perhaps by involving an unbiased third party who would sample and record Hercules' daily food intake—would explain why his diet was not working.

Here is how a related scenario might play out in our world: A student had been progressing well but no longer does. His teacher is considering eliminating the program:

"Wait," she cautions herself. "Let me view some recordings of the days when things were going well and compare them with today's. Uh, oh. I see I've been using the same candy as reinforcers, even though the time of day for this lesson has changed. Now we're working right after snack period. Maybe he's not hungry! I forgot to assess the reinforcers the way I did earlier."

> "The possibility of accepting a powerless program as strong or rejecting a powerful program as having no effect is the ultimate cost of lack of independent variable accuracy." (Peterson et al., 1982)

Conclusion: Even though it seemed as if the teacher had retained a previously successful program, she did omit an especially important step—the reinforcement assessment. She had, therefore, inadvertently compromised the fidelity of the intervention because she changed her teaching procedure. Without careful assessment, she might have unintentionally discarded a promising method.

Don't wait for trouble before finding out if you are using your methods as intended. Instead, verify regularly and objectively by measuring and matching what you are doing against what you intended to do (Peterson et al, 1982, p. 483).[43] DVD and audio taping are good ways to preserve the evidence; so are permanent products like work sheets and still photographs. You may need to enlist the help of a colleague to observe you occasionally. Any objective method is acceptable, as long as it is reliable and valid. Here are some measurement methods popular among educators.

Counting

You can *count* when the behavioral event has a *clear beginning and end*. Examples are the number of:
- words read or spoken correctly
- instructions followed to standard
- pictures chosen or delivered according to guidelines
- correctly solved arithmetic problems
- products assembled or assigned tasks completed to standard
- times the student approaches with a spoken, signed or pictorial request
- times the student brushes his teeth or uses the toilet correctly without prompting
- place settings arranged properly
- sandwiches served

Actions that produce a *permanent product*, like a work sheet, assembled product, the physical placement of an object, or an audio or DVD recording, can ease the recording process and make it more reliable. However, this approach of reviewing products of behavior later means you must allocate extra time to complete the observation and recording process.

Sampling

Counting behavioral events accurately can be difficult when:
- the actions occur too often or too rapidly
- their beginnings and ends are hard to detect
- they vary much too much in length or duration

If any of these challenges are present, *sampling* is a good choice. To see what we mean, try reliably counting the number of cries or breath-holdings in a tantrum or the number of times a child interacts with others on the playground.

---

[43]Peterson, L., Holmes, A. L., & Wonderlich, S. A. (1982). The integrity of independent variables in behavior analysis. *Journal of Applied Behavior Analysis, 15,* 477–492.

You can sample in various ways.[44] One is *time* sampling. You break time up into consistent intervals, the size of which will depend on the frequency and complexity of the performance of interest. You choose a time interval of a size that is:

- large enough to be *practical* and allow observers to see the behavior's *presence or absence*; yet
- small enough to obtain a sufficient amount of data to reveal actual changes

It can be difficult, if not impossible, for a teacher to conduct a lesson while writing down every verbalization made by a student developing competent speaking abilities. A solution would be to break time into 5 or 10 or 15-minute intervals and mark down a plus or minus sign for whether or not the student spoke. Getting agreement from an independent third party observer would be relatively simple, because the very first time the observers heard the student speak during the interval, they could shift their attention elsewhere.

On the other hand, if intervals were too large, say hourly, then detecting subtle changes would be difficult. Any single word spoken would permit the whole hour to be scored with a plus. Conceivably, five utterances, one per hour, would cause one to overestimate, concluding that conversation was going on all day!

Time sampling systems can be adjusted in various ways in addition to interval size. For instance, you can decide to use:

- a *partial interval system* (otherwise called an *"interval spoilage system"*). Here, any instance of the behavior within the interval permits the whole interval to be scored for the response, as in the case above. This system inflates the data by making it seem to happen for a longer duration than it probably did.

- a *whole interval system*. The behavior must continue (or be absent) every moment throughout the interval. An example would be scoring an interval + when the student stayed on task completely throughout the interval. This system can deflate the data because even the shortest pause will cause the scoring to fall in the minus category.

Duration is still one more measure you may select, if the length of time the student continues an action is what interests you most.

- *The concept is simple*: start measuring the time elapsing from the moment the behavior starts until it stops. Length of time on-task or engaged, time participating in social play, or spent at mealtime preparation all illustrate this measurement method. My computer could measure the duration of my writing, especially as it saves automatically and records the time for each save. You could set a similar clock-like device to records when your student starts a process and when s/he ends it.

- *The execution may not be quite so simple*. Depending on the class of behavior you are observing, you may have to remain vigilant to catch any starts and stops. Therefore, you may decide that brief pauses are unimportant and choose to use the duration method.

Regardless of your chosen system, you want to be sure it is dependable or "reliable." You need to show indexes of agreement [A÷(A+ D)] that reach over .80.

Surely by this point in your training you appreciate the importance of precisely measuring and analyzing your students' performance and the conditions under which it occurs. Next we describe the measurement procedure itself.[45]

---

[44] See Mayer, G. R., Sulzer-Azaroff, B., & Wallace, M. (2012) chapter 7, and Bondy, A. S., & Sulzer-Azaroff, B. (2002), chapter 11 for more complete discussions of methods for observing and recording data.

[45] Portions of this material were prepared by Melissa Mackal.

The Measurement Procedure

A measurement procedure includes a definition of a correct response, a definition of an incorrect response, and describes how the data are to be calculated. For example, if your measurement procedure included counting verbal imitations, your measurement procedure would look something like this:

"Data are collected as a per opportunity measure. Data are summarized as percentage correct. A correct response is defined as an unprompted, correctly articulated response. An incorrect response is indicated if the response is prompted, inaudible, inarticulate or another response other than that modeled."

If your measurement procedure included time sampling of on-task during a group activity, your measurement procedure might look like this:

"Data are collected using time sampling. Observers score a plus (+) if the learner is on-task at a specific point in time. They score a minus (-) if the learner is not on-task or is engaged in stereotypic or disruptive behavior. Data are collected every minute on the 1-minute mark for 10 minutes and are summarized as percentage of observations scored for on-task."

Defining your measurement procedure is a critical step to standardizing data collection not only for you and your inter-observer, but for inter-observing via DVD as well.

As always, though, reading, writing and speaking on a subject takes you only so far. The remainder, DOING, is the biggest challenge. So, get ready to start observing and measuring your student's performance.

Activity 19.3 (Estimated time: 1/2 to 2 hours)
Designing a Measurement System [46]

Written Requirements: Form 19.4

Objectives: To generate the measurement design, including method, data collection procedures, criteria and graphing conventions to serve as a basis for evaluating your student's performance.

Instructions

1. Write down your final objective and your reasons for selecting it on the accompanying form.
2. After reading the mini-tutorial on measurement of validity, reliability, and treatment fidelity, select or devise a method for measuring the student's performance as s/he progresses toward the objective. When considering a method, first develop a *practical, objective* plan for *validly* and *reliably* gathering evidence of the effectiveness of your interventions. Generally this involves observing, recording, and analyzing your student's, and sometimes other people's, behavior.

For example, for *on-task during a group activity*, you might write: "Measurement procedure is momentary time-sampling. Data are collected on all children in the group. Observers score a plus (+) if the child is on-task as defined, a minus (-) if off-task or engaged in stereotypic or disruptive behavior. Data are collected every minute on the 1-minute mark, are summarized as percentage of intervals scored on-task, and graphed as percentages."

For measuring a child's use of descriptive adjectives, you might say: "At least once a week, the child will view and be asked to describe a particular set of slides. Observers will use a prepared recording form and will count and graph the number of unprompted descriptors the child uses."

You then will:
- use your method to assess your student's performance.
- independently and simultaneously with another person, conduct dual observations of your student's performance.
- calculate indices of inter-observer agreement.
- decide *whether*, and if so, *how,* to modify your recording method(s) to improve their reliability.
- continue this process until indices of agreement are greater than 80%.
- set up a graph on which to plot your data.

3. Submit the form to your instructor.

---

[46] *Instructors/supervisors*: A rapid turnaround on this assignment will permit your students to move on to testing out their proposed measurement system, as required for next week.

Form 19.3
Designing a Measurement System[47]

| Name _____ | Instructor's Name _____ | Date _____ |

1. Write your final instructional objective(s) here:_____
_____
_____

To insure the objective is complete, break it apart by writing the phrase or portion that indicates:

• The *actions*. What will the student be saying or doing?
_____

• Its *context*. What conditions will be in effect during instruction? Include relevant people, time of day, locations, materials, time since last meal/snack, and so on.
_____
_____

• The *events or stimuli*. What is intended to activate or trigger the actions? Perhaps visual presentations, instructions, introduction, presence of materials, and so on.
_____
_____

2. Describe how you will measure performance during the baseline and instruction phases of your intervention. Include:

• The recording method you will use: ☐ Counting ☐ Time Sampling ☐ Duration ☐ Other explain)
_____

• Who will record the data? Why? _____
_____

• Will you use ☐ *real-time observation and recording* or ☐ *permanent product recording*?

3. Write, your measurement procedure in complete sentences.
_____
_____
_____

4. If you plan to observe and record in real time, who will serve as an independent observer to conduct reliability checks? _____ Describe how they will assist you.
_____
_____

• If no one else will be involved, say how you plan to demonstrate the reliability of your recording. (Maybe you will need to use permanent products, DVD or audio recordings to score later.)
_____
_____

• Over how many days do you plan to measure your student's *baseline* performance? _____

5. Describe your plan for demonstrating *treatment fidelity*. _____
_____

6. On the back, add your questions and submit this form to your instructor.

---

[47] **Instructors**: A rapid turnaround on this assignment will allow your students to move on to testing out their proposed measurement system, as required for next week.

Activity 19.4 (Estimated time: 1–3 hours)
Summarizing a Journal Article

Written Requirements: Forms 19.4 and 19.5

Objectives: To conduct a critique of a research article or synthesize a theoretical review, you will:

1. identify and demonstrate your comprehension of a research article's major components and sections; or
2. prepare a report synthesizing the main premises, questions and issues as presented in a theoretical review

Instructions

In the last unit you began to take a look at some of the research journals available to behavior analysts. Your assignment for Activity 19.3 is to read at least one of the articles you selected last week and complete the attached summary form.

 Note to fast-paced students: All practicum students are expected to read at least five relevant articles by the time they prepare their final report. Of course, the sooner you read your articles, the more refined your procedures should be. So race ahead with your readings. You will be happy you did.

The *Summary of an Applied Behavior Analytic Journal Article,* form (19.4), should be suitable for reporting almost all of the studies you read, summarize, and integrate into your end-of-semester final report. However, for this first assignment, you also may choose an especially relevant group study or a review paper on a specific area of special relevance to your project. An example is a review paper by Scott R. McConnel (2003) entitled *Interventions to Facilitate Social Interaction for Young Children with Autism: Review of Available Research and Recommendations for Educational Intervention and Future Research.*[48] In the latter case, you may find the second form (19.5) more appropriate to your needs.

---

[48] *Journal of Autism and Developmental Disorders, 33*(5), 351–372.

Form 19.4 (p. 1 of 3)
Summary of an Applied Behavior Analytic Journal Article

Your Name _____ Date_____ Instructor's name _____

Author(s)' last name(s) followed by first initials _____

_____

Date _____ Article Title _____

_____

Name of Journal _____Volume _____ Issue ____ Pages ____ to____

Explain why you chose this article. Say how it relates to the teaching you plan to do.

_____

_____

_____

_____

Introduction

List the *main* reasons why the authors decided to conduct this study. _____

_____

_____

What specific questions did the author(s) ask or hypothesis did they want to test? (usually found in the last paragraph of the introduction). You may restate that question in the form of "*If* (or given; a general description for the method used_____

_____

then" (a general description of the anticipated results _____

_____

Methods. Precisely describe:

 The participants, including personnel, students, others

_____

_____

The setting (location, physical arrangements)_____

_____

_____

 What was measured (usually particular behaviors)?_____

_____

_____

How did the researchers conduct their measurement? What materials did they use? _____

_____

_____

What did the authors do to show their measures were *reliable* or dependable _____

_____and *valid* (measured what they were supposed to)_____

_____

Form 19.4 (p. 2 of 3)

Your Name _____ Date _____ Instructor's name _____

Describe the method the authors used to demonstrate treatment fidelity (integrity of the intervention). _____
_____
_____

Describe the *experimental design* the authors used (A-B-A-B; Multiple baseline; Changing Criterion, control group, other)? _____
_____
_____

Describe the *procedures* (*Who* did *what*, *how*, *with whom*, *where*, *when*, *how often*, and for *how long*?) _____
_____
_____
_____
_____
_____
_____

Results

What happened as a result of the procedures that were used? (You may wish to use the attached templates to sketch the graphs.) _____
_____
_____
_____
_____

Discussion

What *main* issues did the authors discuss? _____
_____
_____
_____
_____
_____

Conclusion

Refer back to the specific question or hypothesis the authors posed in the introduction. How did the authors answer the question? _____
_____
_____
_____

Add your own comments and questions here: _____
_____
_____
_____
_____
_____
_____

Form 19.4 (p. 3 of 3)
Your Name _____ Date_____ Instructor's name _____

Templates for Sketching Results. (Optional)

A-B-A-B (Withdrawal design)

| Baseline Intervention | Baseline Intervention | | |

Multiple Baseline Design

Baseline   Intervention

Baseline   Intervention

Baseline   Intervention

Form 19.5 Conceptual Article (p. 1 of 2)

Summarizing a Review of the Literature, Theoretical or Conceptual Journal Article

Your Name _____ Date_____ Instructor's name _____

Use brief, to the point phrases, please.

Author(s)' last name(s) followed by first initials _____

_____

Date _____ Article Title _____

_____

Name of Journal _____ Volume _____ Pages ___ to ___

Introduction
List the *main* reasons why the authors decided to prepare this paper.

_____

_____

_____

Write the specific issues the author(s) wanted to address (often found in the last paragraph of the introduction).

_____

_____

Explain why you chose this article. Say how it relates to the teaching you plan to do.

_____

_____

_____

_____

_____

Main theses. Precisely describe:

the bases for the author's viewpoint._____

_____

_____

_____

the historical background of the topic or issue._____

_____

_____

_____

_____

the evidence the authors presented in support of their position or viewpoint._____

_____

_____

_____

_____

_____

_____

_____

_____

Form 19.5 (p. 2 of 2)

Your Name _____ Date_____ Instructor's name _____

Were any studies or data presented? If so, describe. Otherwise write N/A _____

_____

_____

_____

_____

What arguments did the authors offer to attempt to convince readers of the validity of their conclusions?_____

_____

_____

_____

_____

What additional issues did they raise?_____

_____

_____

_____

_____

_____

_____

Conclusion

State the authors' main conclusions._____

_____

_____

_____

Say what other issues they raised? (limitations, needed related research and so on). _____

_____

_____

_____

_____

_____

_____

_____

Your own comments: _____

_____

_____

_____

_____

Activity 19.5 (Estimated time: 1–3 hours)
Baseline Performance DVD Recording

Written Requirements: DVD Cover Sheet Form 19.6

Objective: To execute a DVD production of your student's baseline performance, you will generate a DVD recording displaying your student engaged in the behavior(s) of interest. (You may use the DVD you recorded for Exercise 19.1 for this purpose.)

Instructions

1. Record a three-minute DVD segment of your student and his/her baseline performance.*
2. Fill out the DVD cover sheet form entitled *Form 19.6 DVD Cover Sheet, Baseline Performance.*
3. Since this is a DVD recording of baseline performance only, answer N/A, (i.e., not applicable) for areas on the cover sheet that are not applicable to your session.
4. It is very important that you attach this form to your DVD. Consequently, to receive a "complete" for this assignment, the DVD cover sheet must be attached.

* NOTE: REMEMBER! When assessing baseline performance, do not provide any prompts, reinforcers, or any other of your treatment components! You want to see what your student can do BEFORE treatment starts.

Form 19.6: DVD Cover Sheet (p. 1 of 3)
Baseline Performance

Date _____/_____/_____	Student's Name
Child's Pseudonym Name of ABA Instructor Brand and Model of Recorder	Location of Recording Site People present (please check) □ Parent □ Regular classroom teacher □ Aide or assistant □ Other personnel (specify) _____ _____ _____
Time Recording Started _____Stopped _____	□ Other student(s) (describe)_____ _____ _____

Any specific operating instructions for the way your instructor will need to play this recording?

_____

_____

_____

Contextual arrangement

Describe below the contextual components as they apply to your recording:

Time of day	General ongoing activity(ies)	Description of physical layout (add sketch)

Form 19.6 DVD Cover Sheet (p. 2 of 3)
Baseline Performance

In what way is the setting natural or arranged? Is the setting intact in its original state or were environmental components changed in any way to facilitate learning? Please describe.

_____

_____

_____

Teaching program components

State your target response and corresponding definition by which your child's performance is to be measured:

_____

_____

_____

From the checklist below, check or list the teaching procedures you will be demonstrating:

- ☐ Discrete trial format
- ☐ Incidental teaching
- ☐ Small group instruction
- ☐ Individual instruction (if different than discrete trial, please explain)
- ☐ Task analysis of sequenced events
- ☐ Other _____

State your teaching procedure:_____

_____

_____

_____

State your measurement procedure: _____

_____

_____

_____

Did you collect data? If so, please place in labeled, sealed envelope and attach to this sheet.
Select reinforcers used:
- ☐ Tangible
- ☐ Social
- ☐ Activity
- ☐ Other _____

Add any further comments here or on a separate sheet.

Form 19.6 DVD Cover Sheet (p. 3 of 3)
Baseline Performance

Your Name _____ Date _____ Instructor's Name _____

Tape counter or footage number		Person teaching	Briefly describe what is happening (include a key word, action or object that will help your instructor find the right passage)	Comments
Started	Stopped			

Unit 19 Discussion Topics

1. Reading about, observing, and actually applying a behavior analysis can be quite different experiences. Say what you learned as a result of participating in Exercise 19.1.

2. Contracts:
   - How did you feel about negotiating a formal contract with key players in this undertaking?
   - What advantages and disadvantages to you see in using contracts of this sort?
   - Where else in your professional and personal life could you see the value of negotiating a contract with key parties concerned with a given set of activities and/or outcomes?

3. Without identifying him or her specifically, tell your classmates about your student and your reasons for selecting this student.

4. Share the instructional objective you selected for your student.
   - Explain why you chose this one.
   - Describe the resources you have available to pursue this objective.
   - Ask your fellow students with what resources they might be familiar related to this topical area.

5. Share the challenges you faced in attempting to design your measurement methods.
   - Explain how you overcame those challenges.
   - If others remain unsolved, explain what they are and the kind of help you would appreciate receiving from the others.

6. Specify the name of the journal article you read. What was the most useful morsel you gained from this experience? How will you put it to use in your teaching program?

7. Ask your fellow students for specific suggestions for your measurement system and/or for titles of articles they feel would be especially relevant to your project. Give the others some in return.

8. Share an example of a situation in which failure to measure human performance or treatment fidelity may have influenced an important educational or life decision.

Unit 20
Spring Trials
Testing Your Measurement Procedures

"Look at those cherry blossoms." Lucy gestures in the direction of a delicate silk scroll hanging on the wall of *Chang's Garden.* "That reminds me—the forsythia bushes are in full bloom at our place."

Dawn and Ginger follow her glance. With the arrival of spring, the three realize that they are mere months away from the beginning of their joint adventure.

"You girls excited?" asks Dawn.

"Can't wait. Hal and I have been budgeting for an adventure like this for years and I'm ready to begin tasting the fruit of all that labor! I think we can scrape by financially," she hesitates, "but any free-lance work we pick up will give us some wiggle room."

"Hmm, I thought I was the only one worrying," replies Ginger. "I need to spend my time gathering the data for my thesis. The grant makes it a bit easier, but I want to enjoy the experience! I can't stop wondering if my financial plan is sound. What do you think, guys?"

Lucy reassures Ginger that with the group sharing expenses and her extra job last semester, she should do fine.

"True," replies Ginger, brushing back her auburn curls, "but you both know how much I tend to fret about finances! I keep thinking that even with all our planning, we're forgetting something important."

Dawn takes a sip of her tea and begins to smile. "Hey, I have an idea. Why don't we have a trial run? We can rent an RV like the one we have on order. It will give us a chance to test out our plans AND…we'll get an extra weekend vacation out of it!"

"What a great idea! Although putting our plans to the test will add an additional cost up front, it may actually save us more in the long run. You know—like finding out if we really need such a luxurious vehicle, and such. A long weekend is coming up and if we suggest it to the guys, they'll probably go for it."

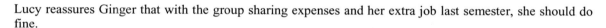

* * * * *

The concept of a trial run does make sense, doesn't it? Knowing that things are in working order before you begin in earnest is important. Imagine that you had developed an elaborate plan of your own. How would you feel if you encountered some clearly avoidable mistakes just because you didn't want to take the time to test it out in advance? (Sound familiar? This kind of avoidance behavior does take extra time and effort, so at least once in a while, most of us act impulsively.)

Examples here are failing to assess our measures for reliability or to collect baseline data. As you know, a baseline is a series of pre-intervention data points to be used to as the standard against which to assess subsequent change. You may *think* your measures are as precise and valid as they can be or that you are sure your student's baseline is so low that measuring it is unnecessary. But you could be wrong. It is better to be certain of your measures and starting points so you will be able to determine exactly how far you have traveled later on.

The dangers of failing to assess baseline are twofold: 1) you may attempt to teach something the student already has mastered; 2) you may be overshooting the student's abilities by making demands beyond those permitted by his or her current skill repertoires. Long ago we had a student who did not talk. In fact, he produced very few sounds; but he spent considerable time viewing and turning the pages in books or magazines. It was only after we wrote some simple instructions on cards: "Put the pencil on the desk," "Go look out the window," and he complied, that we realized he actually could read and comprehend what he was reading. That baseline assessment led us to replace the intended drills in letter recognition with methods to teach him expressive communication skills.

Unit 20 Objectives

Assuming you have completed formal coursework in or otherwise mastered information about analyzing data in published reports, and about designing, graphing and analyzing graphic representations of data, by the end of this unit you should be able to carry out a formative evaluation of your measurement procedure and methodology, critique a research article emphasizing data collection and graphing conventions, demonstrate plotting data, and execute a DVD production of your teaching session by:

1. with the assistance an inter-observer,
   - independently but simultaneously observing your student's performance
   - collecting data
   - calculating agreement indices between you and your associate by dividing the number of agreements by the total number of agreements plus disagreements
   - selecting a graphing convention
   - constructing a graph
   - plotting your student's performance data.

2. Identifying and demonstrating comprehension of a research article's major components and sections, especially the graphic representations of results.

3. Generating a DVD recording presenting your and your student's interactions during a teaching session.

Activity 20.1 (Estimated time: 1–5 or more hours, depending on the clarity and complexity of your measures).
Testing Your Recording Method

Written Requirements: Form 20.1

Objectives: To evaluate your measurement procedure and methodology, you will:

1. conduct an assessment of your student's performance using your methods both individually and with a second independent observer.

2. conduct an observation of your student's performance and collect data *simultaneously* but *independently* of an associate (no peeking).

3. calculate an index of agreement between you and your associate by dividing the number of agreements by the total number of agreements plus disagreements.

Form 20.1
Testing Your Recording Method

Your Name _____ Date _____ Instructor's Name _____

1. Attach the measurement system you and your instructor agreed would be appropriate to use.

2. If you prepared forms to use during observational recording, please attach them.

3. Review your behavioral definitions with the person who will help you collect data for purposes of reliability. Collect your data for a session. Describe the experience below:_____
_____
_____
_____
_____

4. Suggest and justify any changes you feel your system requires so far. _____
_____
_____

5. You can continue to improve upon the system by checking its reliability, preferably with the help of another observer (an aide, parent, sibling, relative, your Field Facilitator etc.). Let us review:

      a) Both observers independently score the same series of episodes (blocks of time or instances) at the same time.

      b) Afterward, look at the score each assigned for the same episode, one episode at a time.

      c) Without discussing your scores, mark each pair as an agreement (A: you both assigned the same score) or a disagreement (D: your scores differed).

         (1) Indicate the total number of agreements _____
         (2) Indicate the total number of disagreements _____

      d) The way to calculate your index of agreement percentage is to divide the number of agreements (A) by the total number of agreements plus disagreements (A + B).

$$\frac{(A) \underline{\quad\quad}}{(\div) \quad (A+D) \underline{\quad\quad}} \times 100 = \underline{\quad\quad} \%$$

      e) Is your index of agreement above 80%? Y/N

6. If you did not achieve at least 80% agreement, re-test, and if necessary revise the system, including response definitions and/or recording approach until you are satisfied that it validly assesses what it is supposed to measure. If applicable, attach the new form.

7. Pose your comments or questions here:_____
_____
_____
_____
_____
_____

Activity 20.2 (Estimated time: 1 to 3 hours)
Broadening your Knowledge of Published Research: Special Emphasis on Measurement and Graphing

Having started planning the methods you will use to measure your student's performance and ways to present them visually, you probably will find it helpful to review the techniques highly skilled behavior analysts have used. This activity will permit you to review data collection and graphing methods incorporated within papers published in journals publishing empirically sound papers. *(Note differences between this and previous forms.)*

Written Requirements: Form 20.2

Objectives: To produce a critique, emphasizing data collection and graphing conventions, of a research article, you will identify and demonstrate comprehension of a research article's major components and sections.

Form 20.2 (p. 1 of 3)
Article on Measurement and Graphing

Your Name _____ Date_____ Instructor's Name _____

Author(s)' last name(s) followed by first initials _____
_____

Date _____ Article Title _____
_____

Name of Journal _____Volume ____ Issue ___ Pages ___ to____

Explain why you chose this article. Say how it relates to the teaching you plan to do.
_____
_____
_____
_____

Introduction
List the *main* reasons why the authors decided to conduct this study. _____
_____
_____

What specific questions did the author(s) ask or hypothesis did they want to test? (usually found in the last paragraph of the introduction). You may restate that question in the form of "*If* (or given; a general description for the method used) _____
_____
*then" (*a general description of the anticipated results) _____
_____

Methods
Precisely describe:

T*he participants*, including personnel, students, others_____
_____
_____

The setting (location, physical arrangements)_____
_____
_____

What was measured? Check the methods(s) the authors used and explain how they used them:
☐ counting   ☐ sampling   ☐ (say what kind)   ☐ other
_____
How did the researchers conduct their measurement? What materials did they use?
_____
_____

How, if at all, did the authors do to show their measures were *reliable* or dependable _____
_____
_____and *valid* (measured what they were supposed to) _____
_____
_____
_____

Form 20.2 (p. 2 of 3)

Your Name _____ Date_____ Instructor's name _____

Describe the *experimental design* the authors used (A-B-A-B, multiple baseline, changing criterion, control group, other?)

_____ -
_____
_____
_____

Describe the *procedures* (*who* did *what, how, with whom, where, when, how often,* and for *how long*?).

_____
_____
_____
_____
_____
_____

Results

1. Say what happened as a result of the investigation.

_____
_____
_____
_____

2. Attach sketches, or use the templates to show the way the authors graphed the results.

3. Try to think of some other ways the authors might have displayed their data. Explain below and attach relevant sketches.

_____
_____

Discussion

What *main* issues did the authors discuss?_____
_____
_____

Conclusion

Refer back to the specific question or hypothesis the authors posed in the introduction. How did the authors answer the question?

_____
_____
_____

Add your own comments and questions here:

_____
_____
_____
_____
_____

Form 20.2 (p. 3 of 3)

Your Name _____ Date_____ Instructor's Name _____

Templates for Sketching Results. (Optional)

A-B-A-B (Withdrawal design)

Baseline Intervention Baseline Intervention

Multiple Baseline Design

Baseline   Intervention

Baseline   Intervention

Baseline   Intervention

Activity 20.3 (Estimated time: 1–2 hours)
Graphing Your Own Data

Written Requirements: Form 20.3

Objectives: To demonstrate your ability to plot data, you will:
1. select a graphing convention.
2. construct a graph.
3. plot your student's performance data.

Figure 20.1

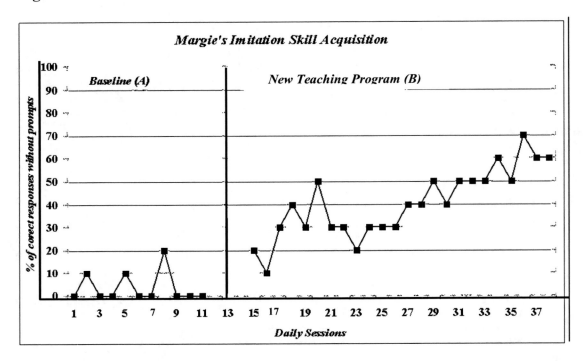

This Unit will prepare you to design an effective measurement and recording method to assess the effectiveness of your teaching procedures. Graphing[49] is a basic tool that behavior analysts use to view and analyze data. Plotting data on graphs allows you to:

- analyze changes in level, trend, and variability in student performance to determine whether, and if so, how effectively our teaching methods are working
- clearly show those results to parents, other team members, administrators, program evaluators and others
- account for the effort and resources we are using to conduct our teaching program
- Figure 20.1 shows what that simple A-B line graph might look like. Initially, most of you will choose to create simple line graphs that show your student's performance during baseline (A) and the data collected during intervention (B). Your measure of performance will appear and be labeled on the "Y" or vertical axis, and days or sessions will appear on the "X" or horizontal axis.

Of course, there are several other options you could use to graph student data. So here we go... let's explore... and start thinking about the best plan for graphing YOUR data!

---

[49] For more extensive information on using graphing as a tool for evidence-based decision making in this field, see Mayer, G. R., Sulzer-Azaroff, B. & Wallace, (2012), pp. 129–151. We also recommend an excellent article on graphing: Dixon, M. et al. (2007). Creating single-subject design graphs in Microsoft Excel, *Journal of Applied Behavior Analysis, 42*, 277–293.

Form 20.3 (p. 1 of 2)
Graphing Your Own Data

Your Name _____ Instructor's Name _____ Date _____

The purposes of this activity are to enable you to:

1. display your data in a form that you and your instructor can readily analyze.
2. construct a picture for you to display to your student's teacher, parent(s) or others participating in the student's program.

Instructions

1. Say how you plan to graph your data:[50]
   Line (frequency) graph _____
   Bar graph _____
   Semi-log graph _____
   Other? Describe.

2. Explain your choice. Does it display your data better than any other type of graph? Why or why not?

3. Attach a copy of what your anticipated graph will look like. (You may find the appended graph paper useful. If you plan to use a withdrawal or reversal design, try out the attached tutorial by Jennifer Crockett.)

4. Provide some actual or fictitious data. Say which you have included:
   Actual data _____ Hypothetical ideal data _____

5. Self-check. Have you included the following?

   _____ A title that clearly indicates what your graph is about
   _____ A label for time (days, weeks, sessions) across the bottom (X line or *abscissa)*
   _____ A label for the scale showing change along the vertical left side (Y line or ordinate)
   _____ Enough horizontal lines to permit the data line or bar to move to its optimal level
   _____ A place on the left for the baseline (pre-treatment or teaching) level
   _____ A dashed vertical line separating the baseline from the treatment phase
   _____ A legend if more than one set of data will be included

5. If you have any questions or concerns, pose them below._____
_____
_____
_____
_____

---

[50] We suggest you review material on graphing methods from earlier courses.

Form 20.3 (p. 2 of 2)

Your Name _____ Instructor's Name _____ Date _____

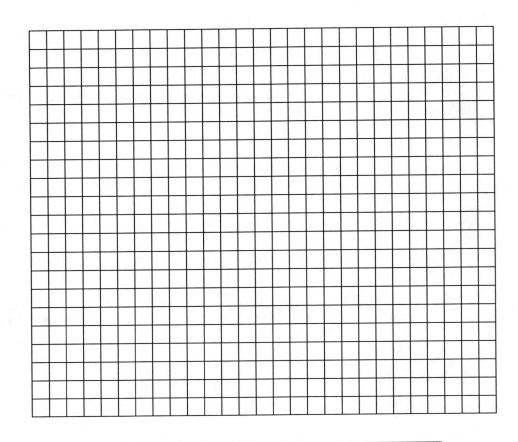

Activity 20.4 (Estimated time: 1 hour)
DVD Recording: You Working With Your Student(s)

The *purpose* of this DVD taping activity is to provide you and your instructor with another glimpse into your student's performance, as you and your student interact.

Written Requirements: Form 20.4

Objectives: To execute a DVD production of your teaching session, you will generate a video recording presenting your and your student's interactions during a teaching session.

Instructions

1. Record a three-minute DVD segment of you and your student working together in the area of your teaching interest.
2. Please fill out the DVD cover sheet form entitled *Form 20.4: DVD Cover Sheet, First Recording: Teaching Session.*
3. To receive your grade you need to send this form along with your DVD.

Form 20.4: DVD Cover Sheet (p. 1 of 3)
First Recording of Teaching Session

Date _____/_____/_____	Student's Name
Child's Pseudonym	Location of Recording Site
Name of ABA Instructor Brand and Model of Recorder	People present (please check) □ Parent □ Regular classroom teacher □ Aide or assistant □ Other personnel (specify) _____ _____ _____
Time Recording Started_____Stopped_____	□ Other student(s) (describe)_____ _____ _____

Any specific operating instructions for how your instructor will need to play this DVD-recording?
_____
_____
_____

Contextual arrangement:

Describe the below components of contextual arrangement as it applies to your recording:

Time of day	General ongoing activity(ies):	Description of physical layout (add sketch)

In what way is the setting natural or arranged? Is the setting intact in its original state or were components in the environmental changed in any way to facilitate learning? Please describe.
_____
_____
_____
_____
_____

Form 20.4 DVD Cover Sheet (p.2 of 3)
First Recording of Teaching Session

Teaching program components

State your target response and corresponding definition by which your child's performance is to be measured:

_____
_____
_____

From the checklist below, check or list the teaching procedures you will be demonstrating:

☐ Discrete trial format
☐ Incidental teaching
☐ Small group instruction
☐ Individual instruction (if different than discrete trial, please explain)
☐ Task analysis of sequenced events
☐ Other _____

State your teaching procedure:

_____
_____
_____
_____

State your measurement procedure:

_____
_____
_____
_____

Did you collect data? If so, please place in labeled, sealed envelope and attach to this sheet. Select reinforcers used:

☐ Tangible
☐ Social
☐ Activity
☐ Other _____

Add any additional comments here:

Form 20.4 DVD Cover Sheet (p.3 of 3)
Teaching Session—First Recording

Your Name _____ Date _____ Instructor's Name _____

Tape counter or footage number		Person teaching	Briefly describe what is happening (include a key word, action or object that will help your instructor find the right passage)	Comments
Started	Stopped			

Unit 20 Discussion Topics

1. Talk about the successes and challenges you encountered in attempting to develop:
   a. Your definitions of the behaviors or student skills you would like to increase or decrease
   b. Your graphing method

2. Share your successes in obtaining assistance from others involved in your student's programming. What advice can you give to your classmates?

3. Talk about any changes in your own attitude in areas of measurement, data recording, establishing a baseline, graphing or other topics included in the Unit's activities.

4. After reviewing the literature:
   a. describe some worthwhile or unique approaches used to collect and /or display behavioral data.
   b. What was different and useful about those methods?

5. Pose related questions that you feel your classmates might be able to help you answer.

Remember to maintain confidentiality conventions.

Unit 21
Trial Runs
Testing Your Teaching Procedures[51]

"Thanks for driving, guys."

Hal and Lucy retrieve the bags from the rack of the RV, hand a few to Ginger, and the three wave as Art and Dawn prepare to drive away.

"Any time. It was a blast, and I think we've learned a lot! Talk to you later," replies Art, as he pulls away.

Heading towards Ginger's apartment, they continue their *post mortem*.

"Am I glad we decided to do a weekend trial run!" exclaims Hal. "All of us took too much *stuff*. We've got to pack more efficiently."

"True, Hal. And we'll need to find a way to plan our stops! Each of us seems to have a different metabolic clock."

"We know we agree about most of the places we'd like to visit," adds Lucy. "But the differences might get us into trouble.

"Like yesterday. Remember, Hal? You wanted to take the RV to the beach. I needed to pick up a few things at Walgreen's, get something to drink and take a long nap. And though you didn't say anything, Ginger, I suspected you really wanted to hike the nature preserve."

Her sister shrugs her shoulders. "It might have been fun."

"I'm convinced," Hal grudgingly agrees. "Much as I would like to fly about, free as a bird, I realize this experience will work better now we've experienced one another's needs. Even though we'll have our bikes with us, we'll have to plan our itinerary more carefully."

✶✶✶✶✶

At this point in your practicum experience, you probably appreciate the importance of preparing and testing your plans before implementing them. Having decided upon a data recording and display system, you will collect sufficient baseline data to supply a picture of your student's pre-intervention performance level. Then, if necessary, you may choose to refine your recording system or even your instructional objective. Afterward, you will focus on designing and maybe even testing the feasibility of your teaching intervention. A few examples of procedures you might consider are:[52]

- Use of powerful reinforcers to *increase the rate* of a simple or complex behavior (examples: speaking, playing, or remaining engaged in an activity for increasingly longer time periods)
- *Shaping* a new skill: bicycle riding, self-feeding, positioning a sentence strip

---

[51] ***Instructor/supervisor***: Depending on the schedule at your site, you may wish to designate this week instead of Week 9 as the vacation week. Whichever one you elect, recognize that your students will need to collect sufficient baseline data and plan their teaching interventions with care. You will need to consider their plans thoroughly and provide them with detailed feedback.

[52] If you need a refresher, we suggest you refer to a basic text on applied behavior analysis or behavioral procedures e.g., Mayer, Sulzer-Azaroff, & Wallace (2012), Alberto & Troutman (1982); Bondy & Sulzer-Azaroff (2003); Cooper, Heward & Heron, (2007), Miltenberger (2001).

- Teaching a simple or complex *sequential task or chain* of behaviors (examples include: dressing oneself, assembling the pieces of a product, carrying on a conversation, boarding, riding and exiting from a bus)
- Use of *differential reinforcement* to teach your student to *discriminate* between two objects or events that are similar but differ in crucial ways, thereby requiring different sets of behaviors
- Use of multiple exemplars, settings, or other methods *to promote generalization of skills* across people, places, objects or events
- A combination of these and/or other behavioral procedures

Once you have conceived a reasonably complete plan, you will be wise to conduct a "trial run." If you plan your schedule carefully this unit (and next unit if you choose to continue during your break), you should be able to locate and fix any elements you feel need adjusting in either the measurement or intervention systems. By then, you should be ready to apply your interventions in earnest.[53]

Now that you have been on-site for several weeks, your instructor probably wants to learn how your hosts view your performance as a professional and how you might work to do even better. We ask your Field Ffacilitator to assess this set of competencies. Please provide him or her with Form 21.4 accompanying *Activity 21.4* and follow the instructions accompanying the assignment.

Unit 21 Objectives

Assuming you have completed formal coursework in or otherwise mastered information about designing lessons or programs in autism education, by the end of this unit you should be able to display your student's baseline data, identify and interpret performance patterns, generate the main components of your teaching plan, and demonstrate an acceptable level of professionalism, by:

1. plotting your student's baseline data.
2. identifying and stating interpretations of performance patterns.
3. stating or listing the main components of your teaching plan, including but not limited to, your teaching objective, relevance, instructional setting, time and duration, resources employed, reinforcers employed, instructional strategies and measurement design.
4. demonstrating your professional skills including, but not limited to, receptivity, flexibility, helpfulness, responsibility, reliability, rate of productivity and timeliness.

Activity 21.1. (Estimated time: 1 hr)
Collecting and Plotting Baseline Data.

Written Requirements: Form 21.1

Objectives: To demonstrate your student's typical performance, you will:

1. plot your student's baseline data.
2. describe the patterns the baseline reveals.

Please proceed directly to *Form 21.1*. It will guide you step-by-step through the process.

---

[53] **Instructor/supervisor**: Your students probably are progressing at different rates at this point. Some may have developed or chosen good, solid objectives, and measurement and/or teaching methods. Others may need considerable coaching and extra time to accomplish those purposes. We suggest you handle this on a case-by-case basis, balancing your own schedule against theirs. If you must choose between the *rate* versus the *quality* of their efforts, we suggest you choose the latter. Teaching your students to do it *right* is more important than getting it done fast.

Form 21.1
Collecting and Plotting Baseline Data

Your Name _____ Date _____ Instructor's Name _____

1. Last Unit you prepared your measurement, data recording and graphing methods. Based on your instructor's feedback and/or your experience, you may have altered the system. If so, describe the changes and reasons for those changes._____
_____
_____
_____

2. Having decided upon your measurement procedures, you should *construct a baseline*. Baseline data are collected to demonstrate a student's ongoing performance prior to your implementing your intervention. Try not to begin your intervention procedures until you have finished collecting several (at least three) baseline data points. If you intervene prematurely, you will be unable to assess the results of your teaching strategies accurately because you will not know where the student was functioning when you started.[54]

3. Plot baseline data on your graph. *Copy the graph, attach it to this form* and turn it in to your instructor for comment.

4. Do the data appear to reveal any patterns? _____ Explain._____
_____
_____

5. Do the data hint that you might have a difficult time achieving your proposed teaching objectives? _____Explain._____
_____
_____

6. Do the data demonstrate that your student's level of performance in relation to your objective is better than anticipated? _____ Explain._____
_____
_____

7. Add any further comments or questions related to this experience.
_____
_____
_____
_____
_____
_____

---

[54] Basic applied behavior analysis texts describe more detailed procedures for establishing baselines.

Activity 21.2 (Estimated time: 0–2 hours)
Rethinking your Instructional Objective (Optional)

Note: If you feel you do not need to amend your instructional objective, you should now inform your instructor accordingly. You can do this by submitting the form with your name and "no changes" written next to Number 5.

The purpose of this activity is to enable you to revise your instructional objective prior to designing and testing your instructional plan.

Instructions

Another week has passed, and during that time you have had additional opportunities to observe your student. You may be having second thoughts about the instructional objective you have proposed. It is possible you found out the student already demonstrates the skill you chose to teach; or conversely, you may realize that necessary foundation skills are not yet in place. If you are reconsidering your instructional objective, review the information provided during Unit 17 and your previous assignments on specifying instructional objectives. Alternative proposals may be submitted on the attached form.

As previously instructed, be certain your objective(s) are stated constructively. Avoid any designed to reduce rates of a behavior directly. Timely submission of new objectives to your instructor are important, to allow time for review and comment and for you to get started.

Form 21. 2 (p. 1 of 2)
Final or Revised Objective(s) (Optional)

Your Name _____ Date _____ Instructor _____

1. Student's name (with permission) or pseudonym of program or family _____

2. Name of field facilitator _____ Phone number _____
   Email address _____

3. Area in which you will be working. Check the relevant box or fill in the portion under "Other."

communication ☐   physical/motor skills ☐
academic skills ☐   recreational, leisure skills ☐
activities of daily living ☐   self-help skills ☐
engagement in general ☐   social skills ☐

Other (describe) _____
_____

4. Reasons for revising objective. (You may conduct and attach another narrative recording to justify the change. Include what you learned from this new recording). _____
_____
_____
_____

5. Assuming you have read the child's individual education plan, state how your objective supports required goals. _____
_____
_____

6. Specify your proposed objective. Be sure to include the *behavior* (what the student will be doing), the *contextual arrangements* (materials, conditions—time, place, physical arrangements etc.—and specific antecedents, if appropriate). Also include a *standard* for judging mastery of the objective.[55]

Given (context and direct antecedents or "discriminative stimuli") _____
_____
the student will (the behavior) _____
(the standards or criteria) _____
_____

7. Print the objective on the attached "Revised Teaching Contract."

8. Speak with and explain your proposed changes to the teacher and parent. Obtain the necessary signatures. (If you are teaching the child at home, the parent's signature will be sufficient.)

9. Submit the signed contract to your instructor.

_____

[55] Refer to Week 3 to review details.

Form 21. 2 (p. 2 of 2)

Revised Teaching Contract

As a student of *Behavioral Interventions in Autism* I, (your name) _____, have been assigned to work with (student pseudonym) _____. His or her teacher (and/or parent) and I have conferred about an appropriate instructional objective for me to try to teach this child. We have agreed that under my instructor's supervision, the objective of this teaching is as follows:_____

_____

_____

_____

_____

Teaching this instructional objective is scheduled to take place (give time, days and location) (student pseudonym) _____

_____ will be taught the skill _____,

using the following teaching procedure:_____

_____

_____

Our reasons for selecting this objective are:_____

_____

_____

_____

I plan to measure _____'s progress toward reaching this objective and report the results weekly to my course instructor. From time to time, I also plan to send DVD recordings of our teaching interactions for my instructor's review. Identifying information will be kept confidential, except in the case of the parent(s) and teacher's future written agreement to share them with specifically designated others.

Signing this contract signifies your consent to the above objective, agreement to the intervention and grievance procedures as explained. You also acknowledge the potential benefits and risks or discomforts of this objective. You may withdraw consent at any time, and the objective will be immediately discontinued.

Parent _____   _____ _____
                 Signature   Print Name   Date

Teacher _____   _____ _____
                 Signature   Print Name   Date

ABA student _____   _____ _____
                 Signature   Print Name   Date

Activity 21.3 (Estimated time: 2–3 hours)
Programming for Learning: The Many W's and an H

WwWwWwWwHs

It is time for you to outline all the essentials of your teaching lesson or behavior change plan. We can help you draft your design by posing a set of Ws, plus a How question.

Written Requirements: Form 21.3

Objective: To generate the main components of your teaching plan, you will state or list its main components including, but not limited to, your teaching objective, relevance, instructional setting, time and duration, resources employed, reinforcers employed, instructional strategies and measurement design

Please remember the importance of:
- choosing and displaying reinforcers meaningful to the student at that time and place
- maintaining a positive and constructive focus
- avoiding unnecessary prompts
- …. and above all, the fact that *the student is always right. If the student is not learning it is because we are not teaching!* (And by *we*, we mean all of us: authors of this manual, instructors who failed to teach you properly, and possibly even you by miscalculating what to teach and how to teach it effectively.) We all are in this together! So, with that in mind, let us begin by completing Form 21.3.

Form 21. 3 (p. 1 of 3)
Programming for Learning[56]: The Many W's and an H

Your Name _____ Date _____ Instructor _____

1. **Who** is your student? Briefly describe the student in terms of
    - age _____
    - gender _____
    - general level of functioning _____
    - past learning successes _____
    _____
    - major challenges _____
    _____
    - family circumstances _____
    _____
    - other historical and current factors that may influence this student's learning
    _____

2. **What** are you planning on teaching? Restate your instructional objective.
    _____
    _____

3. **Why** did you choose this particular objective for this student?
    _____
    _____

4. **Where** will the teaching take place?
    _____
    _____

5. **Why** are you selecting this location?
    _____
    _____

6. **When** will you schedule this teaching?
    _____

7. **Why** did you choose this time block?
    _____

8. **What** materials, furnishings, and other contextual arrangements do you plan to organize?
    _____
    _____
    _____
    _____
    _____
    _____

---

[56] In Bondy, Dickey, Black & Buswell (2002), *The Pyramid Approach to Education: Lesson Plans for Young Children*, Newark, DE: PECS, you will find a set of blank lesson plan forms and a number of developed lesson plans in such areas as communication, community, domestic, recreation/leisure, school, self-help and social skills.

Form 21.3 (p. 2 of 3)

Your Name _____ Date _____ Instructor _____

9. **How** will they be arranged? If you feel it is relevant or informative, sketch the room arrangement here.

10. **Why** did you select these contextual arrangements?_____
_____
_____

11. **What** immediate reinforcers, if any, will occur as *natural consequences* to the instructional interaction?_____
_____
_____
_____

12. **What** immediate reinforcers will you *arrange* that you feel reasonably confident will maintain your student's efforts?_____
_____
_____
_____

13. **Why** did you choose these? (e.g., reinforcer or stimulus preference assessments,[57] and see Preference Assessment Checklist Form 3.1)
_____
_____

14. **How** do you plan to ensure that your student is aware of the reinforcers s/he will receive as a result of his efforts? _____
_____

15. **What** delayed reinforcers can you use?_____
_____

16. **How** will you bridge the time delay? (Check and/or add your own plan)

Tokens? ___ Count-down timer ___ Gradually introduce the delay ___
_____

---

[57] See, for example, Fisher, W., Piazza, C. C., Bowman, L. G., Hagopian, J. C., & Slevin, I. (1992) A comparison of two approaches for identifying reinforcers for persons with severe and profound disabilities. *Journal of Applied Behavior Analysis, 25,* 491–498, Pace, G.M., Ivancic, M.T., Edwards, G. L., Iwata, B. A., & Page, T. J. (1985). Assessment of stimulus preferences and reinforcer value with profoundly retarded individuals. *Journal of Applied Behavior Analysis, 18,* 249–255.

Form 21. 3 (p. 3 of 3)

Your Name _____ Date _____ Instructor _____

17. **What** reason do you have to believe the student will work for those reinforcers?
_____
_____

18. If the reinforcer(s) are not natural consequences of the student's actions, say **how**, if at all, you plan to shift those over to more natural consequences._____
_____
_____
_____

19. If relevant, **how** do you plan to teach *sequentially* (use *chaining*) or to reinforce successive approximations toward the objective (use *shaping*)? _____
_____
_____
_____

20. **What** instructions or other direct antecedents [*Discriminative Stimuli* (S^Ds)] do you plan to use to evoke the responses you are seeking?_____
_____
_____

21. **Why** are those antecedents essential?_____
_____
_____

22. **How** do you plan to fade those S^Ds if the prompts are not natural to the situation?_____
_____
_____

23. **Why**, *in general*, have you organized your instruction the way you did? You may refer to related scientific literature, basic behavior principles and practices or other solid justifications.
_____
_____
_____
_____
_____

24. How will you assess the *fidelity* of your teaching (that you taught the way you specified)?
_____
_____

25. Describe a few alternative methods you are considering, should this plan not work after _____ days/weeks (circle one).
_____
_____
_____
_____

26. Can you think of any other **W's,** or another **H** we might not have included?_____
_____
_____

27. List any of your doubts, concerns or questions here and on the reverse side._____
_____
_____

Activity 21.4[58](Estimated time: 1–3 hours)
Testing the Waters

After planning your instruction, you will want to do a trial run to check out how realistic and complete that planning has been. Go ahead and try it out. Then turn to and complete Form 21.4.

Form 21.4
Testing the Waters

Your Name _____ Date _____ Instructor _____

1. After receiving approval of your teaching plan from your instructor, share the plan and any instructor comments with your field facilitator. Some final negotiating may be needed. Discuss the experience here. _____
_____
_____
_____

2. Assuming all parties agree on the details, you should arrange for one or two opportunities to give your teaching plan a "trial run."

    a) You might ask a fellow student, colleague or friend to role play the student's part, just to double check that you have made all necessary arrangements. If you choose this option, describe your experience._____
_____
_____
_____

    b) Depending on that experience and how confident you feel, you may decide to begin collecting data now. If you have additional questions or concerns, consult your instructor. State your choice and the reason for making the decision._____
_____
_____
_____

3. When you feel ready, practice the whole procedure with your student, including collecting and graphing data:

    a) Describe the results
    b) Attach your graph
    c) Comment on the experience including your comfort level with the proposed program
_____
_____
_____

    d) Add any questions you may have for your instructor. _____
_____
_____
_____
_____
_____

[58] *Students*: If you have altered either your objective or measurement methods, you may wish to negotiate an alternate date for submitting this assignment with your instructor

Activity 21.5 (Estimated time: 15 minutes)
Interim Field Facilitator Assessment

Written Requirements: Form 21.5

Objectives: To demonstrate an acceptable level of professionalism, you will identify and engage in professional skills including, but not limited to, receptivity, flexibility, helpfulness, responsibility, reliability, rate of productivity, and timeliness.

Instructions for Practicum Student

Please fill in the information requested in the heading. Then give the attached form to your Field Facilitator or Field Supervisor to complete. If applicable, request that it be sent to your instructor before the end of the current week and ask for your own a copy of the completed form.

If you are a parent working with your own child at home, you may ask a member of your child's team or another family member to complete the form. If you are working alone, assess your own performance. When you submit the form, please attach an explanation of your circumstances.

Form 21.5 (p. 1 of 2)
Assessment of Practicum Student's Professional Skills

Upper portion to be filled out by ABA Practicum Student

ABA Student's Name _____ Date_____
Field Facilitator's Name _____
Field Facilitator Contact Information:
Phone _____ Fax _____ email ___ _____
ABA Instructor's Contact Information:
Phone _____ Fax _____ email ___ _____

(ABA students working from a distance, should provide the *Field Facilitator* with a stamped envelope addressed to the instructor. Overseas students should use OVERSEAS AIRMAIL stamps.)

Instructions for Field Facilitator

Thank you for your willingness to facilitate our ABA student's participation in your program. We hope this relationship is proving to be productive. At this point, our ABA student has been participating in the field practicum for several weeks. To help guide his or her progress, we ask you to take just a few minutes to complete the form below. Toward the end of the sequence, we shall make a similar request of you, to allow you, the student and the ABA instructor to assess the student's progress in the interim.

This portion to be filled out by the Field Facilitator or Field Supervisor

1) Please **complete** and **duplicate** the form. 2) Give one copy to the practicum student.
3) Send another to the ABA instructor by the end of the week. Keep the original for your own files.

ABA Practicum Student's Professional Skill	5	4	3	2	1	NA
Is friendly (regularly looks directly at, smiles, greets people individually)						
Listens respectfully (waits while they talk; responds to the point)						
Responds to and gives positive and constructive feedback						
Is flexible (adjusts to new conditions)						
Is helpful in the program						
States plans and expectations clearly						
Undertakes responsibilities and plans time carefully						
Meets responsibilities s/he has undertaken						
Schedules time realistically						
Completes responsibilities on time						
Is prepared in advance of instructional sessions						
Strives for excellence in written and oral communication						
Is patient with his or her student						
Works productively with his/her student						
I would recommend hiring this student as a Behavior Analyst						

5 = consistently;   4 = most of the time;   3 = at an acceptable level;   2 = once in a while;
1 = rarely or not at all;   N/A = not applicable

Form 21.5 (p. 2 of 2)

ABA Student's Name _____ Date_____
Field Facilitator's Name _____

Please comment on the best aspect(s) of the ABA student's performance.

_____
_____
_____
_____
_____
_____
_____
_____
_____
_____
_____
_____
_____
_____
_____
_____

Please add any further comments here.

_____
_____
_____
_____
_____
_____
_____
_____
_____
_____
_____
_____
_____
_____
_____
_____
_____
_____

Unit 21 Discussion Topics

 Choose one or more of these items to discuss with your classmates. Add any new related topics. Don't forget to comment on others' contributions to the discussion. Remember our clear intention to focus on the positive and constructive.

1. Changing objectives:
   - If you changed the objective for your teaching:
     - o Were you relieved to see you had an opportunity to modify it?
     - o What were the reasons for your change?
     - o Share your revised objective with the group.
     - o Explain why you made the change and ask your classmates any questions or concerns you might have about this new objective.

2. Describe your reaction to *The Many W's and an H* as an activity.
   - How completely did you feel *The Many W's* activity covered the crucial aspects of your lesson planning?
   - What additional resources did you use, and why?
   - Can you think of other ways you might employ *The Many W's and an H* as a tool (e.g., in reviewing journal articles, summarizing lessons you observe and so on)?
     - o Give one concrete example.

3. Are you familiar with other lesson planning formats? If so, where do you and don't you see any overlap? Discuss the advantages and limitations of each.

4. Share your experience in *Testing the Waters*.
   - How well prepared did you feel about beginning to conduct your lesson/instruction? Why?
   - Who helped you?
   - What were the results?
   - How satisfied were you with the design of the lesson?
   - What kinds of assistance would you appreciate from your instructor or classmates as a result of this experience?

5. How are you planning on spending your break? (Or if you have taken your break already, share some of your experiences with the others.)

6. Of what value is your Field Facilitator's assessment of your professional performance? What other feedback might you have appreciated?

7. Now that you have reached the mid-point of this practicum experience, comment on the aspects you feel have been most beneficial to you and the student(s) and program with which you have been working.

Unit 22

Time for a well-deserved break.[59]

Take a moment to skim through your progress chart and the packet of materials you have prepared to date. You will be impressed with the quantity of your accomplishments!

During a relatively, short amount of time you have studied the literature, observed and analyzed your student's behavior, and planned and tested your teaching program. Upon your return, you will continue to review relevant literature, begin (or continue) your teaching and evaluating, and, if necessary, consider revising your methods. Ultimately, you will prepare and share a summary of your behavioral instructional experiences with your fellow students, instructor, and field facilitator.

Unit 22 Optional Discussion Topics

1. Share your reaction to your own review of your accomplishments to date.
2. Describe how you spent your break.
3. This breather may have allowed you to form some new perspectives. What are they?

---

[59] Instructor: Depending on your academic or program schedule, you may wish to place this break elsewhere or skip it altogether.

Unit 23
Hitting the Road
Analyzing and Reporting Progress

Bubbling with excitement, a few weeks following their "trial run," our adventurers board their RV. Having set the itinerary and stipulated a set of group agreements, they feel confident theirs will be a really grand adventure.

"Wow, 9:00 A.M., as planned, and we're on our way. Good sign!" exclaims Ginger.

Art steers the vehicle away from the curb, singing "On the road again...." The others join in the chorus, "The life I love is making music with my friends, and I can't wait to get on the road again!" With rush hour subsiding, the traffic pattern allows them rapidly to exit the city. A map spread across her lap, Dawn, the official navigator, studies the route.

"If we are able to make good time, we should reach the Berkshire RV Park before dark, in time to settle in and enjoy our *bon voyage* cookout," she predicts.

"And Mirror Lake is on the way. It should be a spectacular spot for lunch," Ginger adds. "I'm sure glad we packed for our picnic last night. It would be a pity to miss hiking along the lake on a day like this, just because we hadn't done that. Boy, our weekend trial run taught us a lot!"

"What on earth (Figure 23.1) do you have on your lap, Dawn?" Hal inquires.

Figure 23.1

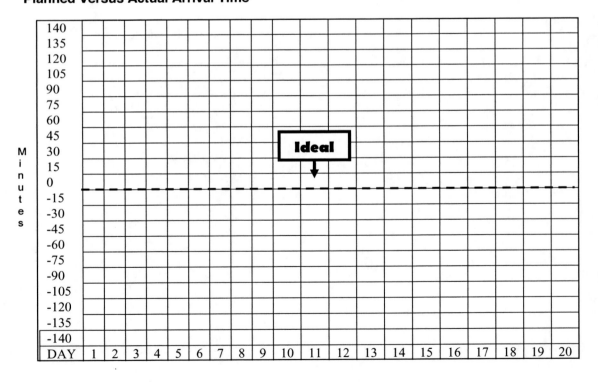

Planned Versus Actual Arrival Time

"After our trial run, each of us agreed that we didn't want to short-change anyone by arriving late, leaving early or by-passing any of our planned stops. I realized our timing would have to be pretty precise if each of us were to get what we hoped for. So I prepared this graph" (she flourishes it with a *"Ta da!"*). We can use it to record and compare our intended against our actual arrival times. That way, we'll be able to arrange realistic departure times and/or driver schedules so we can to fit in all our destinations. The data should help us improve our planning, don't you think?"

"Talk of compulsive…" Art responds.

"Maybe not," Ginger rushes to Dawn's defense. "By tracking data, we'll avoid pitfalls that could cause discord. We all want to enjoy this journey AND for all of us to return home friends!"

"Yep," Dawn concludes. "My aim is to have the line stay flat at the zero mark. Let's see how well we do."

*****

In much the same way, you have designed a precise plan. You have decided on a destination (in the form of an instructional objective), a route (your teaching plan), and a monitoring method (the data collection, graphing and analytic schemes). You are ready to proceed with your plan. The data you have collected will direct you to areas in need of "tweaking." If they indicate that your anticipated results are not being achieved, you may choose to adjust your design. Like our travelers, you will reap the rewards of careful planning, testing and collection of data.

Perhaps your feelings are fluctuating between excitement and apprehension at this point. If so, we commend you. The task you have undertaken is not trivial. Educators need to realize that programming decisions directly affect the lives of their students and the many people who care for them. You have, no doubt, chosen this path because of your eagerness to support student growth and change. Surely you do not want to miss the need to modify your student's educational plan.

Furthermore, the process of assessing your student's progress may reveal some of the subtleties of the impact of your teaching. Is progress rapid enough? Why does performance seem so uneven? If your data do not indicate adequate progress, does that mean you are a poor teacher? These queries are understandable, but remember, teaching is not a "perfect technology." The best laid plans can be influenced adversely by factors beyond your control, such as health problems or home/environmental issues. To balance the scales, variation or fluctuation in data may enable you to identify factors that might otherwise have gone unnoticed.

Suppose you, the teacher, saw the kind of pattern shown in Figure 23.2. The student's rate of reading words correctly appears to be accelerating. Yet some days are better than others. If you study the figure you will see a particular pattern. Go ahead; take a look.

Did you notice the major drop in rate once each five days? Well, it seems that day is always Thursday. "What is there about Thursday," you wonder.

"Oh, I know. We schedule reading daily at 9:45, except on Thursdays. On Thursdays, we plan it for later, right before lunch. That's because the music teacher comes at 9:45."

Usually your student works quite well for access to favorite toys. Why doesn't that work on Thursday? Maybe he is hungry. To test that out, you change the nature of the reward delivered for sets of words read correctly, from toys to small portions of lunch. Lo and behold, the poor performance days are a thing of the past!

Figure 23.2

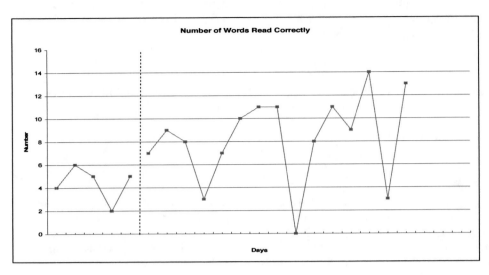

Unit 23 Objectives

Assuming you have completed formal coursework in or otherwise mastered information about analyzing and interpreting graphic data, the value of submitting and receiving feedback on progress reports and of techniques for reviewing technical journal articles, by the end of this unit to be able to generate a progress report, execute a DVD production of a teaching session, and conduct a critique of a research article, you should be able to:

1. re-state your teaching objective (if necessary) and describe the main components related to the progress of your student's performance, including but not limited to curricula used, measurement procedures, instructional setting descriptions, instructional strategies employed, reinforcers used, and performance results.
2. generate and interpret a graphing convention, visually displaying performance results.
3. produce a DVD recording presenting a teaching session with your student.
4. identify and demonstrate comprehension of a research article's major components and sections.

Activity 23.1 (Estimated time: 2 hours)
Ongoing Teaching

Previously, you had the opportunity to try out your procedures to see if they were organized, if data collection methods were effective and manageable, and ultimately, that the whole instructional process was practical and likely to yield positive results. Then you repeated your program, possibly in altered form.

Activity 23.1 Written Requirements and Objectives

Written Requirements: Form 23.1

Objectives: To generate a weekly progress report, you will:

1. re-state your teaching objective, if necessary, and describe the main components related to the progress of your student's performance including, but not limited to, curricula used, measurement procedures, and descriptions of instructional setting, instructional strategies employed, reinforcers used and performance results
2. generate and interpret a graphing convention, demonstrating a visual display of performance results

Instructions

1. For the remainder of this course, you will be required to turn in a weekly "progress report." This will allow you and your instructor to monitor the effectiveness of your instructional methods and make any necessary changes. (*Notice that subsequent forms are modified to reflect activities specific to the current week.*)
2. We suggest that you duplicate, retain and use the attached *Self-Check Form* each week, as it will guide and assure you that you have completed the week's assignments.

Figure 23.3
Practicum Student Teaching: Self-Check Form[60]

□ 1. Organize the environment by obtaining and
arranging furniture, gathering necessary materials
and recruiting help.

□ 2. Conduct your lesson.
- Try to carry out *a minimum of three lessons or
  sessions a week*. This may entail breaking the day(s)
  you are on-site into several sessions; say, three sessions of five-to-fifteen minutes
  each. If you have the option, spread your instruction over several days, rather than
  trying to do it all in one or two days.
- Of course, more than three sessions would be advantageous, but how feasible this is
  must be determined by you, your instructor or supervisor and your hosts.

□ 3. Collect data on your student's performance at least once each week,
though more frequent data collection is preferred.

□ 4. Arrange for dual recording with another person, preferably each week, to allow
you to check the reliability of your recording system.

□ 5. Calculate an *index of agreement* between the two sets of data.

□ 6. Plot the data for all sessions conducted.

□ 7. Draw any conclusions the data patterns might suggest.

□ 8. Pose any concerns or questions to your instructor or supervisor.

□ 9. Complete your weekly progress report.

□ 10. Submit the report to your instructor *by the deadline*.

---

[60] **Students**: You are granted permission to copy and use this form for yourselves on a weekly basis.

Form 23.1
Ongoing Teaching (p. 1 of 3)

Note: By asking you to repeat some information, we are hoping to ensure that you remember to include all the essential elements of your teaching program. Further, it is important that we collectively monitor ANY changes you make to your instructional practices. Feel free, though, to use abbreviations or "same as last time" if agreeable to your supervisor/instructor.

Your Name _____ Date _____ Instructor's Name _____

Identifier for your student (initials or pseudonym) _____

1. Describe your student:
a) gender M/F (circle one)   b) chronological age ____   c) approximate developmental level ____

2. Briefly restate your objective.
_____
_____

Do you continue to feel this is an appropriate objective for your student?
• Circle one: Y/N Why?_____
  _____

• If you answered "no," propose an alternative objective to the student's teacher and/or parent. Assuming they assent, write it here._____
  _____
  _____

3. What *materials* did you assemble in advance?_____
  _____

• Is this a change since the last time? Y/N (circle one) If Yes, explain why._____
  _____
  _____

• Were these materials effective in supporting control by antecedents (technically stimulus control) as well as generalization and maintenance? Explain[61]_____
  _____
  _____

4. Describe:
• the data you collected _____
• How often?

☐ Each session ☐ Each day ☐ _____ times a week ☐ Once a week ☐ Other (Describe)
_____
• Others involved in data collection? _____
• Did each of you independently measure the same thing at the same time? Y/N (circle one)

---

[61] Refer to a basic text in Behavior Analysis for further suggestions.

Form 23.1 (p. 2 of 3)

Your Name _____ Date _____ Instructor's Name _____

 Note: Remember to aim for at least *three* "reliability checks" during the course. If agreement indices fall below .80 you should refine your measures or definitions.

- If you conducted a reliability check this week, how closely did you agree with one another? What was the index of agreement? (Fill in the formula)

    Number of agreements _____ ÷
    Number of agreements plus disagreements _____ = _____

5. *Assistance*
- What other *help* did you arrange in advance?_____
  _____

- From whom? _____

- Describe how it worked out._____
  _____

- Are others conducting the instruction for purposes of promoting generalization?
  Y/N (circle one) Explain:_____

6. *Setting.* Describe *where* instruction took place _____
  _____

- Have you arranged to have your student perform the behavior in *other settings* now or in the future? Y/N (circle one).
  Why?_____
  _____

7. *Sessions*
- How many lessons or sessions did you conduct this week? _____
- What day(s) of the week? M Tu W Th F Sa Su (Circle those that apply)
- How long did each session last? _____

8. *Procedures* If applicable, describe methods of:
- assessing reinforcer preferences _____
  _____
  _____

- reinforcing sequences of small responses to *chain* together and/or *shaping* approximations toward the objective? Describe._____
  _____
  _____

- minimizing and/or gradually fading prompts? Describe._____
  _____

- including *generalization* or transfer of the skill across materials, settings, people, and/or other essential conditions within your instruction?_____
  _____

Form 23.1 (p. 3 of 3)

Your name _____ Date _____ Instructor's name _____

- planning for future *maintenance* of the skill?_____
  _____
  _____

9. *Reinforcers*

- What reinforcers did you use? _____

- What was the basis for selecting these? (Check all that apply)

  ☐ Natural consequence of behavior ☐ Student selected from an array

  ☐ Student selected from series of paired comparisons ☐ Student consistently responsive
  to item or event in the past

  ☐ Token system(s) well established

- The reinforcing value of any given item or event can vary from situation to situation, depending on circumstances. A drink of water tastes so good during recess when the children are hot and sweaty, but might be less satisfying afterward in a cool classroom. How are you adjusting the reinforcers you are presenting to suit the various conditions used to promote generalization training in your teaching?
  _____
  _____

- How did you know your student understood that s/he was working to earn a specific reinforcer?
  _____
  _____

10. *Instructional activities*. Describe:
- What you and/or your associates did., including any evidence of how faithfully you adhered to your instructional protocol (*treatment fidelity*).
  _____
  _____

- What the student did or did not do.
  _____
  _____

11. *Results*
- Describe the results in words and attach your graphs.
  _____

- If your teaching occurs at different times, places, and/or with different, staggered conditions, you should be able to use the multiple baseline graphing format to display those results.

12. *Discussion and questions*. Here is the place to comment on what has been happening in general, including pleasant surprises, and to ask for clarifications and help.
  _____
  _____
  _____

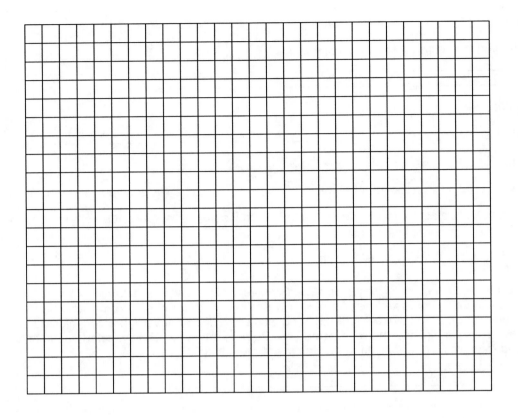

Activity 23.2 (Estimated time: 2–3 hours)
DVD recording

Written Requirements: Form 23.2

Objective: To produce a DVD record of a teaching session.

Note: Remember that the two possible assessments for most of these activities are either a *complete* or an *incomplete*. All students who submit a clearly audible and visible three-minute DVD-recording displaying ongoing instruction should receive a *complete*.

Instructions

1. Check your course policy to recall the equipment necessary to prepare a recording that your instructor will be able to view with his or her equipment.
2. Arrange for a collaborator to film one of your sessions. We suggest you consider using a tripod to keep the camera steady.
3. Practice! Practice! Practice! …until you feel sure you and your associate are sufficiently skilled to take a recording that clearly depicts the ongoing instructional session.
4. Try to schedule the recording to permit the best display possible of your ongoing teaching.

5. You may record for a period of longer than three minutes. If so, you should either
   - delete all but three-to-five minutes of the material
     or
   - in your cover note, indicate the exact beginning and ending footage point for the three-minute portion you want your instructor to view
6. Label the recording with your name and the date and time it was recorded.
7. Fill out the DVD cover sheet form entitled *Form 23.2: DVD Cover Sheet, Teaching Session—Second Recording*.
8. Remember to send this form with your DVD to receive credit for the activity.
9. Add your comments, questions and/or concerns to your cover note.

265

Form 23.2 (p. 1 of 2)
DVD Cover Sheet

Date _____/_____/_____	Student's Name
Child's Pseudonym	Location of Recording Site
Name of ABA Instructor	People present (please check) □ Parent □ Regular classroom teacher □ Aide or assistant □ Other personnel (specify) _____ _____ _____
Brand and Model of Recorder	
	□ Other student(s) (describe)_____ _____ _____
Time Recording Started_____Stopped_____	

Any specific operating instructions for the way your instructor will need to play this recording?

_____

_____

_____

Contextual arrangement:

Describe the below components of contextual arrangement as it applies to your recording:

Time of day	General ongoing activity(ies):	Description of physical layout (add sketch)

Form 23.2 (p.2 of 2)
DVD Cover Sheet

Your Name _____ Date _____ Instructor's Name _____

Tape counter or footage number		Person teaching	Briefly describe what is happening (include a key word, action or object that will help your instructor find the right passage)	Comments
Started	Stopped			

Activity 23.3 (Estimated time: 1–2 hours)
Summarizing a Journal Article

Written Requirements: Form 23.3

Objectives: To critique a research article, you will identify and summarize another journal article of relevance to your teaching program. The paper chosen should support one or more of the strategies you have incorporated within your teaching program.

Instructions

1. As before, you are required to identify and summarize a behavior analytic research article of particular relevance to your practicum project.
2. If you choose a report of a group experiment or conceptual paper, use a copy of the forms included in Unit 17. If none of the templates are appropriate, feel free to use your own format.

Form 23.3 (p. 1 of 3)
Journal Report

Your Name _____ Date_____ Instructor's Name _____

Author(s)' last name(s) followed by first initials _____
_____

Date _____ Article Title _____
_____

Name of Journal _____Volume _____ Issue ____ Pages ___ to____

Explain why you chose this article. Say how it relates to the teaching you plan to do.
_____
_____
_____

Introduction
List the *main* reasons why the authors decided to conduct this study. _____
_____
_____

What specific questions did the author(s) ask or hypothesis did they want to test? (Usually found in the last paragraph of the introduction.) You may restate that question in the form of "*If*" (or given; a general description for the method used) _____
_____

then" (a general description of the anticipated results)_____
_____

Methods

Precisely describe:

T*he participants*, including personnel, students, others _____
_____
_____

The setting (location, physical arrangements)_____
_____
_____
_____

What was measured (usually particular behaviors)? _____
_____
_____

How did the researchers conduct their measurement? What materials did they use?
_____
_____

What did the authors do to show their measures were *reliable* or dependable _____
_____and *valid* (measured what they were supposed to)? _____
_____

Form 23.3 (p. 2 of 3)

Your Name _____ Date_____ Instructor's Name _____

Describe the *experimental design* the authors used (A-B-A-B; multiple baseline; changing criterion, control group, other?)
_____
_____

Describe the *procedures* (*who* did *what*, *how*, *with whom*, *where*, *when*, *how often*, and for *how long*?)
_____
_____
_____
_____
_____

Was the fidelity with which you intervened assessed? If so, describe._____
_____
_____

Results

What happened as a result of the procedures that were used? (You may want to use the attached templates to sketch the graphs.)_____
_____
_____
_____
_____

 Discussion

What *main* issues did the authors discuss?_____
_____
_____
_____
_____
_____

Conclusion

Refer back to the specific question or hypothesis the authors posed in the introduction. How did the authors answer the question?
_____
_____
_____

Add your own comments and questions here. _____
_____
_____
_____
_____
_____

Form 23.3 (p. 3 of 3)
Your Name _____ Date_____ Instructor's Name _____

Templates for Sketching Results. (Optional)

A-B-A-B (Withdrawal design)

Baseline Intervention ┊ Baseline Intervention

Multiple Baseline Design

Baseline ┊ Intervention

Baseline ┊ Intervention

Baseline ┊ Intervention

Unit 23 Discussion Topics

1. Share your experience in conducting your lesson.
   - How did your student respond?
   - Did you receive any assistance from others?
   - How did that work out?
   - Do you think you are on the right track?
   - Why or why not?

2. Tell us about your attempts to collect data.
   - What methods did you use?
   - How valid do you feel the data are?
   - How reliable are the data?
   - What changes, if any, do you think you should make to improve the quality of the data?

3. How informative, valuable are you finding the data?
   - Do you see any patterns emerging?

(You may want to include a copy of your graph with identifying information deleted. If you are working from a distance and the program permits, you may wish to copy and paste the graph onto the discussion board.)

4. To what extent do you find it helpful:
   - to *prepare* your progress report
   - to *receive* feedback from your instructor
   - What aspects of each were especially useful?

5. Share your experiences with this DVD recording assignment.
   - What, if any, problems did you encounter?
   - What kind of help could you use from your classmates?
   - What did you learn from viewing the recording? Selecting the segment to send to the instructor?

Unit 24
Looking Ahead, Behind, to the Left and Right
Generalization and Maintenance

A raindrop sparkles on a pine needle above Ginger's head, drawing her attention away from her laptop screen. "What a magnificent sky. We never see one so blue in the city. And the scent of balsam, especially after last night's rain, umm." She stretches, closes the laptop, folds up the bridge table and returns them to the RV.

"You guys ready?" Art calls out. "If we want a good spot on the lawn, we'd better get our picnic lunch and other gear and head out. The Marsalis Brass Quintet should be terrific."

"Let's be careful, guys," Dawn warns. "Remember to stay in line and well over to the side. Navigating these hilly, curvy roads can be treacherous."

"Yes'm." Familiar with Dawn's cautiousness, Art presents a promissory hand-raise. "I'll be riding 'tail' and won't forget to attach the flag to the back of my bike."

✱✱✱✱✱

 Safe bikers remain alert to road traffic and other potentially hazardous conditions. Effective teachers are similarly vigilant, as they lay out a plan for promoting behavioral change and the conditions needed to reinforce it. In this field we know that when your student's and your own hard work are reinforced, progress tends to accelerate and/or persist. To produce positive change, you must identify and apply powerful reinforcers. So, let's take a look at some of your options.

Is *intrinsic reinforcement* sufficient? Perhaps, under such ideal circumstances as:

- A teaching objective with its own built-in history of reinforcement. In this case, the fun for the student is in the "doing." Think swimming, swinging, singing, baking cookies, playing in the sand, biking, skiing, reading or listening to or making music, producing a work of art, solving a problem or mystery; all sorts of sports and hobbies at which the person has become proficient.
- An activity that can naturally occur under many conditions, at various times, places, with different people and materials: for instance, listening to or singing along with any of a set of musical CD's—at home, in school, with friends, via a portable CD player.
- An activity the teacher enjoys teaching (i.e., finds intrinsically reinforcing). It's probable that the instructor's excitement will be paired with the activity. This can serve as motivation, resulting in increased levels of desired outcome.

Teaching children on the autism spectrum can be more complicated than teaching those who are typically developing. For instance, greater emphasis often needs to be placed on targeting safety skills, such as responding appropriately to a fire alarm or stopping at the end of a driveway or at a curb. Students may require discrete trial intervention to introduce skills in a distraction-free, highly structured environment, delivered via one-to-one instruction. Also common is the need to close gaps in our students' backgrounds skills (imitating speech sounds, observing peer behaviors, and so on). This often requires carefully sequenced learning experiences temporarily supported by contrived reinforcers.

A True Story

Years ago, I taught a class of typically developing fourth graders who spoke only their non-English native languages. One day, I read aloud to them an illustrated story of *Cinderella*, which they enjoyed thoroughly. We then decided to turn the story into a puppet show. The children took great pleasure in making the puppets, costumes, sets, props, drawing the curtains, and practicing the Cinderella script. The experience was extraordinary. The children and I offered to repeat the performance in other mainstream classes. Our audiences were wildly enthusiastic, as were my students and I. The principal got word and came to watch, enjoying the event as much as the rest of us. Puppet shows, arts and crafts skills, and their ability in and confidence with spoken English accelerated accordingly. When my students joined mainstream classes by the end of the school year, they felt comfortable speaking the language.

What we are referring to, of course, is the necessity of including crucial ABA practices (e.g., shaping, chaining, maintenance, and generalization) within your instructional program. This unit we place special emphasis on these aspects, and ask you to address them in your progress report.

Prerequisite Skills

Assuming you have completed formal coursework in or otherwise mastered information about the value of and techniques for promoting generalization and maintenance, the importance of programming essential revisions and methods for reviewing technical journal articles about topics related to complex teaching, you should be able to achieve Unit 24's objectives.

Unit 24 Objectives

To generate a weekly progress report, state shaping, generalization and maintenance procedures and conduct a critique of a research article incorporating generalization and maintenance components, you will:

1. re-state your teaching objective and describe the main components crucial to the progress of your student's performance, including but not limited to curricula used, measurement procedures, instructional setting descriptions, instructional strategies employed, reinforcers used, generalization and maintenance procedures followed, and performance results.
2. update and interpret a graphic representation demonstrating performance results.
3. identify and demonstrate comprehension of a research article's major components and sections, especially as they relate to your project.

Activity 24.1 (Estimated time: 1-2 hours)
Weekly Progress Report.

Written Requirements: Form 24.1

Objectives: To generate a weekly progress report and state shaping, generalization and maintenance procedures, you will:

1. re-state your teaching objective and describe the main components related to the progress of your student's performance, including, but not limited to, curricula used, measurement procedures, instructional setting descriptions, instructional strategies employed, reinforcers used, generalization and maintenance procedures and performance results.
2. generate and interpret a graphing convention demonstrating a visual display of performance results.

Please complete the attached *Progress Report Form 24.1.*

Note: By asking you to repeat some information, we are hoping to ensure that you remember to include all the essential elements of your teaching program. Further, it is important that we collectively monitor ANY changes you make to your instructional practices. Feel free, though, to use abbreviations or "same as last time" if agreeable to your supervisor/instructor.

Form 24.1 (p. 1 of 3)

Your Name _____ Date _____ Instructor's Name _____

Student identifier (initials or pseudonym) _____

1. Briefly describe your student:
a) gender M/F (circle one) b) chronological age ____ c) approximate developmental level ____

2. Please briefly restate your objective._____

_____

_____

Do you continue to feel this is an appropriate objective for your student?
- Circle one: Y/N Why? _____

_____

- If you answered "no," propose an alternative objective to the student's teacher and/or parent. Assuming they assent, write it here._____

_____

_____

3. What *materials* did you assemble in advance? _____

_____

- Is this a change since the last time? Y/N (circle one)   If Yes, explain why._____

_____

- Say how effectively these materials functioned in terms of supporting control by antecedents (technically stimulus control) as well as generalization and maintenance.[62]_____

_____

_____

_____

4. Describe:
- The data you collected _____

- How often?

  ☐ each session ☐ each day ☐ ____ times a week ☐ once a week

  ☐ other (Describe) _____

- Others involved in data collection? _____

- Did you each independently measure the same thing at the same time? Y/N (circle one)f

---

Note: Remember to aim for at least three "reliability checks" during the course. If agreement indices fall below .80, you should refine your measures or definitions.

---

[62] Refer to a basic text in Behavior Analysis for further suggestions.

Form 24.1 (p. 2 of 3)

Your Name _____ Date _____ Instructor's Name _____

- If you conducted a reliability check this week, how closely did you agree with one another? What was the index of agreement? (Fill in the formula)

  Number of agreements _____ ÷
  Number of agreements plus disagreements _____ = _____

5. *Assistance*
- What other *help* did you arrange in advance? _____
  _____

- From whom? _____

- Describe how it worked out. _____
  _____

- Are others conducting the instruction for purposes of promoting generalization? Y/N
  Explain _____

6. *Setting.* Describe *where* instruction took place _____
  _____

- Have you arranged to have your student perform the behavior in *other settings* now or in the future? Y/N. Why? _____
  _____

7. *Sessions*
- How many lessons or sessions did you conduct this week? _____
- What day(s) of the week? M T W Th F Sa Su (Circle those that apply)
- How long did each session last? _____

8. *Procedures*
 If applicable, say how you are:
- Reinforcing sequences of small responses to *chain* together and/or *shape* approximations toward the objective? Describe. _____
  _____
  _____

- Minimizing and/or gradually fading prompts? Describe. _____
  _____

- Including *generalization* or transfer of the skill across materials, settings, people, and/or other essential conditions within your instruction? _____
  _____
  _____
  _____
  _____

Form 24.1 (p. 3 of 3)

Your Name _____ Date _____ Instructor's Name _____

- Planning for future *maintenance* of the skill?

_____

_____

9. *Reinforcers*

- What reinforcers did you use? _____

☐ Natural consequence of behavior　　　　☐ Student selected from an array

☐ Student selected from series of paired comparisons　☐ Student consistently responsive to item or event in the past

☐ Token system(s) well established

- The reinforcing value of any given item or event can vary from situation to situation, depending on circumstances. A drink of water tastes so good during recess when the children are hot and sweaty, but might be less satisfying afterward in a cool classroom. How are you adjusting the reinforcers you are presenting to suit the various conditions used to promote generalization training in your teaching? _____

_____

_____

- How did you make certain the student was aware of the reinforcer toward which s/he was working?_____

_____

10. *Instructional activities.*
Describe:
- What you and/or your associates did. _____

_____

_____

- What the student did or did not do. _____

_____

_____

11. *Results*

- Describe the results in words and attach your graphs._____

_____

- Assuming you are teaching your skill at different times, and/or places and/or with different people or materials, you may wish to prepare separate graphs for each particular condition. If you delayed or staggered those varied conditions, you should be able to use the multiple baseline-graphing formats to display those results.

12. *Discussion and questions.*
Here and on the back are the places to comment on what has been happening in general, including pleasant surprises, and to ask for clarifications and help.

_____

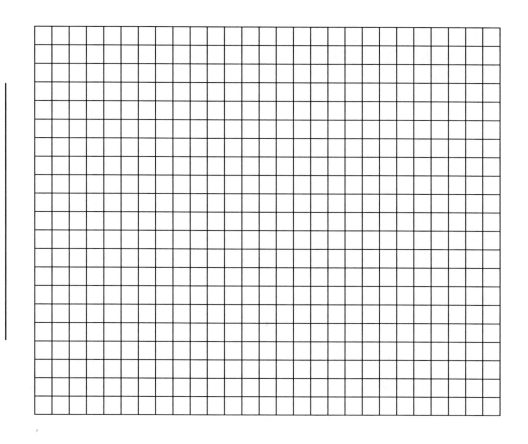

Activity 24.2: (Estimated time 1–2 hours)
Summarizing a Journal Article Incorporating Generalization and/or Maintenance Features

Written Requirements: Form 24.2

Objective: To critique a research article incorporating generalization and maintenance components, you will: identify and demonstrate comprehension of its major components, including generalization and maintenance.

Instructions

This assignment is designed to expose you to ways in which generalization and/or maintenance strategies can be included in ABA program design. When reviewing journal articles, be mindful of the methods used by the authors. This will allow you to gain a greater understanding of how to incorporate these strategies as early as possible within your program.

You already have been required to read an article and summarize what you learned. This week's assignment *concentrates on the way the authors have incorporated generalization and/or maintenance within their programs.*

Instructions specific to locating relevant literature were provided during Units 5 and 6. You may wish to review these. You may find new sources by accessing additional journals or textbooks and reviewing the volume or yearly index. Some resources, for example, *The Journal of Applied Behavior Analysis*, supply a separate index volume covering a span of years.

Remember, your summary should briefly emphasize generalization and/or maintenance.

Form 24.2 (p. 1 of 3)

Your Name _____ Date_____ Instructor's Name_____

Author(s)' last name(s) followed by first initials _____

Date _____ Article Title _____

Name of Journal _____Volume _____ Issue ___ Pages ___ to____

Explain why you chose this article. Say how it relates to the teaching you plan to do.

_____
_____
_____
_____

Introduction
List the *main* reasons why the authors decided to conduct this study.

_____
_____

What specific questions did the author(s) ask or hypothesis did they want to test? (Usually found in the last paragraph of the introduction). You may restate that question in the form of "*If* (or given; a general description for the method used)_____

then" (a general description of the anticipated results_____
_____

Methods:
Precisely describe:

T*he participants*, including personnel, students, others

_____
_____

The setting (location, physical arrangements)_____
_____
_____
_____

What was measured (usually particular behaviors)?
_____
_____

How did the researchers conduct their measurement? What materials did they use?
_____
_____

What did the authors do to show their measures were *reliable* or dependable? _____
_____

and *valid* (measured what they were supposed to)? _____
_____
_____
_____

Form 24.2 (p. 2 of 3)

Your Name _____ Date_____ Instructor's Name _____

Describe the *experimental design* the authors used (A-B-A-B; multiple baseline; changing criterion, control group, other?)

_____
_____

Describe the *procedures* (*who* did *what, how, with whom, where, when, how often,* and for *how long*?).

_____
_____
_____
_____
_____

Describe and comment on the methods the experimenters used to promote maintenance and/or generalization.

_____
_____
_____

Results

_____
_____

What happened as a result of the procedures that were used? (You may want to use the attached templates to sketch the graphs.)

_____
_____
_____
_____

Discussion

What *main* issues did the authors discuss? _____
_____
_____
_____
_____

Conclusion

Refer back to the specific question or hypothesis the authors posed in the introduction. How did the authors answer the question?

_____
_____
_____

Add your own comments and questions here.

_____
_____
_____
_____

Form 24.2 (p. 3 of 3)
Templates for Sketching Results. (Optional)

Your Name _____ Date_____ Instructor's Name _____

A-B-A-B (Withdrawal design)

Baseline Intervention ¦ Baseline Intervention ¦

Multiple Baseline Design

Baseline ¦ Intervention

Baseline ¦ Intervention

Baseline ¦ Intervention

 **Unit 24 Discussion Topics**

1. Have you considered altering your behavioral objective?
   - Why or why not?
   - If you did, what decision did you make?
   - Why?
   - What was the teacher or parent's reaction to your suggested change?

2. Share the new or modified instructional objective you selected for your student.
   - Explain your decision.
   - Describe the resources you have available to pursue this objective.
   - Use this forum to access resource information from your fellow students.

3. Many practitioners work with a student toward an objective for weeks or months before attempting to measure change. Comment on this practice from the viewpoint of the instructor and from that of the student.

4. Specify the name of the journal article you read. Did the authors provide you with helpful insight in areas of generalization or maintenance? Were there strategies described that you could incorporate in your current project or that you would consider using in the future?

Unit 25
Gauging Progress by Monitoring Performance

"Uh oh, I see a blinking blue light in the side mirror," warns Lucy.

Hal presses the break, then glances toward the speedometer.

"Not to worry, Lucy. I wasn't going above 64 and this is a 65 mile-per-hour zone. With the speed control set, we're safe."

As the patrol car passes on its way, all inhale deeply, sit back and relax, appreciating how careful they know Hal to be about regularly monitoring the RV instrument panel.

✷✷✷✷✷

On any trip, instruments serve the essential role of providing information about the vehicle's performance. What is the status of our fuel, coolant, electrical power, and engine temperature? Are the high beams on or off? At what speed are we moving, and are we confident we are moving rapidly enough to reach our predetermined destination?

Similarly, the instruments we use to analyze behavior when teaching children with autism provide us with data about the efficacy of our methods. Last week we concentrated on promoting generalization and maintenance of change. This week our focus turns to *assessing and analyzing:* 1) progress rates, 2) the strength of reinforcing and antecedent stimuli, and 3) any possible side effects. These aspects provide another opportunity for us to assess programming, progress, and if warranted, to make alterations.

Prerequisite Skills

Assuming you have completed formal coursework in or otherwise mastered information about the value of and methods for constructively adjusting teaching strategies and reviewing technical journal articles related to refinement of teaching methods, you should be able to achieve Unit 25's objective.

Unit 25 Objectives

To generate a progress report, state progress rates, reinforcer and prompt effectiveness and alternative instructional strategies and to critique a research article incorporating collateral effects of procedural implementation, you will:
1. re-state your teaching objective and describe the main components related to your student's performance progress, including but not limited to curricula used, measurement procedures, instructional setting descriptions, instructional strategies employed, reinforcers used, progress rate, reinforcer and prompt effectiveness, and alternative instructional strategies.
2. generate and interpret a graphic display of performance results.
3. identify and demonstrate comprehension of a research article's major components, emphasizing collateral effects of the procedural implementation.

Mini-Tutorial on Some Fine Points of Behavioral Instruction

As you continue to implement your teaching plan, we ask that you keep filling out a *Weekly Progress Report.* These reports allow us to make informed recommendations about how to increase your plan's effectiveness, and as a result, increase student achievement. Last Unit, you focused some of your attention on skill generalization and maintenance. This Unit, we turn to:

- *Student Progress Rates*: Behavioral teaching programs are designed to permit our students to learn rapidly while enjoying the experience to the highest degree possible. Prompting and reinforcement procedures are crucial to this process and both require systematic and ongoing review. You begin by looking at how your students are progressing. By examining the association between your graphed student progress data and your procedures, you may identify some promising adjustments in the program. Examples include particular ways to fade prompts, avoid over-prompting, rearrange reinforcer delivery, and so on.

- *Reinforcer Effectiveness:* "Reinforcer effectiveness" describes the extent to which the child sustains his or her work as a function of its consequences. The effectiveness of a reinforcement plan can contribute substantially toward promoting attainment of a teaching objective, as well as to the rate at which the student learns. This area of programming addresses the types of consequences (social, tangible, edible, activity, and so on) that you are using, how you are varying the consequences to avoid satiation, and the timing and frequency (schedule) of reinforcer delivery.

- *Prompt Effectiveness:* As we recognize, we should avoid using artificial prompts whenever possible. If unneeded prompts aren't added, there is nothing to fade! For example, if you wait until a child hands you a picture, and wait longer until she says the word aloud, you are less likely to have to fade verbal prompts. Setting up situations that support child initiation by delaying or omitting prompts should enhance progress. Although using artificial prompts may yield quick results (thereby reinforcing the teacher's prompting), the ensuing process of fading and needing to substitute natural reinforcers can be challenging. You may wish to return to Bondy and Sulzer-Azaroff's (2001) *The Pyramid Approach to Education in Autism*, chapters 8–10, to review sections on prompt hierarchies, delayed prompting, error correction and more.

- *Un-programmed Side Effects:* You may view particular "side effects" as good, bad or indifferent. Valued side effects of teaching might include appropriate generalization (or *transfer*) of skills to new situations, settings or people. An example is seeing a child spontaneously greet or make eye contact with a visiting relative. Familiar examples of undesirable side effects include the student failing to respond in the absence of a prompt (prompt dependency), or trying to escape or avoid the instructional situation by throwing materials, screaming, or engaging in self-injury.

Activity 25.1 (Estimated time: 1–4 hours)
Progress Report: Summary of Instructional Experience

Written Requirements: Form 25.1

Objectives: To generate a progress report and state progress rates, reinforcer and prompt effectiveness and alternative instructional strategies, you will:

1. re-state your teaching objective and describe the main components related to the progress of your student's performance, including but not limited to curricula used, measurement procedures, instructional setting descriptions, instructional strategies employed, reinforcers. used, progress rate, reinforcer and prompt effectiveness, and alternative instructional strategies
2. generate and interpret a graphic display of performance results.

Instructions

Complete the attached *Progress Report Form 25.1* and give it to your instructor. Note the emphasis on analyzing subtleties in the teaching process. Perhaps by viewing a DVD of your own teaching or with the help of an observer, try to identify any reinforcers and prompts you may be using intentionally and unintentionally.

As you know, for the remainder of the course, each unit we will ask that you to turn in a "progress report" from the previous unit. Although similar, these Progress Reports *may focus on different elements of instructional practice. You should complete the attached form and submit it to your instructor by the end of the week.*

Form 25.1 (p. 1 of 4)

Your Name _____ Date _____ Instructor's Name _____
Student identifier (initials or pseudonym) _____

1. Briefly describe your student
    a) gender M/F (circle one)
    b) chronological age ____
    c) approximate mental or developmental age ____

2. What is the *objective* toward which you are working?_____
_____
_____

3. What *materials* did you assemble in advance? _____
_____

• Are they different from last time? Y/N (circle one) If Y, how did you use them?_____
_____

4. *Assistance*
    a) What *assistance* did you arrange in advance? _____
    _____

    b) From whom? _____

    c) Describe how it worked out. _____

5. *Setting.* Describe *where* your lessons took place._____

6. *Sessions*
    a) How many lessons or sessions did you conduct this week? _____

    b) On what day(s) of the week? M Tu W Th F Sa Su (Circle those that apply)

    c) How long did each session last? _____

7. *Reinforcers*
    a) What reinforcers did you use? _____

    b) What was the basis for selecting these? (Check all that apply)

        ☐ Natural consequence of the behavior being addressed

        ☐ Student initiated action toward obtaining

        ☐ Student selected from an array displayed

        ☐ Student selected from series of paired comparisons

        ☐ Student consistently responsive to item or event in the past

        ☐ Use of token system(s) well established

        ☐ Other? (Explain) _____

Form 25.1 (p. 2 of 4)

Your Name _____ Date _____ Instructor's Name _____

c) How are these reinforcers working?

- If you have been recording and graphing data *within* a session (i.e., across two minute or five-minute blocks of time), good for you! Look at a few of those recent graphs or if you have not been graphing data within sessions, look at your recent *daily data sheets.*

- Review the rate (unit of change per unit of time) *during sessions* within which the behavior of concern is changing and comment on whether it seems to be accelerating (moving faster) or decelerating (slowing down) over time. If the rate either is accelerating or remaining at a high steady level, you can feel confident the reinforcers are functioning well. If you see the rate of correct responses slow down or become quite irregular during the session, the power of the reinforcing event may be failing.

- Based on the rate of behavior change, comment on the effectiveness of the reinforcers you are using. _____
  _____
  _____

- Now take a look at your *session-by-session* graphs or recent daily data sheets and comment on whether the behavior is *accelerating, decelerating* or remaining at a *steady* low, medium or high level._____
  _____
  _____

- If the rate of the behavior is remaining at or dropping to an unacceptably low level, either during or between sessions, you might consider altering the reinforcers you are using. Comment on the plans you have for doing this. (If not applicable, indicate N/A)
  _____
  _____
  _____

d) What else, if anything, do you plan to do to keep reinforcers as powerful and effective as possible? This could include changing events in the environment, changing the daily schedule or even changing your instructional objective. _____
  _____
  _____
  _____

e) What are you or will you do eventually to fade any artificial or contrived reinforcers?

☐ deliver them less and less often

☐ make them less and less artificial and more and more natural to the situation

☐ other (describe) _____
_____
_____

Form 25.1 (p. 3 of 4)

Your Name _____ Date _____ Instructor's Name _____

f) Describe your *reinforcer first* method; that is, how you are trying to make certain the student is aware of the reinforcer for which s/he is working. You will

☐ display it ☐ ask the student to choose it ☐ point to it

☐ ask the student to point to the current activity, word, or picture, then the next word or picture depicting a preferred activity

☐ other (describe)

_____
_____
_____

8. *Instructional activities.*

a) Describe cues that are natural to the situation (e.g., picture displays next activity; bell signals time to clean up; teacher instructs "find a partner;" words in book cue spoken words; and so on). These, therefore, would not need to be faded or eliminated.

_____
_____
_____

b) Identify and describe below the prompts you and/or your associates supplied to help the student to give the correct response.

Note: You may be using these prompts intentionally or unintentionally. To check this out, try watching a DVD recording of your teaching or ask an observer to watch and comment on subtle prompts you or others may be using.

☐ Full spoken prompt
☐ Partial spoken prompt (might include changes in volume, pitch and so on.)
☐ Fully gestured prompt
☐ Partially gestured prompt
☐ Visual prompt (e.g., instructor looks at correct choice)
☐ Full pictorial prompt
☐ Partial written or pictorial prompt, as in errorless discrimination training
☐ Other (describe)

_____
_____

c) What did the student do or not do in response to those prompts?

_____
_____

d) If you have been using artificial prompts, describe methods you plan to or have been using to gradually eliminate or fade them?

_____
_____
_____

Form 25.1 (p. 4 of 4)

Your Name _____ Date _____ Instructor's Name_____

9. *Results.* Describe:

    a) the data you collected _____

    b) how often?

       ☐   Each session
       ☐   Each day
       ☐   _____ times a week
       ☐   Once a week
       ☐   Other. Explain _____

       _____

    c) What was the basis for deciding on the schedule you identified above?

    _____

(**Note**: Have you done at least three "reliability checks" yet? Are agreement indices remaining above .80 or do you still need to refine your measures/definitions?)

    d) What were the indexes of agreement in each case so far? _____

Please attach a copy of each of your graphs.

10. What *un-programmed side effects* have you noted that appear to relate to your teaching program?
transfer of skill to

☐ new settings   ☐ new people   ☐ new situations   ☐ avoidance attempts

☐ actual escape from situation   ☐ other side effects. Please describe _____

_____
_____
_____
_____

11. Propose any changes to your program that you feel would be supported by the evidence provided above.

_____
_____
_____
_____
_____

12. *Discussion and question.* Here is the place to
    a) comment on what has been happening in general, including pleasant surprises
    b) ask for clarifications and help

_____
_____
_____
_____
_____

Activity 25.2 (Estimated Time: 1–3 hours)
Summarizing a Journal Article

Written Requirements: Form 25.2

Objectives: To conduct a critique of a research article incorporating collateral effects of procedure implementation, you will identify and demonstrate comprehension of a research article's major components and sections, emphasizing effects collateral to the procedural implementation.

Instructions

In this unit you are concentrating on elements of your teaching plan that may be affected by the way reinforcers and prompts are delivered. For this assignment we ask you to locate and report on another journal article: one that analyzes the results of an intervention in terms of planned and unplanned procedural factors that may have influenced those outcomes *indirectly*. These issues will often be reviewed in the *discussion section* of the article.

The index in some journals may specify articles that address indirect effects of teaching procedures. Many journals include an index in their final yearly issue. Others, including *The Journal of Applied Behavior Analysis*, supply separate index volumes covering a span of years.

Form 25.2 (p. 1 of 3)

Your Name _____ Date _____ Instructor's Name _____

Use brief, to-the-point phrases.

Author(s)' last name(s) followed by first initials

_____

_____

Date _____ Article Title _____

_____

Name of Journal _____ Volume _____ Pages ___ to ___

I. Introduction

a) List the *main* reasons why the authors decided to conduct this study. How did they justify what they did?

(1) _____

(2) _____

(3) _____

b) What specific questions did the author(s) ask or what was the hypothesis they wanted to test? You may restate that question in the form of "*If* (or given; a general description for the method used) _____

_____

then" (a general description of the anticipated results) _____

_____

c) Explain why you chose this article and how it relates to the teaching you are doing.

_____

_____

_____

II. Methods

Precisely describe:

a) *the participants*, including personnel, students, others

_____

_____

b) *the setting* (location, physical arrangements) _____

_____

_____

_____

c) What was measured (usually particular behaviors)? _____

_____

_____

d) How did the researchers conduct their measurement? What materials did they use?

_____

_____

_____

_____

Form 25.2 (p. 2 of 3)

Your Name _____ Date_____ Instructor's Name _____

e) What did the authors do to try to convince readers the measures were *reliable* or dependable

_____

and *valid* (measured what they were supposed to) _____

_____

f) Describe the main procedures (w*ho* did *what, how, with whom, where, when, how often,* and for *how long?*).

_____
_____
_____
_____
_____

g) Explain the approach the authors took toward promoting generalization and/or maintenance of the target behavior(s).

_____
_____
_____
_____

III. Results

Describe what happened as a result of the methods being used.

_____
_____
_____
_____

(Optional) Sketch the most interesting graphs below.

Form 25.2 (p. 3 of 3)

Your Name _____ Date_____ Instructor's Name _____

IV. Discussion and Conclusion

a) List the *main* issues the authors discussed. _____
_____
_____
_____

b) Refer back to the specific questions or hypotheses the authors asked in the introduction. Based on their findings, what conclusions did they draw? _____
_____
_____
_____

c) Summarize the author's analysis of factors that might have influenced reinforcer effectiveness, and/or the impact of unintended prompting or other factors. _____
_____
_____
_____

d) Are there other factors that you feel might have influenced the results? _____
_____
_____

e) What did the authors suggest might improve the outcome in the future? _____
_____
_____

f) Now add your own comments.
_____
_____
_____
_____
_____
_____
_____
_____
_____
_____
_____
_____
_____
_____
_____
_____
_____

Unit 25 Discussion Topics

1. Share any lessons you learned by looking more closely at your prompting methods.

2. Did you decide to alter your teaching methods as a result of the work you did last week? Explain why or why not.

3. Given your experiences to date, do you wish you had identified a different instructional objective?
    - If so, what would that be and why?
    - If not, what has contributed to your level of confidence?

4. In a sentence or two, briefly summarize the article you read.
    - Offer reasons for choosing this particular paper.
    - Describe what you learned, especially in terms of the participants' progress rates, the effectiveness of the reinforcer used, intentional and/or unintentional prompting and side effects.

5. Share your perspective and/or ask questions related to your practicum experiences.

Unit 26
A Tale to be Told
Reporting Your Methods and Results

"What on earth are those creatures over there?"

"Deer. No, not deer; too big around the middle. Necks too long and thick."

"If I didn't know better, I'd say they were llamas."

"Pretty weird, but, I think you're right. I thought llamas were native to South America."

The car slows down while everyone looks more closely. All agree.

"Who would believe this? Llamas! Quick, Hal take a picture."

"It's amazing how things happen sometimes. Remember Sunday? If we hadn't started talking to those students from overseas at the picnic ground, we'd never have taken that side trip to the chasm. It would have been a pity to have missed that!"

"I'll bet Ginger remembers Sunday for more than that. You really seemed to have hit it off with the guide—the one who coincidentally turned out to be in charge of Continuing Ed at your school. Did I see him writing down your number? Now you've decided to go back, you might run into him."

Ginger blushes, looking pointedly off in the distance. "Yup! This llama story will be another good one to add to the list of wonders we've seen."

******

As we journey through the field of autism education, our own stories also unfold. Personnel needs and roles change; many further their educations and move into more challenging roles. Because each student brings unique qualities to each lesson, you will find yourself continually fascinated and challenged by their changing requirements. Careful observation and chronicling of teaching procedures and resulting student behaviors will permit you to:

1. Record procedures that have enabled your student to meet with success, so teachers that follow can capitalize on that information when designing future lessons.
2. Review and analyze procedures to discover what specific aspects accounted for successes and failures.
3. Over time, discover general relationships and patterns and adjust your methods accordingly. The association between increased communication skills and decreased deviant/aggressive behavior is an example. Such information can be used to form hypotheses, which then would warrant experimental testing to assess generality across behaviors, individuals or settings. In fact, this is the way many of the formal behavioral procedures you have learned about actually evolved! Consequently, this week we concentrate on narrating the details of our teaching methods and outcomes.

Assuming you have completed formal coursework in or otherwise mastered information about preparing a report according the APA style, you should be able to achieve Unit 26's objectives.

Unit 26 Objectives

To generate a *preliminary* report of your lesson and produce a DVD, you will:

1. write your lesson's justification, purpose, method and results to date, plus factors that may have influenced the outcomes and preliminary conclusions.
2. produce a DVD recording of a teaching session.

Activity 26.1 (Estimated time: 3–6 hrs.)
Detailed Outline for Final Report

Written Requirements: Form 26.1

Objectives: To generate a *preliminary* report of your lesson, you will include your lesson's justification, purpose, method and results to date, plus factors that may have influenced the outcomes and your preliminary conclusions.

Instructions

Attached is a form designed to help you prepare the report you will submit during the final unit of this course. In general, it is, organized according to the publication guidelines of the American Psychological Association,[63] but also incorporates features of an applied behavior analytic report. The amount of writing space provided on the form is designed to give you a general sense of how much material is called for, but not meant to restrict or to compel you to expand on concise answers. The assignments you have completed earlier in the practicum will ease this process. After referring back to each previously completed relevant activity, you need only to update and further develop your descriptions and interpretations and *there you go.* You have the ingredients for the item.

Please closely inspect your technical writing—grammar, spelling, and word usage—as these aspects will be among the bases for assessing the quality of your final report. Attention to these details will save you time during final preparation.

To minimize pressure, we purposely have allowed an extra week between this assignment and the due date for your final report. We suggest you submit this material as soon as possible, to allow sufficient time for a thorough review.

During Unit 27 you will update your graphs; for Unit 28 you will narrate a completed report, without using any forms or additional supports. You will combine all the pieces you generate in this and next week's assignment, edit it as your instructor suggests, and produce a cohesive report worthy of submission for final grading. Afterward, you should give a copy of the revised report to your field facilitator, your student's teacher and parents. You may, if appropriate, provide additional copies for the site administrator, to file along with the student's official records.

---

[63] *Publication Manual of the American Psychological Association, 5th ed.* (2001). Washington, DC: American Psychological Association. www.apa.org.

Form 26.1 (p. 1 of 6)

Your Name _____ Date _____ Instructor's Name _____

Detailed Outline for Final Report

1. Title: Write a concise title for your report that includes phrases telling what was done with whom for what purpose:

_____

2. Your name (author) and affiliation (place you work or school where you are studying)_____

_____

3. Abstract: We suggest you outline the abstract this week. Next week you will be asked to provide a full abstract._____

_____
_____
_____
_____
_____
_____

4. Introduction: Why did you do the study? Include:

    a) A general review of information specific to your area of study. Include as references the relevant research reports you have summarized in earlier assignments and any others you have read.

_____
_____
_____
_____
_____
_____
_____
_____
_____
_____
_____
_____

    b) Why you decided to do this particular project at this time. Refer back to earlier assignments, especially Unit 16, in which you identified a student and began to discover how s/he and the environment were influencing one another, and Unit 17, as you began to focus on an instructional objective.

_____
_____
_____
_____
_____
_____
_____

Form 26.1(p. 2 of 6)

Your Name _____ Date _____ Instructor's Name _____

      c) Specify the purpose of your instructional program. Often this is stated as an if-then relation: If (the general method or procedure), then (the anticipated outcome and relevance of what you did and hoped to find). You also may include the specific objective of your lesson in this section.

_____
_____
_____
_____

5. Method
      a) *Participants*: Include demographic information (gender, age, educational background etc. as relevant),
          (1) *Student*: You can use your student description from Unit 2 and the more detailed information you supplied in Unit 5.

_____
_____
_____
_____

          (2) *Staff, parents and other people significant in your student's life*: You will find some valuable material in assignments from Units 2 and 4.

_____
_____
_____
_____
_____
_____
_____
_____
_____

          (3) *Yourself:* Describe your background and skills in this field, as well as short- and long-term aims.

_____
_____
_____
_____
_____
_____
_____

      b) *Setting*: Say something about the geographical location of your project; include a description of the instructional site along with the kind of information that was requested in Units 4 and 5. Be sure to describe the arrangements of furnishings, regular sources of distractions, as well as anything else in the environment that might impact your teaching or the student's learning.

_____
_____
_____
_____

Form 26.1(p. 3 of 6)

Your Name _____ Date _____ Instructor's Name _____

c) *Materials, equipment*: When planning a vacation, it's often helpful to compose a "packing list"; by doing this you can avoid forgetting items. The list can also be a valuable resource when packing for the next trip. Similarly, when you report on a method used to teach, you want to be sure every item used in the process is listed in case you or others want to replicate the project.

_____
_____
_____
_____
_____

You may wish to sketch out the way furnishings and materials are organized here.

d) *Specify your instructional objective*. This should include the *act* (behavior or performance) you are teaching, the *conditions* under which it should or should not occur, and the *standards*—how you *assess correctness* (as in the number of correct responses in a row for how many days in a row). Refer back to Unit 5 or the most current version of your objective and state it below.

_____
_____
_____
_____
_____

e) *Measures*: In Unit 6 you designed your measurement system. Perhaps you have modified this. In reality, many do when they find out how difficult getting good reliable data can be. You may have added new measures or dropped old ones. Regardless, (1) explain how you measured each bulleted item below, and (2) describe the tools used.

- the main behavior(s) of interest

_____
_____
_____
_____

Form 26.1 (p. 4 of 6)

Your Name _____ Date _____ Instructor's Name _____

- any indirect responses

_____
_____
_____

- the reliability of scoring (indexes of agreement)

_____
_____
_____

- documentation that you and/or others followed procedures as designed (*treatment fidelity* or *intervention integrity*)

_____
_____
_____

f) *Procedures*: Detail *who* did what with whom; *how*; *where*; *when* and *why*—the kinds of information we requested during Unit 21. Return to your materials for that week, revise and update your procedural section below. This section should be written in a way that would allow others to precisely duplicate your project, with the intention of getting similar results.

_____
_____
_____
_____
_____
_____
_____
_____
_____
_____
_____
_____
_____
_____
_____
_____
_____
_____
_____
_____

g) *Replication*: Due to time constraints, *we* have not required you to repeat your methods across other behaviors, in other places, at other times, or with other students. That is something you would need to do if you were conducting a full experimental analysis of behavior. However, in the event that you have had the opportunity to carry out such replications, here is the place where you would detail them.

_____
_____
_____
_____
_____

Form 26.1 (p. 5 of 6)

Your Name_____ Date _____ Instructor's Name _____

6. *Results.*

What happened as a consequence of your intervention?

    a) Attach the most recent version of your graph(s).

        (1) Be sure to label each one with a clear title, indicating where baseline began and where your intervention started by placing a vertical dashed line between those phases. (That could be all on the same day for purposes of this assignment, but ordinarily baseline probably would continue for several days.) You also should disconnect the lines connecting data points between one phase and the next.

        (2) If you changed your procedures, disconnect the data lines and draw a dashed vertical (phase) line between one procedure (or variation) and the next. Write a title for each phase above its data.

    b) As if you were a camera, report exactly what the data are telling you. (Omit any rationale or interpretation for now. Your turn to do that will come very soon.) This could be in the form of a statement like the following: When the teacher (or "I") did such and such, my student did such and such. Specify areas of the graph to which you are referring.

_____
_____
_____
_____
_____
_____
_____
_____
_____
_____
_____
_____
_____

7. *Discussion*

    a) *You will have the opportunity to interpret your results soon.* But before doing that, provide a general summary of how well your original question seemed to have been answered and/or its purpose achieved. Refer to both the methods you used and the results you recorded.

_____
_____
_____
_____
_____
_____
_____
_____
_____
_____
_____
_____
_____
_____

Form 26.1 (p. 6 of 6)

Your Name _____ Date _____ Instructor's Name _____

b) Now speculate about why things have been turning out the way they have. Consider unusual events, such as illnesses of the student, teacher or classmates, or disruptions or distractions such as weather changes. Did you run out of particular rewards? Were materials or furnishings unsuitable? Did things happen at home that may have calmed or set him or her off? How about the time of day? Could the student have been hungry, tired, or thirsty? Did s/he need to use the toilet or have a toileting accident? Was there a schedule change? Undoubtedly, you have thought of other reasons why the data look the way they do. Here you also might suggest follow-up investigations to test your hunches.

_____
_____
_____
_____
_____
_____
_____
_____
_____
_____

8. *Conclusion.*
Again, refer back to your original question or purpose. Briefly summarize your findings and any solidly supported (documented) reasons for those results. Comment on the significance of these findings, both in terms of this particular study and ways the information could be used with other students or in future projects.

_____
_____
_____
_____
_____
_____
_____
_____

9. *References.* List all the publications mentioned in the paper. Do not include references to papers to which you did not refer. Remember to use the APA guide to set up your reference list.

References

_____
_____
_____
_____
_____
_____
_____
_____
_____

Activity 26.2 (Estimated time: 1 hour)
DVD Recording

Written Requirements: Form 26.2

Objectives: To produce a DVD recording of a teaching session you will:

1. prepare a three-to-five minute DVD recorded sample of your ongoing teaching.
2. use the *Teaching Performance Checklist* to guide your preparation of the DVD-recorded session.
3. fill out the form entitled *Form 23.2 DVD Cover Sheet, Teaching Session—Second Recording* (to receive credit for this activity, you need to send this form with your DVD).
4. use the DVD recording to self-assess your instruction privately (though you may pass along your comments, you are not required to give or send those to your instructor).
5. use the instructor's comments and suggestions to improve your teaching performance.

Form 26.2 (p. 1 of 3)
DVD Cover Sheet

Date _____/_____/_____	Student's Name
Child's Pseudonym	Location of Recording Site
Name of ABA Instructor Brand and Model of Recorder	People present (please check) □ Parent □ Regular classroom teacher □ Aide or assistant □ Other personnel (specify) _____ _____ _____
Time Recording Started_____Stopped_____	□ Other student(s) (describe)_____ _____ _____

Any specific operating instructions for how your instructor will need to play this DVD recording?
_____
_____

Describe below, the components of the contextual arrangement as it applies to your recording:
_____
_____
_____

Time of day	General ongoing activity(ies):	Description of physical layout (add sketch)

Form 26.2 DVD Cover Sheet (p.2 of 3)

Describe the procedures used to teach the skills, or target responses, (e.g, what shaping procedures were employed?)

_____

_____

_____

_____

What reinforcers were used, and how did the children respond to them? Please describe.

_____

_____

_____

Explain other pertinent ongoing activities that may have affected learning conditions (e.g., lunch was currently being prepared on the other side of the room).

_____

_____

_____

On the attached page, please identify the specific time and number on the tape counter or footage number and write a brief phrase to indicate what is happening during the DVD recording.

Add any further comments or questions you may have for your instructor.

_____

_____

_____

_____

_____

_____

_____

_____

_____

_____

_____

Form 26.2 (p.3 of 3)
DVD Cover Sheet
Your Name _____ Date _____ Instructor's Name _____

Tape counter or footage number		Person teaching	Briefly describe what is happening; include a key word, action or object that will help your instructor find the right passage.	Comments
Started	Stopped			

Unit 26 Discussion Topics

1. This unit you have had an opportunity to gather all the facets of your program and organize them into a meaningful whole. How do you feel at this point? If you had it to do over,
    a) what would you keep ?
    b) what would you do differently?

2. Talk about the general value of integrating each of the aspects of a ABA program into a "story" written according to the suggested format.

3. Share the story with your group about how the foundation for your project was built by the efforts of others. Explain how those accomplishments helped lead you in the direction you have taken in designing your teaching program.

4. Now that this practicum experience is nearly over, how well prepared do you feel you are to be able to:
    a) read the research literature in the field?
    b) make use of what you read?

5. In considering your project, share aspects that were the most
    *   interesting
    *   exciting
    *   entertaining
    *   unexpected
    *   fulfilling

6. What teaching objective(s) are you especially eager to tackle next? Why?

Unit 27
Postcards from Afar
Displaying and Interpreting Your Graphs

"Right! We *know* all of us had planned to visit the Fine Arts Museum and do the Freedom Trail today. But that was before the Sox started jockeying for first place. I just called Stan, our college buddy—you remember the one who covers the game for *Sports Illustrated*. He assured us he could get us tickets. So we're going to get together in about an hour over at the park entrance."

The women look at one another and shrug.

"Why don't you ladies go do your thing? I'll call on the cell phone and we'll meet you after the game's over."

"Well," Ginger sheepishly announces, "actually I sorta made a tentative date to meet someone at the Starbucks on Harvard Square at three and was going to ask you if you minded my begging off on this one. I've done the Freedom Trail before and can catch up with you later."

"Anyone we know, Ginger?"

"Uh—remember that guy who was touring those foreign students? We've been chatting back and forth on the Internet. It's not anything, but since I let him know we'd be in the area, he did ask if we could get together."

"Your choice, folks. Anyway, Lucy and I can take a side excursion to the Prudential Center. I hear they've got some great shops and I really need some new hiking boots. All that climbing has worn mine out. And, Ginger, you be good."

Lucy and Dawn head off to visit the Boston Gardens; then to pick to up the Freedom Trail. One of their early stops is the New Statehouse.

"That's really something. They call it "the New Statehouse," but it's over 200 years old. Too bad we don't have the camera. The guys will be sorry they missed this. And we won't have a slide to show and tell about it to our friends and families."

"I think our problem is solved," Dawn points. "There's a souvenir stand selling picture postcards."

They examine the display and choose several.

"At least we'll be able to share the experience a bit this way, don't you think?"

******

Now that you are well into this field sequence, surely you have had experiences of your own you are ready to share with your instructor; then later with your student's teachers, parents and other key people. As you already know, the final project requires you to prepare and submit a formal written report of your program. Your earlier practicum assignments were designed to lay a foundation for this report, so it should not be a grueling task. By now, you have read several journal articles whose content helped justify and probably clarify the way you have approached your teaching. Last week you actually prepared a complete outline of your report. This Unit we ask you to design your own "postcards": the *picture* is your data, displayed in its final form; your *message* will be the written abstract plus a few paragraphs of introduction justifying 1) why you did what you did and 2) how you did it. We also request a written description of your results.

Your instructor's suggestions will allow you to complete the report in its final form for the next—and last—unit's assignment.

Prerequisite skills

Assuming you have completed formal coursework in or otherwise mastered information about the value of and techniques for writing a formal research or case report, you should be able to achieve Unit 27's objectives.

Unit 27 Objectives

To clearly and accurately describe, display and interpret your student's performance over time, as presented in your graph, you will:

1. generate a graph including, but not limited to, independent and dependent variables, labeled axes and phases of your intervention, and a legend.
2. describe and analyze the graphic results in paragraph form, including levels of performance, events, and other pertinent data.
3. compose an abstract of 120 words or less describing the project, including the problem addressed, procedures used, results, and implications for future work with your student.
4. compose an introduction to the final report that includes reported empirical evidence, and a justification for your teaching approach, and your purpose.

Notice, you will have no forms to fill out this unit. Instead, you use your own materials to prepare each of these assigned activities.

Activity 27.1 (Estimated time: 2–6 hrs)
Preparing Your Final Graph(s)

Written Requirements: Your own data display

Objectives: To generate a graphing convention that clearly and accurately displays your student's performance over time and describes and interprets your student's performance as presented in your graph, you will:

1. generate a graph including but not limited to independent and dependent variables, labeled axes and phases of your intervention, and legend.
2. write, in paragraph form, a verbal description of your student's performance as displayed in your graph(s).

Purpose

They say a picture tells a thousand words, and in conveying applied behavior analytic results, this is certainly true. The first activity for this unit asks you to update and/or revise your graph(s). You may wish to add supplementary graphs necessary for clarifying the conclusions you draw in your final report.

The *main data* should show how your behavior analytic teaching practices—what you did—influenced student learning.

Supplementary graphs may help explain your outcomes. For example, you may wish to display the influence of reinforcing items or events as a function of time of day; or to plot data to demonstrate differences in rates of student responding as a function of specific materials, weather conditions, instructors, or environmental distractions. Maybe you will refer to your graph to justify reassessing and/or adjusting your teaching practices or objectives. Any or all of those would be reasonable and acceptable.

So… your current task is to prepare your main graph. Then, as suggested, we hope you will try to include at least one supplementary graph. These graphs should be in their final form, ready to be attached to your final report.

Instructions

1. Prepare your main and preferably one or more supplementary graphs in their final form. Remember to include:
   - a title containing your teaching method (the independent variable) and what you measured (the dependent variables)
   - the labels of the vertical and horizontal axes and each different phase (e.g., "baseline," "intervention 1" or a more descriptive phrase, and so on).
   - vertical dashed lines separating procedural changes
   - breaks in the lines that connect one data point to the next when phases change
   - legends
   - other features of a well-constructed graph, about which you learned in earlier courses

3. Submit the graph to your instructor. Write your name on the back.

4. Write one or two paragraphs describing what each graph shows. Identify events that occurred on given days that may have influenced results, but avoid the temptation to explain or interpret the results until you prepare your final *discussion* section.

Activity 27.2 (Estimated time: 1–2 hours)
Writing Your Introduction: Making a Case for Your Intervention

Purpose: This unit you have the opportunity to alter or elaborate further on the reasons why you conducted your teaching program the way you did. Throughout your studies of ABA, you have learned the value of using methods based on research or *empirical* evidence of effectiveness. We have asked you to review journal articles that support your own teaching approach and serve as a guide for improving your program. Now we ask you to prepare the final summary of what you have learned from the experience and use that information to justify the approach you used in your teaching plan. Consider: 1) How the articles you have read justify your teaching program. 2) What you have learned from your reading. 3) How you have applied that information.

Written Requirements: Referring to the current edition of the *Publication Manual of the American Psychological Association,* use your own materials to prepare the introduction to your final report (double space, please). Be sure to include your name, the date, and the name of your instructor.

Objectives: To compose an introduction of your final report, you will include empirical evidence, a justification of your teaching approach and your purpose.

Instructions

1. Refer to the summary of the research literature you prepared for last unit's assignment, "The *Preliminary Project Report.*" Now you should begin the actual writing by detailing the background for your project. List and discuss the conclusions of each research report you read, recognizing the work of others as a basis for the specific methods you chose to use. Taking into consideration your instructor's comments and your own review of the preliminary report, add any other sources that further support or otherwise relate to your procedural choices. Mention the most pertinent findings, methodological issues and key conclusions.

2. Develop the sequence of logic between what has come before and what you have done, using language understandable to a lay audience. Lead up to your hypotheses or, purpose. You may choose to summarize with a statement such as: "If _____," (the method you used), "then, we would anticipate that _____" (the results you would expect). The concluding statement in the introduction should clarify the relation between the conclusions drawn in scientific research reports and the focus and methods you have selected.

3. You now have your opening paragraphs.

4. Submit this *introduction to your final report* to your instructor.[64]

---

[64] ***Instructors***: A rapid turn-around time should permit your students to prepare a more finely-polished final product for next week.

Activity 27.3 (Estimated time: 1 hour)
Preparing an Abstract of Your Report

Written Requirements: Original composition

Objectives: To compose an abstract of your final report, summarize what you did in 120 words or less, describing the project, including the problem addressed, procedures used, results, and implications for future work with your student.

Here you provide a clear advance summary, or *abstract,* of your report. An abstract provides a brief, comprehensive overview of your project and results. The current *Publication Manual of the American Psychological Association* indicates a good abstract contains accurate, self-contained, concise material of no more than 120 words, and is specific, nonevaluative, coherent and readable. If you need to shorten your abstract, refer to the published papers you have reviewed for inspiration.

> **Note:** If you are working with a group of fellow field practicum students, you will want to share your results with those peers. Please be sure to omit any identifying information about your student and his or her family.

Instructions

Consider general guidelines as you revise your abstract on the basis of your instructor's feedback. Each item listed below is an important component and, if appropriate, should be included. Remember, an abstract is designed to be a brief overview, so limit each item to a phrase or at most a sentence or two. Detailed description of your project is to be included in the body of the paper.

1. Describe the challenge facing your student, plus the objective you selected.

2. After reviewing your notes, say how research supported your methods.

3. Describe your method, including a brief account of the student, setting, personnel, materials, observational recording methods, procedures (*who* did *what* to *whom, how, why, when* and *where*—sound familiar?).

4. State the results to date.

5. Speculate about why things turned out the way they did and what you might do more of or differently in the future.

6. Write a concluding sentence.

7. Review your abstract for clarity, spelling accuracy and grammatical correctness.[65]

---

[65] Most word-processing programs provide spelling and grammar check functions.

Unit 27 Discussion Topics

1. If you were to choose or design a picture postcard depicting one of your experiences in this course,
    *   what would the picture look like?
    *   what message would you write on the reverse side?
    *   to whom would you send it? Why?

2. Spend a while thumbing through your ABA notes and materials.
    *   Jot down five *behavioral principles* (*general* rules or guidelines based on scientific evidence) you consider most important.
    *   Comment about where you saw those principles illustrated in the design and conduct of *this* practicum course.
    *   Comment on how effectively those applications functioned.
    *   Add any other ways those principles might be used to improve the quality of the course.

3. Do you think it would be a good idea to base part of your grade on your student's progress? (Notice we currently do not.) Why, or why not?

4. Compare and contrast your attitude toward data collection and analysis between the beginning and end of this and your other ABA courses. Has it changed? If so, how? If not, why not?

5. Post a draft of your abstract for the others in your group. Ask them to comment on its clarity, and suggest ways you might revise it.

Unit 28
Taking Stock
Evaluating Performance and Products

As the mists spiral gently off the granite boulders, our adventurers gaze out at the rocky bay. The golden glow of dawn enthralls them as it begins to transform into brilliant sunshine.

"Look at the fir trees in silhouette. They seem almost afire."

"And watch, over there—the lower mountains. It's almost as if something is peeling away their protective covering. I never imagined how vivid the textures and colors of rocks could be: bronze, rust, deep gray, slashes of white!"

"What I find so fascinating is the way the sea is gently lapping against the rocks—a remarkable transformation after the smashing and crashing of last night's storm."

"Yep, we did the right thing coming here. We all needed a place to chill out and regroup."

"Think about me," Ginger sighs. "I've got to submit the first draft of my THESIS when I get back to school tomorrow. You guys really need to count your blessings! You get to enjoy the nature of this unspoiled country; throw a few lobsters on the fire, and fall asleep to the sound of the surf."

"Or the storm!" quips Art.

"We know what you mean, Ginger. Too bad you have to get back to the grind. We all want time to stand still for a while, so we can reflect, sum up our experiences, and consider our next destinations."

They chat about the small towns and villages of inland New England they plan to see during fall foliage; then zigzagging down the coast, catching historic sights, museums, county fairs and sports events along the way.

"Yeah, right. Then rest and recover in Florida." Dawn envisions the time-share they've secured for late winter, while Art spins silent fantasies of catching the Red Sox at spring practice.

"So, after Florida, what then?" Ginger questions.

"We've agreed to take stock at that point to decide whether to continue, and if so, when, where, why and how," Art responds. " And thanks for all the great food and sharing your recipes."

"Don't forget to send us the very first draft of your book," Ginger reminds Hal and Lucy. "What a brilliant idea for the two of you to collaborate! I love the title: *The Sensualists' Guide to the Eastern States*."

"Hmm," Hal whispers to his wife. "I wonder who the 'us' can be. Better not ask. We'll find out if and when the time is right."

*****

Our travelers have come to realize that the journey through life moves along in stages. Each experience can enrich, but the most valuable ones are carefully orchestrated, monitored and evaluated.

The same happens for those of us threading our way through the challenges of educating children with autism. In fact, in our understandable frenzy to capitalize on the fleeting opportunities of children's younger years, we often are inclined to rush from one focus to the next with nary a backward glance. Like so many other temptations, the wiser option is to postpone gratification long enough to address the important questions: "Are these the most optimal objectives to pursue at this point or would others be preferable?" "Did this method work?" "If so, how well?" "Might there be a better way?"

Now this unit is yours to sum up and to pause and reflect. Besides fulfilling your "civic duty" to abet the continuous improvement of this field practicum, your formal appraisal of this experience also will remind you how much you have done and how far you have traveled along the path toward competence in applying behavior analysis within the field of autism.

Prerequisite Skills

Assuming you have completed all the assignments in this program to your instructor's and/or supervisor's satisfaction, you should be able to achieve Unit 28's objectives.

Unit 28 Objectives

By the end of this unit, you should be able to justify, describe and discuss the method and results of your program to date in your final report, and to demonstrate an acceptable level of professionalism, execute a DVD production, and evaluate your field experience, you will:

1. compose a final *methods* section that describes your teaching intervention, participants, relevance, setting, time and procedures.
2. compose a *results* section, including your graph(s) and a verbal description.
3. compose a *discussion* section that includes, but is not limited to, your conclusions and future implications and recommendations.
4. request feedback on your professional skills including, but not limited to, receptivity, flexibility, helpfulness, responsibility, reliability, rate of productivity and timeliness.
5. produce a DVD recording of your final teaching session.
6. evaluate your field experience.

Activity 28.1 (Estimated time: 4–6 hours)
Completing Your Final Report

Written Requirements: Your own composition

Objectives: To generate the final account of your project report, you will compose:

1. a *methods* section that describes your teaching intervention, participants, setting, time and procedures and any other essential elements.
2. a *results* section.
3. a *discussion* section that includes but is not limited to your conclusions and future implications and recommendations.

The time has come to narrate the details of your journey through this practicum… to update your instructor, your fellow students, your Field Facilitator, and perhaps your student's parents.

Instructions
1. Refer to the materials you competed for *Units 25* and *26* and the feedback you received from your instructor. Those contain practically everything you will need to construct your final report.

2. Write your report according to the format suggested in the current edition of the *Publication Manual of the American Psychological Association*. Its author guidelines are followed by most educational and scientific journals. The best way to learn a new skill is to do it correctly the first time. At a minimum, we expect your report to use:
   - double spacing
   - correct grammar, spelling and punctuation
   - use of past tense (except, as appropriate, in *the discussion and summary* section)
   - coverage of each of the following sections listed, including
     - o Your revised **abstract**
     - o An **introduction**. Include your revised brief review of the literature. Tie it together as it relates to your project and end with a summary question or hypothesis.
     - o The revised **methods** section, containing descriptions of:
       - the participants
       - the setting(s)
       - the materials
       - the measures, along with
       - evidence supporting
         - reliability
         - the fidelity with which the procedure or treatment was implemented
       - the teaching procedures (what you did)
     - o The **results**
       - your graphs
       - your own written description

> **APA Format**
>
> - *Title Page*
> - *Abstract (separate page)*
> - *Introduction*
> - *Methods*
> - *Results*
> - *Discussion*
> - *Summary*
> - *References*

> The *Methods* section should be objectively written, without any rationales or explanations as to why things did or did not happen. Those belong in the *Discussion* section.

- o The *discussion*. This should include:
  - An explanation of what did work and why (you may refer to some of the papers you have read)
  - An explanation of what did not work and why
  - What should be tried in the future
- o A *reference list*. This should include all journals and texts you cited in the paper and *not* those you *did not* cite.

3. There are no length requirements. Try to keep wording as direct, simple, and clear as possible. As a general guideline, most manuscripts will contain about 8 to 15 pages.

4. Submit this report to your instructor by the end of the unit.

Activity 28.2 (Estimated time: 30 minutes)
Final Field Facilitator Assessment

Written Requirements: Form 28.1

Objectives: To demonstrate an acceptable level of professionalism, request that your Field Facilitator or Field Supervisor review your professional demeanor in the practicum setting. The information they provide should enable you and your supervisor to identify specific professional skills you will want to preserve and those you probably will want to refine.

Instructions

1. Fill in the information requested in the attached form.

2. Prepare as many copies as you will need.

3. Early in the week, give the form to your *Field Facilitator* and/or Field Supervisor and any others from whom you would appreciate receiving feedback, along with stamped envelopes addressed to your instructor. Ask them to
    *   complete the form
    *   make a copy
    *   mail the original to your instructor, if applicable
    *   give you a duplicate copy.

4. If you wish, schedule a meeting with the *Field Facilitator* and/or Field Supervisor to discuss any of the ratings, especially the positive ones. This should help reinforce your constructive efforts as well as to identify opportunities for improvement.

5. Do the same with any others who have completed the form.

6. Send your instructor a short paragraph describing your plan to maintain and improve your professional skills.

7. *... and this is critical:* Write and distribute notes of thanks to everyone in your setting who has assisted you in any way. Be sure to recognize how much time they spent and provide examples of ways they invested it in helping you to do a good job. Send copies to your instructor.

Form 28.1 (p. 1 of 2)
Assessment of Practicum Student's Professional Skills

Upper portion to be filled out by ABA Practicum Student

ABA Student's Name _____ Date_____ Field Facilitator's Name _____

Field Facilitator Contact Information:
 Phone _____ Fax _____ email _____

ABA Instructor's Contact Information:
 Phone _____ Fax _____ email _____

(If working from a distance, ABA student should provide the *Field Facilitator* with a stamped envelope addressed to the instructor. Overseas students should use OVERSEAS AIRMAIL stamps.)

For Field Supervisor or Facilitator:

We thank you for your willingness to facilitate our ABA student's participation in your program and hope this relationship has proven to be productive.

This portion to be filled out by the Field Supervisor or Facilitator

1) Please **complete** and **duplicate** the form. 2) Give one copy to the practicum student, and another to the ABA instructor within the week. Keep the original for your own files.

ABA Practicum Student's Professional Skill	5	4	3	2	1	NA
Is friendly (regularly looks directly at, smiles, greets people individually)						
Listens respectfully (waits while they talk; responds to the point)						
Responds to and gives positive and constructive feedback						
Is flexible (adjusts to new conditions)						
Is helpful in the program						
States plans and expectations clearly						
Undertakes responsibilities and plans time carefully						
Meets responsibilities s/he has undertaken						
Schedules time realistically						
Completes responsibilities on time						
Is prepared in advance of instructional sessions						
Strives for excellence in written and oral communication						
Is patient with his or her student						
Works productively with his or her student						

5 = consistently   4 = most of the time   3 = at an acceptable level
2 = once in a while   1 = rarely or not at all   NA = not applicable

Form 28.1 (p. 2 of 2)

ABA Student's Name _____ Date_____
Field Facilitator's Name _____

Please comment on the best aspect(s) of the ABA student's performance.

_____
_____
_____
_____
_____
_____
_____
_____
_____
_____
_____
_____
_____
_____
_____
_____

Please add any further comments on here.

_____
_____
_____
_____
_____
_____
_____
_____
_____
_____
_____
_____
_____
_____
_____
_____
_____
_____
_____

Activity 28.3 (1 hour)
Final DVD-recording Session

This is your final DVD-recording assignment. The purpose and value of DVD-recording in this course was introduced in Unit 4, along with practical guidelines concerning equipment and recording methods. Please refer back those guidelines if you need a refresher. As with your other DVD-recordings, this assignment also asks you to use the *Teaching Performance Checklist* to focus specifically on observable aspects of your teaching.

Written Requirements: Form 28.2

Objective: To produce a DVD recording of your final teaching session.

Instructions

1. Follow earlier guidelines for producing this final DVD-recording of an ongoing teaching interaction.

2. Carefully review the *Teaching Performance Checklist* and plan the logistics of your teaching session so your DVD-recording will capture as many as possible of the listed aspects of your teaching.

3. Arrange for a collaborator to DVD-record one of your sessions, or use a tripod. Record a three-to-five minute segment that displays you and your student interacting now, at the end of the course.

Remember….
You may record for a period longer than five minutes. If so, you should either:
*   Delete all but three-to-five minutes of the material, or
*   Indicate the exact beginning and ending footage point for the three-to-five minute portion you want your instructor to view.

4. Complete form entitled "*Form 28.2: Teaching Session—Fourth Recording*," summarizing what the recording displays and how well it reflects both your and your student's progress. Submit it to your instructor along with the DVD package ***by the end of the week***.

5. *Be sure to include form 28.2 with your DVD to receive credit for this requirement.*

Form 28.2: DVD Cover Sheet (p. 1 of 4)
Teaching Session—Fourth Recording

Your Name _____ Date _____ Instructor's Name_____

Please provide the requested information and submit this form along with your last DVD-recording.

1. *A brief statement* of your teaching activities as seen on the DVD recording.

_____
_____
_____

2. *A brief description* of your student's responses as they appear on the recording.

_____
_____
_____
_____

3. Other important features or events that happened beforehand or appear on the recording, and might have affected your student's performance.

_____
_____
_____
_____

4. The extent to which you feel your teaching has improved from the earlier recordings to this one.

_____
_____

5. The extent to which your student has made progress from the initial recordings to this last one.

_____
_____
_____

6. How you plan to improve your teaching interactions in the future, with this child or other children with whom you are or will be working.

_____
_____

7. Write additional comments or questions here and on the reverse side.

_____
_____
_____
_____
_____
_____

Take heart! Your grade does not depend on your student's progress; even if it has not been as rapid as you hoped. Numerous factors influence those outcomes, many of which may be beyond your control. What we have been seeking is your very best effort.

Form 28.2: DVD Cover Sheet (p. 2 of 4)
Teaching Session—Fourth Recording

Date _____/_____/_____	Student's Name
Child's Pseudonym	Location of Recording Site
Name of ABA Instructor	People present (please check) □ Parent □ Regular classroom teacher □ Aide or assistant
Brand and Model of Recorder	□ Other personnel (specify) _____ _____ _____
Time Recording Started_____Stopped_____	□ Other student(s) (describe)_____ _____ _____

Any specific operating instructions for how your instructor will need to play this DVD-recording?
_____
_____
_____

Contextual arrangement

Describe the below components of contextual arrangement as it applies to your recording:

Time of day	General ongoing activity(ies):	Description of physical layout (add sketch)

Form 28.2: DVD Cover Sheet (p.3 of 4)
Teaching Session—Fourth Recording

In what way is the setting natural or arranged? Is the setting intact in its original state or were components in the environment changed in any way to facilitate learning? Please describe.

_____
_____
_____

Teaching program components

State your target response and corresponding definition by which your child's performance is to be measured:

_____
_____
_____

From the checklist below, check or list the teaching procedures you will be demonstrating:

☐ Discrete trial format
☐ Incidental teaching
☐ Small group instruction
☐ Individual instruction (if different that discrete trial, please explain)
☐ Task analysis of sequenced events
☐ Other _____

Briefly summarize your teaching procedure:

_____
_____
_____
_____

State your measurement procedure:

_____
_____
_____

Did you collect data? If so, please place in labeled, sealed envelope and attach to this sheet.
Select reinforcers used:
☐ Tangible
☐ Social
☐ Activity
☐ Other _____

Add any further comments on a separate sheet.

Form 28.2 DVD Cover Sheet (p.4 of 4)
Teaching Session—Fourth Recording

Your Name _____ Date _____ Instructor's Name _____

Counter or footage number		Person teaching	Briefly describe what is happening (include a key word, action or object that will help your instructor find the right passage)	Comments
Started	Stopped			

Unit 28
Discussion Topics

1. *For all participants*:
   - Share the abstract of your final report, along with your main graphs, if possible
   - Comment on any one or more of the following:
     a) What was the most important lesson you learned from your project?
     b) What would you be sure to do again in the future?
     c) What would you do differently?
     d) What did you find most surprising?

2. Comment on the abstract(s) of others in your group.
   a) What was especially impressive about one or more of the abstracts?
   b) What questions would you like to pose about one or more of the abstracts?
   c) What did you learn from any one or more of the abstracts that you feel you will be able to capitalize on for yourself?

3. Reflect on this practicum experience.
   a) What aspects would you definitely retain? Why?
   b) What aspects would you adjust—in what way, and why?

4. Did your previous coursework prepare you for this practicum?
   a) What aspects were most helpful in preparing you. Why?
   b) What aspects were least helpful? Why?
   c) Describe how and why would you alter the latter.

5. Comment on any other aspects of your ABA experience that you wish to.

Activity 28.4 (Less than 1 hour)
Student Evaluation of Your Field Experience

Written Requirements: Assessments to be administered by your instructor or field supervisor

Objectives: To produce an evaluation, you will complete an assessment form prepared by your university, training program, instructor or supervisor.

Instructions

1. At the end of this course, your instructor, supervisor or assessment team should supply you with one or more forms for you to complete.[66]

2. Follow the instructions accompanying the assessment(s).

3. Notify your instructor or supervisor that you have submitted those forms, as requested.

And congratulations. You did it![67]

---

[66] **Instructors or field supervisors** should use their organization's general course evaluation form, if one exists, and/or prepare one of their own to fit their unique circumstances.

[67] The authors would appreciate receiving a summary copy of the course evaluation results; also reports of successes and constructive suggestions from instructors and students for revising future editions of this manual. Please use Bazaroff@comcast.net and the phrase "Comment on *ABA Across the Autism Spectrum*," in the *subject line*.

References

Alberto, P. A., & Troutman, A. C. (1982). *Applied behavior analysis for teachers.* Columbus, OH: Merrill.

Bondy, A., Dickey, K., Black, D., & Buswell, S. (2002). *The Pyramid Approach to education: Lesson plans for young children*, Newark, DE: Pyramid Educational Products, Inc.

Bondy, A., & Sulzer-Azaroff, B. (2002). *The Pyramid Approach to education in autism.* Newark, DE: Pyramid Educational Products, Inc.

Cooper, J. O., Heron, T. E., & Heward, W. L. (2007). *Applied behavior analysis* (2nd ed.). Upper Saddle River, NJ: Prentice Hall.

Dixon, M. et al. (2007). Creating single-subject design graphs in Microsoft Excel, *Journal of Applied Behavior Analysis, 42*, 277–293.

Dyer, K. (2011). A-B-C analysis. In F. Volkmar (ed.) *Encyclopedia of autism spectrum disorders.* New York: Springer.

Fisher, W., Piazza, C. C., Bowman, L. G., Hagopian, J. C., & Slevin, I. (1992). A comparison of two approaches for identifying reinforcers for persons with severe and profound disabilities. *Journal of Applied Behavior Analysis, 25*, 491–498.

Mayer, R. G., Sulzer-Azaroff, B., & Wallace, M. (2012). *Behavior Analysis for Lasting Change*, 2nd ed. Cornwall-on-Hudson, NY: Sloan Publishing.

Koegel, R. L. & Koegel, L. K. (1995). *Teaching students with autism.* Baltimore, MD: Paul H. Brookes.

Peterson, L., Holmes, A. L., & Wonderlich, S. A. (1982). The integrity of independent variables in behavior analysis. *Journal of Applied Behavior Analysis, 15*, 477–492.

Publication manual of the American Psychological Association, 5th ed. (2001). Washington, DC: American Psychological Association. www.apa.org

McConnel, S. R. (2003). Interventions to facilitate social interaction for young children with autism: Review of available research and recommendations for educational intervention and future research. *Journal of Autism and Developmental Disorders, 33*(5), 351–372.

Miltenberger, R. G. (2008). *Behavior modification: Principles and procedures.* Belmont, CA: Cengage.

Pace, G. M., Ivancic, M. T., Edwards, G. L. , Iwata, B. A., & Page, T. J. (1985). Assessment of stimulus preferences and reinforcer value with profoundly retarded individuals. *Journal of Applied Behavior Analysis, 18*, 249–255.

Whalen, C. & Schreibman, L. (2003). Joint attention ffor children with autism using behavior modification procedures. *Journal of Child Psychology and Psychiatry, 44* (3), 456–468.